Rhetoric of Modern Death in American Living Dead Films

Rhetoric of Modern Death in American Living Dead Films

Outi Hakola

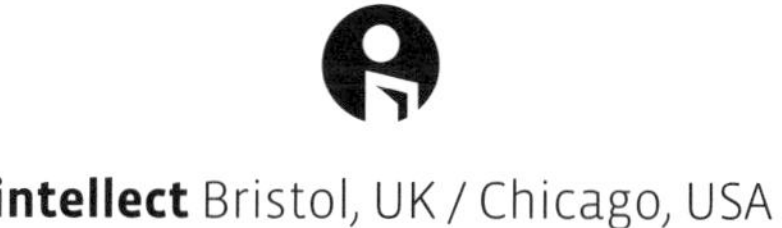

intellect Bristol, UK / Chicago, USA

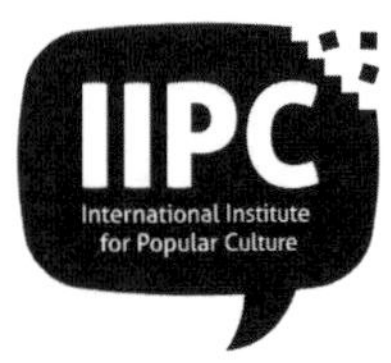

First published in the UK in 2015 by
Intellect, The Mill, Parnall Road, Fishponds, Bristol, BS16 3JG, UK

First published in the USA in 2015 by
Intellect, The University of Chicago Press, 1427 E. 60th Street,
Chicago, IL 60637, USA

A catalogue record for this book is available from the
British Library.

Series: Part of the *Studies on Popular Culture* series
Series editors: Bruce Johnson and Hannu Salmi
Series ISSN: 2041-6725
Electronic ISSN: 2042-8227
Cover designer: Stephanie Sarlos
Copy-editor: Paul Nash
Production Manager: Tim Mitchell
Typesetting: Contentra Technologies

Print ISBN: 978-1-78320-379-6
ePDF ISBN: 978-1-78320-381-9
ePUB ISBN: 978-1-78320-380-2

Printed and bound by Hobbs, UK

Contents

Studies on Popular Culture

Series Editors' Preface

In academic institutions there is increasing interest in the meaning and place of 'the popular' in the definition of modernity and postmodernity. In particular, in the twenty-first century, it is through popular culture in its various forms that the tensions between the local and the global are acted out most immediately, not only through the content of popular cultural forms, but in their means of production, distribution, and reappropriation through consumption. Indeed, a study of the evolution of the term 'popular' is an essential analytical key to the understanding of the various confrontations – class, race, gender, place – that define contemporary power relations. The study of popular culture helps us to understand the contradictions in the contemporary sensibility. It gives us a more direct understanding of how we invent ourselves, how we imagine the possibilities of the world we live in, its ethical and moral dimensions and specific social practices.

The International Institute for Popular Culture (IIPC) is a multi-disciplinary research unit, concerned not only with issues in contemporary popular culture but also in its history and transformations. The Institute places special emphasis on the questions of popular culture as heritage and the social role of popular culture. The Institute was developed during 2005 at the Department of Cultural History, University of Turku, Finland, and was formally inaugurated in 2006 with an international conference under the title *The History of Stardom Reconsidered*. Apart from continuing regular conference activity the Institute maintains a refereed online publication series for monographs and conference proceedings (http://iipcblog.wordpress.com/publications/) and presents its monthly IIPC Debates featuring international speakers, available online at http://iipcblog.wordpress.com/iipc-debates/. IIPC facilitates international scholarly collaborations, offers its own doctoral programmes, and fosters engagements with private sector stakeholders in the culture industries. The series *Studies on Popular Culture* is a collaboration between IIPC and Intellect Books, presenting contributions to a critical understanding of popular culture and its history in all its forms. The series is particularly open to comparative and international approaches, and it places special emphasis on the transdisciplinary nature of popular culture studies. Its objective is to present leading research in the field, with a particular emphasis on work in and from what may be thought of as 'off-centre' research areas.

Bruce Johnson and Hannu Salmi, Series Editors

International Institute for Popular Culture
University of Turku http://iipc.utu.fi

Chapter 1

Introduction

Death is but the doorway to new life. We live today. We shall live again. In many forms shall we return.

These are the words from the opening of *The Mummy* (1932), a classic horror film. The citation from the Scroll of Toth foretells the following scene of the ancient mummy returning to life to haunt the living. The words also open the door to a specific American horror film genre. As the mummies rise from their tombs, so the corpses of zombies walk the earth, and the vampires honour the dark nights. In these living dead films of undead monsters, death is not where the narration ends. In the words of a tagline of the mummy films of the 1990s and 2000s: 'Death is only the beginning.'

In these films, by returning to life, the undead force a renegotiation of how life and death are understood. However, there is no singular phenomenon that could be defined as death. Death is more than just the biological processes of dying: it always has cultural, social, religious and philosophical dimensions. Even the medical definitions of death are culturally constructed in certain historical situations; for example, they have been changing from the lack of heartbeat to the permanent loss of brain function (for example, Kellehear 2009). Since the birth of the living dead films in the early twentieth century, the modern ideals of medicalized, institutionalized and marginalized death have been dominating the Western cultural sphere. Still, the practically compulsive repetition of death in the living dead films proclaims the continued cultural need to encounter death and dying. The cinematic undead figures connect with the complexity of death-related cultural attitudes and fears, articulating and addressing in medium-specific ways the biologically natural and inevitable fact of death, which is socially, culturally and personally disturbing.

Through the very repetition of death, the living dead films of different decades and generations create – more or less as a by-product – a picture of the changing values and attitudes related to death in American society. In this study, I will approach these films and discuss how they negotiate modern ideas of death, and how they articulate and address changing perceptions of death for and with their viewers.

1.1. Cultural Context: Change of Death-Related Attitudes

A number of scholars, Philippe Ariés, Norbert Elias and Zygmunt Bauman among them, have suggested that the role of death changed in Western societies with the onset of modernization, industrialization and medicalization. In the late eighteenth century, death and the dying began to be marginalized and removed from public space into hospitals and other specialized institutions – to be dealt with by professionals. By the mid-twentieth century, the process had taken death away from the social sphere, replacing the public experience of death with experiences of the private (Ariés 1977; Elias 2001; Bauman 1992). I will refer to the idea of death as marginalized, privatized, scientific and medicalized through the concept of 'modern death'.

Tony Walter contrasts modern death with both traditional death and neo-modern death. Traditional death relates to the pre-modern era (such as the Middle Ages) when death was quick, frequent and tackled by religious authorities (Walter 1994: 10, 47). In the course of the eighteenth century, in the modern era, death began to retreat from the public gaze, and the medical staff now assumed final authority. In the first half of the twentieth century, the scientific apparatus of the West sought to explain and control death, which led to its further modernization in Western societies. By the mid-twentieth century, this process had come to its head: death and dying people had been taken away from homes to hospitals, and encounters with death and corpses had been handed over to professionals. However, in the late twentieth century, the extreme medicalization drew different responses, when dying people and their relatives started to demand specialist and dignified care for the dying. The hospice and palliative care movements, for example, concentrated on the privacy of death from a different perspective. This process is part of what Walter calls a neo-modern death, which gives more room to the personal experience on the public agenda, even when modern ideas are still part of these practices. He argues that the prolonged and personal dying processes have led to a slow revival of death (Walter 1994: 1–24, 39–62).

While such broad definitional changes of death in Western culture are oversimplified and, although several changes have taken place in different areas and at different times, these definitions nevertheless give a general idea of the cultural atmosphere in which cinema started to imagine and represent death around the turn of the twentieth century. Cinema is, indeed, one of the most expressive technological innovations of modern society and life in the twentieth-century United States (for example, Charney & Schwartz 1995: 1–10). Interestingly, cinema has been seen to be part of the modern processes of preserving life and conquering death by such scholars as the French film theorist André Bazin. He talks of a 'mummy complex' where the film has the power to freeze time and humanity to a certain moment, quite like embalmment in ancient Egypt, and bring the past alive on the screen (Bazin 2005: 9–16). In fact, Elias E. Merhige's *The Shadow of the Vampire* (2000) discusses whether the cinema is more powerful as a form of immortality than being an undead. This film imagines that the main role in Murnau's *Nosferatu* (1922), the pioneering Dracula film, was played by a vampire. The director of the film persuades the Count to participate in the filming by arguing:

> Our battle, our struggle, is to create art. Our weapon is the moving picture. Because we have the moving picture, our paintings will grow and recede; our poetry will be shadows that lengthen and conceal; our light will play across living faces that laugh and agonize;

and our music will linger and finally overwhelm, because it will have a context as certain as the grave. We are scientists engaged in the creation of memory … but our memory will neither blur nor fade.

Although Bazin's mummy complex discusses the rather modernist tendency of denying the finality of death as part of cinema in general, the living dead remain as reminders of it as they give form, embodiment and life to death. Throughout Hollywood horror productions, the living dead films have continued to address modern society's tension between distancing and obsessing about death.

Indeed, even in modern society, the marginalization of death has never been total. With repeated stories and images, the birth of the new reproductive media (such as cinema) created alternative public images of death and dying – exaggerated and visual. As Vicki Goldberg (1998: 30) argues, deaths in the media served as 'a substitute for experience'. Charlton D. McIlwain takes this argument a step further by claiming that the mass media and entertainment industry function as the missing link between the periods which openly embraced death. To him, the media have actively forced death back into the public domain by allowing people communally to discuss and give meanings to it (McIlwain 2005: 3–20, 39).

The living dead films can also be seen to participate in this transformation from modern death to the revival of death. This is not to say that films always promote the neo-modern revival of death at the ideological level of the stories but rather that the films' narration makes death and dying part of public discussion. As several film scholars have argued, cinema is essentially a collective, communal and public space, and form of communication and reception. Its publicness hinges not only on the movie theatre as a (semi-)public place, but also the viewing experiences themselves become collectively shared and, thereby, public processes (Hansen 1991: 2–19; Hansen 1995: 137–40; Denzin 1995: 6; Donald & Hemelryk Donald 2000: 114–15). In particular, when the modernization of death led to underlining the personal level of experience (one's own death and the death of loved ones), the cinema provided a place for personal experiences and public images to meet. Participation in the revival of death is how the living dead films, too, participate in public life by creating socially constructed experiences and effects.

The management of death has also changed in the 'more public' or 'realistic' mediums like television and the news media. Based on his work on American television programmes, McIlwain argues that death has been given more discursive space in both magazine shows and television dramas, as well as in the fan communities and web discussion pages of these shows, such as *Six Feet Under* (2001–05) or *Crossing over with John Edward* (1999–2004). The increasingly open relationship with death and mourning in television has reframed 'privacy of death' as 'death as a public spectacle' (McIlwain 2005).

Folker Hanusch also draws on his research on death in journalism to claim that the news media, especially since the Internet's arrival, is now filled with mourning, memorials and the visuality of dying. At the same time, he argues that there is nothing new in the news' representations of death. There have been times when these representations have been even more graphic and cruel than they are today. In this way, the news responds to cultural desires and participates in hiding death when it has not been appropriate to go into details (Hanusch 2010). All in all, the Western media is more aware of the emotional impact of death, both through personal emotions and social anxiety.

Because the media has taken an active role in the revival process, McIlwain demands that it is not enough to recognize the media as an alternative public or refuge for death. Rather, we should study how the restoration has been embedded through mass-mediated articulations of death (McIlwain 2005: 49). This is the goal of my study. I suggest that by analysing the ways in which films such as American living dead films fantasize and address death, we can gain a more comprehensive picture of death's role in Western societies.

Living dead films are mostly overlooked in this discussion of changing cultural perceptions of death, which is problematic for at least two reasons. First, although horror films in general are marginalized in American culture, it is this marginalized position together with horror's dramatizing possibilities that highlight the genre's intense view of death. Unlike some non-fictional modes of representation or more realistic traditions of cinema, the living dead films use their fantasizing potential to play more freely with our understanding of death. Their productive power and social force lie in creating images of death and dying that challenge existing cultural practices. Because living dead films combine the horror genre's transgressive and countercultural possibilities with the centrality of death in themes, narration and images, these films hold an exceptional position of acceptably debating modern death (for horror's transgressive potential, see Bourget 1995: 57; Wood 1984: 171–72; Wood 1995: 62–63).

Instead of being openly political, these films have more freedom to approach such themes as death. Adam Lowenstein (2005: 8) recognizes that horror films' ability to deal with social issues is often created through allegories. He writes that, unlike representations, 'the allegorical moment attempts to shift cinema's relation to history from compensation to confrontation' (Lowenstein 2005: 8, see also Clover 1992: 231). While films that deal with the politics of the United States, for example, can be read as immediate representations of events, allegorical films, such as living dead films, can choose indirect links to confront sociocultural issues differently. Therefore, by looking into the ways in which living dead films encounter death, the competing cultural tendencies can be detected in different ways from the realistic media representations of death which are bound to the dominating cultural understanding of it.

Second, because in living dead films death is present at multiple levels, they should not be overlooked in death studies. Death is visible in the events of death, the themes of the films and, most importantly, in the main monsters on which the narration focuses. The living dead embody death in their presence and their most important feature is a culturally unnatural relationship to death. They are socially recognized as dead, yet they are at least physically animated. Their transgressing corporeality contradicts modern death by threatening the biological definitions of death, but more importantly, the liminal state of the undead challenges the modern understanding of death which supposes that the two spheres – life and death – can and should be separated and kept apart with the help of knowledge, science and professionals. These films represent the return of that which has been repressed. The undead's existence cannot be explained with reason or science; instead, they are unexpected, magical even. Thus, in these films, the mere existence of undead monsters, the sources of both chaos and fascination, challenge the limits of modern death. Therefore, it is of crucial importance to analyse the ways in which these films invite American audiences to conceptualize death.

In this study, my hypothesis is that American living dead films portray the change from modern and alienated death to the revival of death, and further, I argue that these films have not only reacted to, but also actively participated in the sociocultural change in death-related attitudes and values. The films' repetitive structures of producing death-related experiences and the ways in which the films have relentlessly challenged the possibilities and limits of modern death have heralded and encouraged the major cultural change from the marginalization to the revival of death.

1.2. The Material: Living Dead Films

The medium-specific features of cinema enable us to fantasize and experience death in effective ways; films imagine, define and give a visible and audible form or shape to death. Death has been one of the key themes in horror films, and because their intention is to cause fear, death is most often constructed as monstrous and horrifying. The genre takes its name from the Latin *horrere*, 'to bristle' or 'to shudder', and this, as Anna Powell (2005: 8) notes, highlights the affective dimension of the horror genre. A film is a horror film if it aims (and succeeds) to cause horror in the viewer. The chosen themes, motifs and aesthetics are always bound to the viewer's experience.

This disposition where horror's recognizable features are connected to the genre's intentions as opposed to its attributes can be labelled as the 'dominant feature' of horror. Steve Neale argues for naming the dominant features, because genres cannot be defined in any other way than at this basic and descriptive level. Even the most formulaic and generic story can only repeat a certain amount of all the possible conventions of each genre (Neale 2000: 220). In the horror genre, the aim is to generate terror, frequently with narrative techniques that rely on anxiety, shocks and special effects. The macabre themes, the probing of taboos, fears and the unknown, as well as pushing the limits of what is 'normal' and accepted, and the use of certain iconography and monsters generate the genre's discursive repertoire. However, there is no single film that could possibly include all the different dimensions in one and the same story. As David J. Russell (1998: 234–38) claims, no one convention can define the horror genre by itself, because the genre is a combination of these.

The dominant feature of horror encourages the films' contribution to shocking and culturally controversial issues, such as violence and death. The use of terrifying effects also entails that dying is rarely a natural, beautiful or peaceful transition from life to death.

Rather, the conventions of the genre frame dying in an exaggeratedly dystopic manner, representing it as unnatural, disturbing and violent. Such deaths do not reflect or directly imitate the everyday reality of viewers; what they offer are dramatic and narrated spectacles. They rather reflect and imitate the cinema's and the genre's own history of expressing death (see also Cawelti 2004: 153–54; Grønstad 2003: 74–79; Leffler 2000: 197–227, 262–64).

At the same time, these films are part of a culture, and their meanings are negotiated in relation to society. Christine Gledhill, for example, writes more generally that genre films tend to repeat generic motifs over and over again – compare this to horror's repeated death – and by doing so they create dialogism over the topic, providing struggles over the understanding of the topic in changing sociocultural contexts (Gledhill 2000: 238). Similarly, the unabated balancing of horror films on the fine line between terrifying yet fictitious death and socially acceptable uses of death imagery demands constant re-evaluation of death-related values and practices.

I will approach this struggle with the notion of death through an examination of American living dead films, paying particular attention to the films' monster characters – vampires, mummies and zombies. These characters are located on the borderline of the living and the dead, threatening the living through their very existence. It is not an unproblematic task to define the living dead precisely, as there are multiple cinematic characters that are former humans but whose unnatural relationship to dying and death has turned them into appalling and unnatural creatures. Some definitional limits can, nevertheless, be set for the living dead as a certain kind of monster in the horror genre. I will return to this task in more detail in Chapter 2, but as a starter, Richard Greene and K. Silem Mohammed (2006: xiv) define the undead as 'corporeal beings who are physically or mentally dead, but are in some way not "at rest"'.

The living dead make a rewarding object for the study of death-related values because not only do they symbolize the threat of death but their grotesque corporeality also embraces and embodies it in a most concrete and impressive way. Indeed, as a medium, cinema does more than discuss death-related issues: it shows them. The technological nature of the filmic medium takes advantage of the sensual aspects of death and dying. Death is embraced both at the story level and by giving it an affective visual and audible form. The medium-specificity of cinema highlights death's corporeal dimensions. In modern zombie films, for example, the detailed disintegration of the body has become an important part of the dying process – screams accompanying body parts being torn off and entrails falling on the ground. Death is not simply a theme, as it inextricably intertwines with the films' material-technological aspects. Embodied images make death an integral part of the embodied cinematic experience.

I will concentrate on American genre films, not because I wish to suggest the originality or superiority of Hollywood films, but because Hollywood's genre system is perhaps the best known and most influential, and even if American horror films' primary audience is national, these films also make up the genre's international mainstream. Death, as represented in American films, clearly participates in the negotiation over death not only in the United States, but also elsewhere.

Since the First World War, Hollywood (including its horror films) has had a leading market position in Western countries. In addition to the internationally distributed products, Hollywood films are often produced internationally as well, and Hollywood has attracted film-makers, screenwriters, stories and shooting locations from different parts of the world. On top of this, American audiences are far from homogenous, with a mix of different cultural, ethnic and national backgrounds. It can also be argued, as Barry Keith Grant does, that it is these culturally complex audience and production constructions that make American genre films interesting. The formulaic audiovisual stories have gathered wide audiences despite differences of language, nationality, geographical area and class. In this sense, genre films can be seen to serve as an ideal melting pot of American culture where perceptions of what American culture constitutes are transmitted and transformed (Grant 2007: 5).

Norman K. Denzin argues further that the United States is a cinematic society in that the cinematic imagination has become an organic element of the country's societal fabric. The popularity of cinema makes it not only a commercial institution but also a collective and socially shared self-reflection of society (Denzin 1995: 14–34). This is an interesting claim if we take into consideration the complex and pluralistic American sociocultural contexts. Still, the United States presents itself and acts as a nation, and as a nation it participates in the creation of a cultural community and shared narratives, or at least shared processes in the creation of public opinion. Similarly, while Hollywood can present a certain image of American death, it does not reflect the sociocultural contexts as such, because there is no homogenous American way of death, rather a diversity of death-related values and practices (see, for example, Corr & Corr 2003: 39).

I have selected vampires, mummies and zombies, the three most common and most recognized undead characters of Hollywood films, to represent the question of death-related issues and discussion. As I study the historical change in relation to modern death, I have chosen films from different eras. I will refer to five different Hollywood periods: early horror films (c. 1908–29), classical period (c. 1930–49), transitional period (c. 1950–75), post-classical period (c. 1975–94) and digital period (c. 1995 onwards). Although I discuss several films, I have chosen set films for closer analysis of each monster – vampire, mummy and zombie – from sound-film eras (classical, transitional, post-classical and digital).

As early horror films rarely included undead figures, this period is excluded from my study. The undead characters did visit the silent screens of the United States and elsewhere, but horror films were more or less isolated productions before the sound era. The best-known early horror films came from Germany, including the influential undead film *Nosferatu* (1922), but this period also included some American short films and silent films. Many were fantasies or comedies of such undead characters as mummies and vampires. The living dead features became part of the horror genre with the advent of sound, at the same time as the ideals of modern death became rooted in American culture.

Films from the 1930s are the first widely spread cinematic versions of vampires, mummies and zombies. From the classical period, I have chosen Tod Browning's *Dracula* (1931), Karl Freund's *The Mummy* (1932) and Victor Halper's *White Zombie* (1932). To be able to explore the changing genre conventions in both reception and production, I have taken *The Return of Dracula* (1958) by Paul Landres, Edward L. Cahn's *Curse of the Faceless Man* (1958) and George Romero's *Night of the Living Dead* (1968). The post-classical period exploits the earlier horror stories while also challenging the horror genre's boundaries and traditions: Frank Agrama's *Dawn of the Mummy* (1981), Dan O'Bannon's *The Return of the Living Dead* (1985) and Francis Ford Coppola's *Bram Stoker's Dracula* (1992). And last, the digital films, which introduce new digital aesthetics to Hollywood and focus on market synergies and the branding of films, include Stephen Sommer's *The Mummy* (1999), Paul W.S. Anderson's *Resident Evil* (2002) and Catherine Hardwicke's *Twilight* (2008).

The chosen films include both well-known and B productions. They show horror's internal tension: a repetitious tradition finds the occasional big-budget film and produces a bigger bang for the themes of the genre. The films are also in one way or another connected. They tap into discussions with earlier folklore and literature traditions of the undead, and build on a repetition of films with the same topic. These films can, therefore, be considered to be adaptations, remakes or comments. Scott A. Lukas and John Marmysz, for example, argue that the cinematic remaking, repetition and recreation take advantage of technological innovations, but even more importantly, that they react to cultural changes. The cultural need and desire to repeat certain stories, formulas and themes reveals the existence of such timeless issues as death, but every new version, even the 'bad' or 'not-too-interesting' versions, imply that a desire has arisen to rework and negotiate these issues within this genre with other cultural products and with society (Lukas & Marmysz 2009: 2–5, 12, 16). Similarly, I will approach the individual films from the premise that the different characters and films provide repetition and recreation, which makes comparison all the more interesting. And, yet, these characters and films emphasize certain new dimensions in their relationship to death and in the ways they address death for the viewer.

Comparing the similarities and differences of vampires, mummies and zombies is an opportunity to identify some more general features and interesting contradictions in the broader cinematic context of negotiation and representation of death. As the society and generations of viewers have changed, so the living dead films produced over the decades have changed as well, and with every new film, negotiations over death have been made and remade in their generic, narrative and sociocultural contexts.

1.3. Theoretical Departure Points: Understanding Textual and Generic Addressing

My study of how modern death is addressed in living dead films is informed by two major theoretical and methodological sources: post-classical narratology and socio-semiotic understanding of genre. Post-classical narratology offers a model of textual spectatorship and complements this viewpoint with a perspective into analysing the addressing of death at the level of film narration. Genre theory accounts for the ways in which formulaic films, of which horror films are claimed to be a prime example (Clover 1992: 212), create standardized yet constantly evolving models for communicating certain themes, such as death. Despite the differences in their theoretical premises and ambitions, these approaches overlap in several questions raised in this study. They approach films through the films' semiotic elements and they also widen the perspective from aesthetic and representational questions to encompass issues of the communicative aspects and social implications of cinema.

The narratological theories give insights into the ways cultural narratives and their specific elements are constructed. Where the formalist/structuralist approaches of classical narratology pay attention to the narrative form, techniques and elements, post-classical narratology concentrates on the contextual elements of the narrative: its goals, reception strategies, the viewer's role and different sociocultural contexts (see, for example, Prince 2008: 115–21). However, in cases where the structural and formalist approaches are separated from the narratives, the post-classical approach to narratology has been criticized for simplifying and emptying the concept of narration in ways that assimilate into other approaches and discourses (Kindt 2009: 44; Prince 2008: 122; Chatman 1990: 309–23). The structural elements of the narrative, or how stories are narrated, need to be included in the post-classical approaches, even though the emphasis would be on the communicative and contextual dimensions.

In my analysis, I will refer to concepts of classical narratology, such as narrative perspective or character construction, but I will deploy these to study the themes of death, not to describe the content of the films as such. Similarly, Ansgar Nünning argues that classical narratology offers field-tested analytical tools to which post-classical narratology adds contextual meanings. This shifts narratology from content description to vital contributions to the different cultural and interdisciplinary debates (such as understandings of death) (Nünning 2009: 52–56, 60–63).

Furthermore, post-classical narratology is not a unified field but an area of multiple approaches. Mine is a cultural approach where narration is considered a way of dealing with human experiences. For example, Mieke Bal argues that the narrative should not be seen solely as a selection of semiotic objects that can be arranged in certain ways. Instead, it has a role as a cultural and discursive phenomenon (Bal 1999: 9, 14, 222). Her cultural studies approach highlights narratives as active cultural modes and forces which work beyond fiction, too, and provide wider cultural models for making sense of experiences. Accordingly, I will ask how the narration of living dead films fulfils the purpose of encountering death. I will then look into the ways in which these narratives of death participate in death-related cultural processes. Finally, how are the two levels – narrative purposes and cultural processes – linked through the process of textual addressing of American living dead films?

Because of this combination of semiotic, communicative and social questions, my approach can be described as rhetorical, in the footsteps of such scholars as Seymour Chatman and Wayne C. Booth. Booth, for instance, defines rhetoric fairly broadly as 'the entire range of resources that human beings share for producing effects on one another'. Rhetoric can thus be applied to all fields, so long as the methods and goals of communication processes constitute the core of the study (Booth 2004: xi). For his part, Michael Kearns contends that rhetoric is interested in the 'interaction between text and audience', in how the text works as an act of communication and how textual elements affect the audience. His rhetorical approach brings into the spotlight how the receiver should 'take the text', as opposed to just focusing on what the story's cultural effects are (Kearns 1999: 2–18). Similarly, by approaching the rhetoric of death in living dead films, I intend to highlight the communicative elements of these film texts.

Film is never an empty spatial structure – it actively engages in the process of signification in its technological apparatus and viewer orientation. Films are both viewed objects and subjects that offer themselves to be viewed. As such, the film text always presupposes a viewer and requires an embodied response (see also Williams 1995: 9; Sobchack 1995: 37; Dixon 1995: 2–7). There are several analytical labels to describe the process whereby a film text presupposes the existence of a viewer – and not just any actual viewer, as Franco Casetti (1998: 46) says, but the possibility of one. These labels include positioning, point-of-view and enunciation, but I prefer to use the term 'addressing' because it includes a component of activity: addressing is not in itself a textual position, but refers to a shifting process between multiple possible positions offered for the viewer. This approach combines film with the dynamics of reception.

Addressing thus pertains to the multi-staged and dynamic process in which text prescribes meanings in medium- and genre-related ways, invites viewers to read these meanings, and also assumes certain responses and experiences (see also Frow 2006: 72–76; Ridell 1998: 127–28; Mayne 1995: 157; Casetti 1998: 9, 44). Moreover, Irene Kacandes defines 'address' as a narrative act that identifies the receiver. This direct recognition of the viewer also demands the receiver to become involved in the narration, and invites the receiver to experience the events at a personal and emotional level (Kacandes 2005: 4–5). Addressing is tied to the ways in which the film both imagines and offers itself to the viewer without determining a priori the readings and experiences of an actual viewer. It foregrounds the rhetorical communicativeness of films and emphasizes the role of film texts as central parts of this communication. Here, addressing hence refers to the processes by which the living dead film texts invite viewers to read out and embody the articulated death-related meanings and experiences in certain preferred, or suggested, ways.

We can dissect the communicative specificity of film texts by using Stuart Hall's well-known and influential encoding/decoding model. Hall formulated his model as an answer to the critique of rather linear understandings of communication. Contrary to linear designs of 'sender–message–receiver' structures, he does not assume that encoded and decoded messages are the same. Rather, the effects of decoded meanings cannot be dictated, although some preferred or dominating meanings can be proposed. The actual viewers have, in principle, the power to choose from among the available meanings according to their background, competences, uses and gratifications, or even to oppose the offered meanings altogether (Hall 2001: 166–75).

Similarly, the encoding of meanings in films is guided by Hollywood's production practices, modes and technologies, as well as by cultural and genre conventions. Moreover, encoding decisions do not exclude intertextual elements, or extra-textual factors such as age limits, distribution strategies, advertisement and institutional criticism, which touch the expectations both film-makers and viewers have of genre films. Furthermore, sometimes, encoded meanings can also be contradictory. They can be used to create – intentionally, accidentally, intertextually or because of a historical perspective or genre hybridization – confusion to the text, which challenges the addressing modes. The uncertainty is a source of ambivalence and presupposes an active spectatorship even at the textual level. In decoding, the viewers also have internalized generic conventions and cultural contexts. Instead of speaking of any dominant position, then, the viewing processes are fluid with negotiated meanings and multiple positions (see also Landsberg 2009: 223–24; Mayne 1995: 172–75).

Understood in this multidimensional manner, Hall's encoding–decoding model assumes a viewer who is actively engaged in the decoding. Thus, already the understanding of a textual viewer presupposes an active viewer. The viewer is needed to complement the film in the process of cinematic circulation of meanings. The same idea of complementing is evident in one of the most pervasive models of narratology, the Russian formalists' classification between *syuzhet* (discourse) and *fabula* (story). *Syuzhet* is the 'how' of the story, how it is presented and expressed through narration and other discursive strategies in the film material, while *fabula* is the chronological reading of the events and cause–effect chains put together by the viewer. The story can be seen as a product of the viewer's active participation which is cued by the film material (Bordwell 1985: 49–57; Bal 1999: 5–7; Chatman 1978: 9). Although these terms have been translated into English in many different ways, I have adopted Seymour Chatman's concepts of discourse and story, mostly because of his rhetorical emphasis of the division. His 'discourse' gives prominence to the expressiveness of narrative elements. Chatman (1978: 9, 19, 37, 43) contends that in the communication process of the (generic) narrative, the discourse is the performance and the story is the abstract level to be read out of that performance. This separation between story and discourse is meaningful in analysing the film/viewer relationship, because it reminds us that the film material itself is not the story, but the story must be read out of it (see also Smith 1995: 74; Ryan 2004: 9).

Several reception studies, including those made within the field of cultural studies, have been interested in how an actual viewer creates the story from the discourse, but my emphasis is on how the text invites the viewer to read itself and how the text, as part of this addressing activity, proposes the story to be created in reception. Drawing on Hall's understanding of his model, Seija Ridell (1998: 127–31) argues that audience members may interpret the text in diverse ways, but they are not able to control how the text is constructed as an industrially produced object. Or, following Dennis Giles (1984: 38–39), the 'final' meaning in this negotiation process is neither wholly identical to the one encoded in the film by the producers nor a completely individual experience. Instead, as a shared experience with other viewers ('imagined community'), the film experiences enter the public domain.

In short, both the encoding–decoding model and the tension between story and discourse presume that there are certain meanings built into the text that are suggested as primary for the viewers and introduced into public debate. In the living dead films, the relationships with deaths are not random, but the death scenes in horror texts suggest certain experiences, emotions and interpretations over some others. However, the horror genre, in particular, plays on expectations of confusion and doubtfulness, and it doubles as part of the film experience and cinematic narrative constructs. David Punter (1996: 117) captures my point: these films can 'use images of terror to provoke powerful tensions between different interpretations'. The narration of living dead films can quite freely provide alternating, contradictory and even ideologically (or morally) questionable positions. Yvonne Leffler presents the complementing view that in the horror genre, where unrealistic and often violent images can overwhelm the viewer, the whole communication process depends on the viewer's generic knowledge and skills. At the same time, the generic competences help the viewer to keep in mind the constructed nature of the material presented (Leffler 2000: 236). A horror film can, therefore, intentionally offer several and even conflicting or uncomfortable positions to choose from.

After all, films within the same genre not only share certain conventional themes and narrative structures, but they also use similar strategies of addressing, which means that their social implications can be gainfully compared. The offered reception modes of the horror genre invites its viewers to participate in specific communities, whether imagined or real, and enables communal negotiations over understandings and expectations of the genres themselves (see also Altman 1999: 158–65; Ridell 1998: 130–31). It is not for nothing that living dead films keep returning to questions of death. By standardizing their generic narration, the films end up using similar strategies of addressing death for their viewers. As Seija Ridell and John Frow maintain, it is, therefore, important to notice the societal force implicated in the genres' addressivity. The structural relationship established through the generic mode of address is reciprocally linked to the single elements included in the genres. Generic addressing does, indeed, generate through textual elements, and textual elements become socially forceful because of their generic mode (Ridell 1998: 131; Frow 2006: 72–75, 102, 129).

As a concept, 'genre' enables comparisons between different films with similar features, such as the living dead films which deal with death-related topics, embodiments and experiences of death. However, the classificatory dimension of genre does not alone provide the whole picture of the concept and its analytical potential. For example, in the case of horror films, it is difficult to find an adequate definition that would allow the dynamic, historical and changing manifestations of genre while still maintaining some of the notion's classificatory uses. Purely classificatory uses of the concept easily end up simplifying the dimensions and functions of genre. I therefore agree with Frow, who argues that individual films do not belong to genres, but rather participate in generic processes (even in several genres at once). Films use generic processes for some purpose and formulate genres (Frow 2006: 2, 28). Each and every new living dead film takes part in its genre by negotiating the meaning of both death and the cinematic manner of its cultural representation, and by inviting the viewers to join in the negotiation. This invites an alternative definition of genre: more than a classification system, genre is cultural practice. This broader and more dynamic view incorporates the classificatory function but emphasizes social and historical processes where industrial mechanisms, genre aesthetics and cultural forms of signification are formulated in relation to one another.

Also, socially and semiotically inclined thinking on genre makes provision for the sociocultural and historical contexts where these negotiations over genre boundaries, genre-related meanings and generic addressing take place (Neale 1995: 180; Moine 2008: xvi, 166; Jenkins & Karnick 1995: 8–9). Genre theory thus brings to the fore not only the shared characteristics and conventions recognized and negotiated by both production and reception, but also gives prominence to an individual genre's sociocultural dimensions and processes in history, emphasizing that films participate in the constant making of the genre and its role in society (Moine 2008: 63–65, 71; Gledhill 2000: 241).

Within cinema studies, the dynamic and processual viewpoint to genre has been well developed by Rick Altman (1995, 1999), Steve Neale (1995, 2000) and Richard Maltby (2003). They have insisted on genre as a communicative process in which meanings are built into and read out of the text. While their approach to genre is textual and semiotic, it nevertheless stresses historically varied textual structures in the communication process. They all discuss how changes in the production practices have affected the fictive world of each genre, how an individual genre's strategic goals are visible in the textual (semiotic) structures of films and how these structures are signalled to the historically specific audiences. Also, several other theorists have stressed genre's nature as a process in which the film text, production and audiences participate (for example, Tudor 1989: 5–6; Grant 1995: 115; Gledhill 2000: 223; Frow 2006: 10; Moine 2008: 89–92).

In this study, I will use the socio-semiotic understanding of genre, because the dynamics of genre-specific address – or, more briefly, addressing – can be identified as overlapping with all three dimensions at some point. Addressing functions at the textual level, but it gravitates towards reception, which is both presupposed in the text and guides its construction. It should be stressed that textual presupposing and actual meaning making can differ from each other. In any case, because of the overlapping of texts, reception, production and sociocultural contexts, the question of generic addressing opens up an intriguing world on the relationship between the horror film's spectatorship and cinematic-specific textual constructions of death.

One way of approaching the rhetorically created, maintained and non-determining relationship between genres and their audiences is through the terms of standardization and differentiation. These derive from analysis of Hollywood's studio system, describing how Hollywood has an enduringly recognizable style and a rather stable construction of production and ideological practices while, at the same time, it adapts to new situations and ideas (Bordwell, Staiger & Thompson 1996: 88, 97). Genre films are part of this very process. The standardization of genre formulas enables studios to produce formulaic films cost-efficiently, helps genre narration break the general causal structures of Hollywood narration and concentrate instead on the dominant features of a certain genre, and assists the viewer in interpreting genre films. For its part, differentiation makes it possible to individualize products (with new monsters, for example) and try out innovations within more or less stable formulas (Grant 2007: 8–11; Ryall 1998: 328; Jenkins & Karnick 1995: 10–11).

The dual dynamic of standardization and differentiation can explain how the makers of genre films are able to choose from a wide array of conventions and even expand these traditions. John Cawelti links the idea of constant play with repetitions and exceptions to the sociocultural uses of genres: the viewer must recognize the film's form which corresponds to their expectations and provides emotional security with the repetitive and predictable modes. Genres also have to permit some alterations to keep up with social and cultural changes, which guarantees that the formulas are not totally static (Cawelti 1976: 6–9, 35–36).

Standardization and differentiation are integral to the process of connecting the living dead films to wider society and culture. By conventionalizing certain aspects of death – notably the predisposition to alienate death in narration – the living dead films, in fact, emphasize the cultural meanings of modern death. However, through continuous differentiation and search for an original filmic expression, these films provide options to alienating death and thereby challenge the role of modern death as well. They not only respond to changes in death-related attitudes, but they can also challenge or comment on death-related sociocultural practices.

The commenting is interestingly pronounced in the horror genre, because it has more flexible possibilities for commentary than most other Hollywood products (Neroni 2005: 27; Wood 1984: 171–72). Despite their occasional popularity, horror genre films are not part of the mainstream, and their repertory of generic conventions includes chaos and ambivalence. Certain experimenting is, therefore, allowed, enabling the crossing of cultural borders, different definitions and new perceptions of death. In fact, every new living dead film renegotiates genre boundaries, including some features of death and excluding others, and expands the generic understanding of death with new features. This constant negotiation with standardized practices of how death is represented and the adjustments to different sociocultural situations and conventions of both production and reception (such as censorship requirements) make living dead films a powerful part of cultural and historical processes of death.

As both encoded and decoded messages are part of the struggle and negotiation over meanings and genre boundaries, including struggles and negotiations over modern death in the living dead films, it makes sense to take a closer look at the film texts in the middle of these processes. I will, therefore, analyse how the film text engages with the struggle over death-related values and attitudes and how it suggests a relationship with the viewer. However, my analysis should not, therefore, be read as an attempt to explain any actual viewer's experiences, but rather as a mapping of the possibilities offered to an actual viewer by the text.

Through the selected examples, I will ask how modern death is addressed for (horror) audiences in the American living dead films and how this addressing has changed over the decades. Before turning to the analysis of the films made in each era – classical, transition, post-classical and digital – I will examine the typical features of living dead films. These typical features, or modalities, provide the basic understanding of why vampire, mummy and zombie films should and could be studied together. I will discuss the typical characteristics of the undead, their generic uses in the film narration and the symbolical meanings they often encourage. In addition, I will look at the ways death is used as part of narration in living dead films, or in other words, how death events function as narrative turning points and give some form or structure to death and dying. Later on, I will use these modalities to compare the films from different eras and discuss how they have been used in the processes of standardization and differentiation. By comparing films from the classical, transition, post-classical and digital eras, I will study the evolving processes of living dead films, their generic addressing and the ways in which (modern) death has been negotiated and offered for viewers to interpret. This will show how American living dead films have contributed to the negotiating and challenging of modern death, and how they have invited their viewers to do so, too.

Chapter 2

Modality of Living Death

We have no reliable information of death as an experience. For example, Zygmunt Bauman (1992: 2–4) argues that while it is the most trustworthy experience in human life, death still remains inexplicable and unknown. People, therefore, need to encounter the death experience in other ways, such as by watching and following the death of others, as well as with the help of fiction, imagining how it will feel. Living dead films explore the dimensions of violent, physical, and horrifying death by both articulating and deconstructing death at the level of cinematic expression and by placing the expressions of death at the core of the audience's experience and reception. As a vampire in *The Return of Dracula* (1958) promises: 'There is only one reality, Rachel. Death. I have come to bring you death, a living death.'

Such an exploration of possible relationships with death can be called genre modality, which refers to the different expressed cultural meanings and aesthetic articulations of a genre. Paul Simpson defines modality as a 'capacity to shape narrative worlds – and its potential to produce stories'. Modality thus connotes the idea of possible worlds and the ways in which different patterns of modality are used differently in varied genres (Simpson 2005: 313). Living dead films respond to one kind of cultural task in relation to encountering death or, because 'fear and denial' are still part of the American 'collective attitude about death and dying', as McIlwain (2005: 10) argues, the horror film's approach to negotiating with death has preserved its importance. Indeed, the horror genre, and within it living dead films, have concentrated on perfecting the cinematic expression of violent death and the depiction of the dying process.

Living dead films' affective, physical and experiencing relationship to death works the traditions of death not only for their own generic uses, but for other films and other genres as well. The specific articulations perfected by a genre can be borrowed by other genres and other media as well, when a need for a certain effect and expression arises (Frow 2006: 75; Gledhill 2000: 229, 232–36, 240; Hallet 2009: 129, 149). This borrowing further increases the sociocultural importance of the genres. As Paul Watson argues, a film genre's power lies in its intertextual relationships, not in any individual practices. Any film genre is a 'metaphorical' process that explores specific dimensions of cinematic expression (Watson 2007: 110–20, 124–26). The ways in which living dead films (and other horror films) create models of terrifying death and dying can be employed in other media images, too, and the recognizable form of these images provides viewers with familiar social experiences, embodied sensations and moral perceptions. This process is visible also in those living dead films that transgress the limits of the horror genre. For example, the digital film

The Mummy (1999) combines horror to action and adventure film conventions, and *Twilight* (2008) mixes horror characters with romance. As genre hybrids, even these films continue to debate with the horror genre's understanding of death and dying, and they open the genre's death-related values and attitudes for different audiences as well.

When death is understood as one of the central modalities of living dead films, its intertextual and sociocultural influence is heightened. It is precisely this that makes it important to study how this modality is communicated to audiences. In living dead films, death creates a thematic or symbolical dimension, and it is embodied by the undead characters to whom other characters react, as well as acted out in death scenes throughout the story. In this way, living dead films are constantly conscious of the presence of death. Catharine Russell refers to this kind of continuing presence of death with the term 'narrative mortality', which describes death's narrative and discursive role in Western fiction. She argues that although in many films death is used to bring meaning for the story by providing a beginning, an ending or both, narrative mortality is more than just formalist perceptions of death. Narrative mortality is an allegorical structure or constant consciousness of death that involves 'the return or the repressed fear of death', which has been highlighted especially in the films of the late twentieth century (Russell 1995: 2–7). Similarly, in living dead films, death is constructed centrally in narration and made present at multiple levels.

First, death is constructed at the level of discourse or, as Altman (1987: 336–37) phrases it, at the level of immediate spectatorship where cinematic techniques are used to engage the viewer with the characters and events. Narratological theories construct characters as important elements of narrative films not only because of their functions and actions, but also because of their personal essence, and events as building blocks of the plot, defined as changes of state, or transitions from one state to another (Bal 1999: 5; Chatman 1978: 43–44, 111–13). Death, too, is a veritable change in state, a transformation from one kind of being to another kind of being or non-being, and as with any narrative element, death happens in a certain place and at a certain time. Consequently, as a narrative event, death both affects the characters (and viewers) and leads the story in a certain direction.

Second, the symbolic meanings are another important dimension of death-related addressing. Symbolic spectatorship is founded on the story level and remains as an actual viewer's reading of the text, as his/her individual decoding process. In Altman's (1987: 336–37) terms, analysing the implied symbolic spectatorship may help to explain how the viewer can interpret often generically conventionalized, recurring and cumulative sociocultural problems in the text. After all, symbolic readings of living dead films are not random. Because they are founded on the discursive level, on generic uses of death events and undead characters, they can also generate socially shared or debated meanings. Both characters and events play an important role in the embedding of symbolic references, but symbolic spectatorship crosses the limits between text and reality. The addressing of death-related symbolism invites the viewer to participate in the negotiation over these meanings. It is through this process that living dead films attempt to force viewers to realize their viewing position and participation in the cinematic and cultural processes.

In the following section, I will discuss how living dead films have created death-related modalities at the level of characters, events and symbolic dimensions. First, I will argue that the living dead are embodiments of death who make both other characters and viewers react to them, often in a way where other characters' reactions signify an exemplary relationship to death. Second, I will emphasize that in living dead films, death events are important narrative turning points where different types of deaths create models of modern dying processes. Furthermore, the ways in which death events are either hidden from or revealed to the viewer create a style of images and movements that construct (violent) death. By doing so, living dead films can provide fantasies of death for the viewer to experience and understand something that is/has been hidden in and rejected from the legitimate cultural sphere. Third, I will argue that in living dead films, death and its embodiments are used to express different social values and cultural allegories. By emphasizing certain dimensions of death more than others, these films offer different interpretative dimensions of death for viewers. In living dead films then, the modalities are related to (horrifying) death, and the generic commentary takes place through characters, events and allegories.

2.1. Embodying Death

The film characters offer important positions for the viewer to attach to the story. For example, Murray Smith (1995: 18) contends that the viewer's "'entry into" narrative structures is mediated by character'. This viewpoint leads to the hypothesis that if characters are important entries into the film text, they are also an important means of addressing the viewer. If death can be confronted and experienced by watching the deaths and responses of others, then the possibilities of engaging with different and multiple character positions invite the viewer to try out varied and even conflicting positions related to death. There are two prime positions of modelling and experiencing death through the characters of living dead films: through the undead, who both embody death and represent the existence and the threat of death in diverse and (partially monster-)specific ways, and through the living, whose relationships to the undead reflect multiple attitudes towards death.

The relationships between viewers and characters should be seen as an engagement where the viewer imagines the character's situation and emotions, but does not necessarily adopt them or experience exactly the same emotions. The term 'engagement' makes it possible to recognize several different processes (not just 'identification' – a term often used in film studies) that take place between viewer and different characters. Smith recognizes such phases of engagement as recognition, alignment and allegiance. Here, 'recognition' applies to the ways in which the characters are structured for the viewer's engagement. He argues that the characters' physicality presents a body to which both iconic and indexical meanings can be attached. The existence of any character already provides some sort of embodiment of the film's thematic motifs. Second, 'alignment' refers to the points of view which the film offers for a viewer. The narration and cinematic devices provide different points of access to the different characters and their feelings, thoughts and actions. Although narration can align the viewer with any character, this positioning does not automatically produce empathy or sympathy towards that character. It is, therefore, necessary to differentiate between alignment and allegiance. 'Allegiance' includes a moral evaluation of the characters, as the viewers decide whether they can evaluate a character to be worthy of sympathetic reactions (Smith 1995: 6–20, 73–84, 187–90).

These three more refined dimensions of character engagement also open up more refined avenues to a discussion how living dead films create relationships to death through their characters. First, recognition brings forward how the living dead embody death, how these genre- and monster-specific embodiments create overlapping, comparable and yet multifaceted aspects to the addressing of death-related attitudes and how the viewer can experience different dimensions of death through such embodied thinking. The recognition of the undead relates to the realization of death's continuing existence in the world and provides some insights into the addressing of death to horror audiences. However, the exterior character recognition is a tentative process with many other dimensions, too, affecting the addressing.

At the level of the characters, the viewer is positioned or aligned with several characters through their exterior features, actions, knowledge and emotions. Smith sees such access to the character's point of view as a process where the film guides the viewer's perception through the character's perspectives. Even more so, the film alternates between different perspectives, creating interesting patterns for the viewing process (Smith 1995: 83, 142, 156). While the term 'alignment' is used here, narratological theories often label such focusing action as 'focalization', which takes place when narration is restricted to someone's point of view. Focalization thus selects and channels perception, cognition and emotions (Kuhn 2009: 263; Horstkott 2009: 172; Jahn 2005: 172). Bal further stresses that focalization is a process where someone's vision of something is addressed for a viewer. In other words, when someone is allowed to narrate or present reactions to the events, this selection addresses the nature of both the character and the object of his/her focalization (Bal 1999: 142–50). The complexity of changing narrative viewpoints creates an effective means of addressing different reactions to death, when attention shifts from one scene and one character to multiple scenes and characters within a movie, and the viewer may also have a certain character he/she prefers over others.

Although alignment, or focalization, is often connected to the positive characters of the story, the position of the monster is also available and even underlined in certain scenes. Such different positions are important because they have different functions. In horror films, as Leffler (2000: 159) argues, positive characters are intended to represent how to react to threat (death) and how to encounter threatening situations, whereas the monsters represent primitive, threatening and uncontrollable facets of humanity. In fact, Daniel Shaw (2003: 11) claims that this potential for dual alignment – of trying out different positions and perspectives in the battle for mastery between the human and the monstrous, between life and death – is a source of pleasure for the viewer of horror.

The difference between alignment and allegiance makes it possible to observe why horror films also present the monsters' point of view to certain events, although the monsters rarely provide morally positive entries to the story. The viewer can experience emotions triggered by death through other characters and this experience can be made more complex if or when the monsters' vantage point is included in the experience. Through a more complex relationship with the viewer, these films force the viewer to evaluate death-related practices from multiple and even contradictory perspectives.

Furthermore, the relationships between viewers and characters are not only cognitive experiences of recognition and moral evaluation, but also embodied, affective and sensual. The phenomenological trend in film and horror studies has called attention to the affective and material relationship between film text and viewer, where materiality of the film calls for bodily reactions and challenges the ideas of physical passivity (see, for example, Sobchack 2008: 196–97; Shaviro 1993: 59–61). Most notably, the theories of Gilles Deleuze (1989: 139) have encouraged affective readings, apparent in his formulation of the film/viewer relationship: 'power to affect and be affected'. Following in Deleuze's footsteps, Anna Powell argues that the cinematic experience can be understood as embodied thinking. While horror films often affect human bodies, both the bodies and minds of the viewer are threatened as well. Therefore, as Powell indicates, horror films' potential lies with the viewer's incorporated mind/brain/body/text and transformation with the image (Powell 2005: 110–16, 201–08). Through these transformations, living dead films, too, provide multiple and varied bodily positions for the viewer to both conceptualize and experience death.

Living dead films, whose stories and narrations revolve around monsters, make the undead the most important means for the addressing of death. While not all horror films depend on monster centrality, living dead films appear to do so. They all have such central monsters as vampires, mummies and zombies, and they create a threat which calls for a reaction by the other characters. For example, not only have monsters given their names or marketing edge to the films in my study, but also the very openings of the films already highlight their centrality. *The Mummy* (1932) unfolds with an archaeological set of the mummy's corpse coming alive again; the first thing that *The Return of Dracula* (1958) does is introduce Dracula by voice-over accompanied with an image of an empty grave, whereas *Night of the Living Dead* (1968) opens on a graveyard, where the leading lady is being attacked by a zombie. In these films, narration starts from the locations where the dead are stored and whence they unexpectedly return. The post-classical and digital films, in particular, are more curious about the birth of their monsters: *Bram Stoker's Dracula* (1992) invites the viewer to witness Dracula's past and transformation, and *The Mummy* (1999) opens with a prolonged sequence of ancient Egypt and the mummification of the future monster.

Living dead films, then, typically start with acknowledging the monsters and their undead state. For example, the local driver of *White Zombie* (1932) argues that 'they (zombies) are not men, they are dead bodies'. The reactions and recognitions spotlight the monstrousness of these walking corpses and also provide clues of the characters' fear, cringing in terror at the undead monsters. They invite the viewers to share their experiences. In this sense, the films accord with Noël Carroll's influential horror identification theory, where horror is marked by the characters' emotions towards the monster. Through identification processes, the characters' emotions work as mediators between the film text and a viewer's experience. Quite plainly, horror seeks to horrify the viewer, and the ways in which the other characters react to the monster create the appropriate emotions for the horror genre – horror, terror and disgust (Carroll 1990: 16–17, 60–86). The undead figures of living dead films elicit certain responses from the characters, and it is these reactions that mediate the death-related attitudes and values to the viewer.

Carroll's idea has been particularly influential because it emphasizes that viewers are not afraid of monsters as such, but rather they fear what these monsters can do to the film characters. For example, Leffler (2000: 165–66) maintains that the horror genre demands an (actual) viewer's participation and emotional commitment to characters: the viewer is encouraged to share the feelings of the characters and worry about their fates. Then, the characters carry possibilities for mediating an experience of horror. In a rather similar way, several other writers have argued that this engagement enables emotional and social learning in teaching how to respond to depicted situations, such as encounters with death. The constructed positions in the text may thus provide such perspectives and attitudes to death which viewers would not encounter in their everyday lives, and the films can give birth to an understanding of rejected or difficult issues, such as violence or death (Gaut 1999: 213–16; Cohen 2001: 246, 249, 259; Landsberg 2009: 221–28; Giroux 2002: 5–11).

However, these arguments also have a flip side. The learning and modelling experiences can also be negative. Jonathan Cohen argues that emotional involvement with a film decreases the critical perspective towards it, and may, therefore, increase the film's effect on a viewer. With violence and horror, the effects are not always seen as wholly positive (Cohen 2001: 260). Carroll has sought to avoid this conclusion by stressing that allegiance takes place only with the positive characters. Indeed, the main criticism towards Carroll's theory has questioned the narrow perceptions of available relationships with the characters and the exclusion of monsters as alignment positions (Hills 2003: 143; Knight & McKnight 2003: 213–19). Carroll's premises simplify practices of cinematic experience, making the undead merely triggers of reaction, not characters in their own right. This is problematic, because monsters are not only central characters but also they are often given sympathetic characteristics. Thus, although the living dead can be considered to trigger the characters' mediating and addressing role in the viewing process, the undead themselves are also part of the addressing of death and death-related experiences.

Smith argues that characters, including living dead characters, are always constructions for narrative purposes. Although they can and should be regarded as persons, characters are always abstractions that embody the necessary themes and purposes of a story (Smith 1995: 20). Thus, the monsters are constructed positions, created to cause terror, and also the monstrosity of undead characters is not given, but produced. The genre conventions of living dead films – such as the grotesque features, discursive use of sound effects, anticipative sounds and visual shocks – label living dead characters as monsters. In the addressing of monstrousness for a viewer to recognize, says Jason Grant McKahan (2007: 137), the monster's actual presence or actions are not as important as is their narrative position as monster. This discursive position is dehumanizing and invites the interpretation of the monster as unsympathetic. Because in living dead films the embodiment of threat is a monstrous figure with an intimate connection to death, the dehumanization of the undead also dehumanizes death: the relationship between the undead and death is represented as unnatural.

As cinematic figures, living dead characters provide abstractions and embodiments of death. As Karl S. Guthke (1990: 4, 13) claims, despite multiple alternatives, Western art and folklore have chosen to give the abstract concept of death a human form, to personify death. The living dead are part of this tradition, and death marks not only their existence, but their physical and mental traits as well. Although living dead characters are widely recognized monsters in the horror cavalcade, the term 'living dead films' is not a firmly established subcategory (Waller 1986: 9; Bishop 2006: 201–05; Davies 2005: 146). These characters, including vampires, mummies, golems (such as Frankenstein) and zombies, are more often dealt with separately as appearing in 'vampire films' or 'zombie films'. Yet, they share similar features, including a corporeal crossing of boundaries between life and death. Thus, it makes sense to compare the different undead characters whose similarities and differences introduce new dimensions of undeadness.

The vampires, mummies, zombies and other monsters are known as the living dead or the undead, for they are born when a living person enters death either by dying or reaching a death-like state. Yet, these concepts carry slightly different philosophical meanings. The living dead are reanimated and corporeal figures which are alive after death, while the undead have an unsolved relationship with death. They appear to be dead but have not necessarily died as such. However, in Hollywood films, these terms can be considered if not synonyms at least referring to the same monsters. Many of the films use both terms in their dialogue and advertising, and none of the monsters strictly obey these ontological categories. Some zombies are not re-animated corpses, as they can also be in a death-like state, hypnotized or infected; some vampires have died before their transformation, others have not; some mummies are revived, others are unnaturally kept alive for thousands of years. As K. Silem Mohammed (2006: 91) notes, it is not merely the technical death that makes a person a living dead, but it may be that a person is forced to act as if dead. Similarly, in this study, I use both terms, the living dead and the undead, to refer to these characters who challenge our understanding of death. More generally, I refer to this (sub)genre as living dead films, partly because of its common use, but partly because this label highlights the corporeality and separates these figures from a wider problematic of such post-mortem characters as (immaterial) ghosts.

In other words, living dead films portray undead characters as their central sources of deadly threat. At times, such characters appear in genre hybrids and other genres as well. These films offer interesting intertextual debates between the undead figures of horror and other genres. The debates also highlight the importance of modality or the standardized ways of presenting the living dead in Hollywood. Whereas the horror genre concentrates on death-related images and stories, genre hybrids and other genres, too, can borrow, comment on and challenge these stereotypical images of death. Still, even within the horror genre, there are several different undead forms, and I will concentrate on the three most common characters: mummies, vampires and zombies.

I have chosen these three figures, as they not only embody death, but by definition also challenge and contrast the idea of modern death. They are all magical creatures questioning the rationality of science. In comparison, as a combination of different humans, Frankenstein, for example, discusses the 'possibilities of science', as John Browning and Caroline Picart (2009: xii) argue. Therefore, although Frankenstein is a famous undead creature, I have excluded him from this study, not because I would deny his undead nature, but because he is a creation of a mad scientist and a combination of different humans, instead having an explicit relationship to a certain person. Thus, Frankenstein would introduce rather different questions of modern death than those raised by the three other living dead creatures.

However, mummies, vampires and zombies also articulate a slightly different relationship to death. Their varying histories in folklore, literature, film and other sources, as well as their different character traits, produce crucial diversities. Yet, conventionalized generic narration and the functions of monstrosity create tendencies similar to the ways in which these characters are approached in living dead films. Also, over the years, there has been a great deal of mutual borrowing between the monsters and the films. For example, it appears that the idea of consuming infection was borrowed from vampirism: the zombie's bite and the vampire's kiss cause death in a similar way. Also, the idea of renewing bodies comes from the vampire world. While the digital mummies become younger and less corpse-like figures through consumption of others' bodies, some vampires have, in return, taken to accentuating animality, borrowing the corpse-like appearances and aggressive behaviour codes from zombies, in particular. For example, the vampires in *Priest* (2011) and *Stake Land* (2010) are rather zombie-like creatures, and in the three cinematic adaptations, *The Last Man on Earth* (1964), *The Omega Man* (1971) and *I Am Legend* (2007), based on Richard Matheson's post-apocalyptic novel *I Am Legend* (1954), the monsters resemble either vampires or zombies.

Due to the repertoire of undead characters, from their wide use in different genres, and from the differentiation between different eras and films, it is challenging to define the living dead at a detailed level. For example, even among vampires, the 1930s Dracula is unable to endure daylight, but the vampires of the *Twilight* saga (2008–12) are not limited by the darkness. However, drawing on the three specific monster characters analysed in this study, I have recognized five advisory characteristics of the living dead: transgressing death, unexpectedness, corporeality, consumption and the capability to transform others. Each of the undead characters articulates these five characteristics differently according to their traditions and film-specific discourses. Applications are often comparable, even hybrid at some points, and yet they manage to introduce new points of view to death-related narrations and discourses.

First, the living dead have an unnatural relationship to death in that they refuse to end existing; they refuse to die. What is disturbing in their death or death-like states is that they threaten the existing categories of life and death. For example, Jen Webb and Sam Byrnand (2008: 83, 85) contend that although the zombies – and other living dead for that matter – have many ambivalences, their singular ambivalence is the state of being undead, the way they hold the door slightly open to the other side and refuse to become exiled from community, returning to bite back at humanity and defying social control. This dimension is widely used, not only in twentieth-century cinema, but the undead have transgressed limits in different cultures and times. Western folklore presents the returning dead as horrifying, infectious and barbaric results of failed transition rites (Bell 2013; Barber 1988: 197). Many disciplines, too, such as medicine, politics and philosophy, discuss the living dead either metaphorically or directly. For example, living dead films have been interpreted as debating the effects of Alzheimer's disease (Behuniak 2011), while in philosophy the undead offer interesting possibilities for arguing metaphysical questions of subjectivity, consciousness and morality (Greene & Mohammed 2006: xiv–xv; Hauser 2006: 54; Jacquette 2006: 106).

In all these cases, and similarly to the use of the living dead in the fantastical images of popular culture, the animated bodies challenge the definitions of death. The first edition of *Encyclopaedia Britannica* in 1768 defined death plainly and dualistically as the separation of soul and body (Kastenbaum 2003: 224). The definition has since grown more complicated. For example, the medical definition of death that was based on the absence of heartbeat and breathing was in the late twentieth century replaced by lack of brain function. But even this demarcation is problematic, as coma patients and the brain-dead show (Gervais 1986: 3; Kastenbaum 2003: 226–28; Singer 1994: 1–5; Bell 2013). For instance, Elizabeth Hallam, Jenny Hockey and Glennys Howarth (2001: 63–72) argue that instead of a singular 'truth' of death, there is a need to speak of a multiple system of different deaths with complex physical and psychological processes.

A purely medical or biological definition of death is thus not an adequate map. Moral and ontological questions have become as important, and some researchers claim that a person should be pronounced dead if he/she no longer has a chance to live (Gervais 1986: 4–10, 45, 162; Singer 1994: 191). The exact definition of death with strict borders has, therefore, become increasingly hard to formulate, and it is this alarming uncertainty which living dead films address. As Lisa Badley (1995: 71) argues, the modern fear of death does not concern death as an event, but it is a fear of "'deadness" and the possibility of a "living death"'. Corporeal continuity after a death-like state, or death, questions death's existing definitions. Similarly, the transgressing and anarchic state of the living dead threatens and confuses such existing cultural categories as the legitimacy of medical definitions of death, which work as the foundation of modern death. Thus, by paying attention to the wavering of definitions, the living dead in themselves challenge the notion of controlled and modern death.

Second, the crossing of the border between life and death has to be unnatural and unexpected. The living dead create a threat that is unanticipated and often impossible to understand or accept by the other filmic characters. For example, as Matthew Walker observes, people in George Romero's zombie films strive to reason the existence of the zombies, but each of his zombie films gives a slightly different reason for their being, and their appearance remains a mystery. Walker adds that it may be enough to explain their origins with their eagerness to live – their 'unlimited desire for life' (Walker 2006: 85).

Third, even if the living dead have physically transformed into something appalling, unnatural or supernatural and discriminated, they are still first and foremost corporeal creatures. I have, therefore, excluded from my analysis immaterial figures such as ghosts, who create their own version of post-mortem existence. However, some writers, such as Adrian Poole, consider ghosts to be the most traditional undead characters, who are similarly terrifying because they have crossed the boundaries of life and death. Still, Poole also acknowledges that ghosts do not always materialize in flesh, nor are they a random or unexpected threat, but are linked to personal retributive justice and revenge (Poole 2004: 33–38).

The living dead, instead, personify death, not through symbolical elements, but because they are corpses, and as corpses they are always related to society. As the anthropologist Douglas J. Davies (2005: 150) argues, corpses are never plain objects, not even in the age of a marginalized death: corpses carry different meanings and social significations. Also, McIlwain (2005: 16) argues that corpses, or mediums of death, serve as an important link between the bereaved and the departed, and Margrit Shildrick argues that corporeal monsters are always more than bodies – they are also discursive and mediated practices. Monstrousness is not separated from humanity, although it is often distanced from it (Shildrick 2002: 1–5, 9–11). Similarly, the undead corpses of living dead films still bear the signs of the human body and by doing so they participate in ongoing cultural and social practices, as well as meaning making. Their physical bodies do not refer to an afterlife but rather to the continuance of a bodily existence in this life, as a recognizable and undeniable influence on the society of the living. These monsters do not narrate what happens when one dies, but rather they show how death is present in the world as we know it.

Vampires, mummies and zombies highlight the exceptional relationship with death in their varied cinematic and embodied appearances. As Manuel Vargas (2006: 42) argues, the undead do not make one harmonious class of monsters, but they appear to have different relationships to death and the dead body. Mummies are ancient relics with preserved bodies, which serve to emphasize their mystical power over death and decaying processes. Their aged corpses are enough to cause horror in modern societies, which have marginalized the dead and idolize the bodies of the young and the beautiful. The renewing bodies of vampires fit this idealized image, but their unnatural bodies rather mock such values by using them against themselves. They employ artificially maintained beauty and overtly sexual bodies to deadly seduction, and vampires' bodies are constantly fighting ageing. This denies death its power to change the body. In contrast, zombies do not renew, but decay. They underline the inevitable frailty of the human body, anti-idealizing the desire for immortality. To cite Kyle Bishop (2009: 20), zombies' relationship to death and dead bodies is more unashamed in its explicitness of decaying and less romantic than, for example, in the case of the vampires. In a similar fashion, Frann Michel (2007: 392) interprets vampire bodies as fantasies of immortality, comparing them to the bodies of zombies, which do not hide their close relationship to death, but stress dread and loss.

However, despite such differentiation, all living dead characters deal with the bodily changes that death necessarily brings. Paul Wells (2002: 10) writes that the images of corpses remind the viewer of mortality but the undead cause true anxiety, because they resist the finality of death either by remaining animated while the body is rotting or by resisting the bodily changes altogether. They embody death, because the bodies of the undead are not just dead bodies – they are transformed bodies which have traits of death in them. In their transforming corporeality, the living dead challenge the body's limits. In accordance with the conventions of horror monstrosity, the transformation tends to exploit grotesque and graphic corpses. Through the addressing of the corporeal embodiments of death and their freakish features of the unclean, incomplete, swelling, dismembering, disparate, unstable, loud and the parodying, for example, the film text also triggers bodily reactions in the other characters and in the viewer. It forces them to experience death through such emotions as amazement, curiosity, loathing and disgust.

The visualization of transformed human bodies has been part of living dead films since the first cinematic horror stories. By making the undead look appalling and monstrous, cinema highlights the horrific effect. However, the range of bodily changes is wide: at the one end of the spectrum, we have modern rotting zombies who are missing organs, flesh and skin, while at the other end there is Madeleine in *White Zombie*, whose body remains intact and whose transformation becomes apparent in her empty stare and slow movements. The comparison shows that undead bodies have always been exploited as raw material for living dead films and the viewer's experience, but because these characters have been consumed in so many films, they and their embodiments need variation over time. The changes in the generic monster images are necessary in terms of the logic of generic processes which combine repetition to differentiation. Similarly, those elements which were new and frightening to the viewers of the 1930s have become horror standards, and new frightening elements are created when former conventions lose their effect.

Such an intensive relation to embodiment is further highlighted in the fourth dimension of the living dead's monstrosity – consumption. The living dead are corporeal creatures with bodily needs such as hunger and sexual urges. To satisfy these, they consume the bodies, blood or flesh of the living. Even when a living dead is part of a crowd (zombies), they remain extremely self-serving and seek to fulfil their own needs. As Phillip Cole puts it, we are not scared of the undead only because we fear death. Death can be a peaceful event or an attractive state. Instead, we are more afraid of the dead who come back to destroy and consume us. For the living dead, humans are reduced into prey of blood and flesh (Cole 2006: 186–88).

However, consuming is not the only threat posed by the living dead, who also have the power to transform those they encounter. This is the fifth defining characteristic of these monsters. Indeed, Shildrick (2002: 68–73) argues that the monstrous body is both anomalous in itself and startling precisely because it always carries a risk of contamination – if not at the material level, conceptually at least, because the improper body threatens to reveal the constructed nature of the 'proper' bodies. In living dead films, the risk of contamination is both conceptual and material. A vampire's kiss, a zombie's bite and a mummy's curse bring transforming death to others, challenging the viewer's relationship to death and corpses through monster-specific embodied narration. This possibility for monstrous transformation underlines, Leffler (2000: 156) claims, the threat to identity: one may die, but the monster refuses to go away. For example, Rain, a wounded character in *Resident Evil*, worries about her destiny and what her animated body might do after her death. She begs Alice to kill her if she turns into a zombie: 'I don't want to be one of those things, walking around without a soul'.

Furthermore, the living dead are a plague that keeps spreading. The idea of contagious death is not unique to horror films, but rather a common idea in folk beliefs where death was feared for causing more death, a belief that was well justified by infectious diseases. For example, several 'real-life vampire' cases have been explained as misunderstood contagious ailments, when several deaths within a short space made a community blame vampires for the misfortunes (Bell 2013; Davies 2005: 146–47). The idea of contagious death is, similarly, central to living dead films. Together, the consumption and the possibility of transforming others represent the fear of what happens if death is not alienated from society.

The undead signify the urgent force of death, insisting to be noticed in modern society. The living dead foreground our problematic relationship with death on two levels, at least. To begin with, we are afraid of the unknown, which is investigated through the transgressiveness and unexpectedness of the monsters. We are also afraid of the horror of the corpse, which is investigated through a consuming and contagious corporeality of the undead cadavers. All in all, what is culturally and socially troubling with the cinematic living dead is that they force viewers to encounter marginalized questions of death and the materiality of dying and dead bodies. Such cinematic and graphic embodiments of death demand modern society's attention: these transforming and consuming corpses create an immediate threat to both the characters and viewers.

2.2. Narrating Death

Through discursive solutions, living dead films produce generic and narrative knowledge of death. As with character engagement, the dramatization of death events helps to comprehend and fantasize about death. Through a systematic use of death events, these films can model dying processes and experiences related to them. The films not only emphasize death's role in the narration, but also give an audible and visible form to death, which enables an analysis of the nature of death as an aesthetic experience. Deaths in living dead films are always constructed and artificial creations, articulated in narration, which gives death both space and time, as well as causality.

In fact, in post-classical narratology, storytelling has come to be understood as a fundamentally human way of comprehending the world (Kreiswirth 2005: 380–81;

Kreiswirth 2000: 305–06, 314–15; Prince 2008: 118; Herman 1997: 1048–57). For example, in her empirical study of the importance of narrative models in the understanding and telling of violent encounters, Rachel Louise Shaw compares film and real-life experiences of violence, concluding that both are framed by narrativization. Moreover, the cinema's narrative models are borrowed to make real-life occurrences comprehensible (Shaw 2004: 131–32, 144–49, 148). The narrativization of death in living dead films likewise deconstructs death into smaller, more comprehensible parts. Exposing and studying death in living dead films, then, functions as a substitute for encountering death in the modern world.

In general, living dead films suggest a certain process of dying to occur, to be processed and accepted. These films can be seen as revealing and fighting the unknown, of which death is a prime example. In these films, the monstrous embodiment of death is created, exposed and finally dealt with before balance is returned to society by extinguishing that which is threatening (see also Carroll 1990: 97–108). For example, *The Mummy* (1932), where the undead character is revived and threatens the lives of the living and is killed in the end, can be read from this perspective: the true identity of the mummy has to be first questioned and confirmed, and it is only then that it can be encountered victoriously. And so it happens that the main characters refuse to believe fully that the mummy has been revived, insisting instead that his body has been robbed. After suspicious deaths, concerns arise, and once the suspicions are confirmed, the team successfully arrives at the correct protective procedures against mummies. The mummy can thus be destroyed in the final scene of the film, linking horror films' use of death to the question of causality: death (or undeath) can be defeated, when there is an underlying cause.

In this standardized narration of death, three different types of death are recognizable: transformative, social and final. Transformative death transforms a person into an undead monster; in social death, the character's transformation is realized and accepted by others; and in final death, the undead monster is violently destroyed. In a certain way, transformative deaths serve as the beginning and escalation of the story, while social deaths function as the story's middle section, where the otherness is processed, and final deaths act as a closure. Together, these three create a formula or a narration of death which living dead films apply.

A similar trilogy is recognizable from different folklores and death rituals around the world. Many cultures, as folklorist Paul Barber (1988: 196) argues, distinguish between the moment of death, the time of burial and the time when the memories and dreams of the deceased have faded away. Cultural anthropologist Victor Turner labels these phases as detachment from earlier social structure, then the liminal period and, finally, the reincorporation in the end when the ritual subject again reaches a stable state. The liminal state, or in other words the time between a person's death and society's readjustment to this death (through burial, for example), threatens the social order, but by definition it is also understood as a limited period – a time within which society adjusts to the loss (Turner 2008: 94–95). This death pattern is quite similar to the one introduced here. Both of these structures describe how death affects a person and society, how the bereaved survive both loss and acceptance of death, and how the parting with the dead is carried through.

In living dead films, death is not an end but rather a cause for some other form of existence. Even when the undead are physically alive, they have been defined as dead, for something crucial has changed in them. They are not the same as they were before, and the person who they used to be dies. In transformative death, the living dead have lost some or all of their human identity. Hallam, Hockey and Howarth (2001: 65) argue that whereas identity is thought to be a construction of both body and self, the death that affects the body necessarily affects the self as well.

Interview with the Vampire (1994) introduces Louis, a vampire who describes his transformative death in detail. He narrates how after the deaths of his wife and child, he longed for death. His wish is granted, when Lestat the vampire changes him. Louis describes the new sensations: 'That morning I was not yet a vampire, and I saw my last sunrise … And then I said farewell to sunlight, and set out to become what I became.' And, later: 'The world had changed, yet stayed the same. I was a newborn vampire weeping at the beauty of the night.' However, the beauty of the new senses come with a bloodlust that drives Louis insane. He cannot come to terms with his changed identity and bodily needs. Thus, transformative death affects both body and mentality, and despite the continuance between two existences, the personality changes. In a way, transformative death is not death as such, but rather the birth of something else. Interestingly, David J. Skal (1993: 287) argues that all monsters can be seen as expressions of birth, no matter how weird or unnatural. Similarly, in transformative death, when a person dies, an unknown otherness (often understood as monstrousness) is born, which is a new beginning and a distinct narrative turning point.

The birth of a monster is reflected in the transforming body. James Dadoun (1989: 49) connects the decomposing and reformulating bodies of horror to the need to link the outer and inner appearance of monstrous characters. The generic (and political) use of ugliness and bestiality is often related to the idea of the beauty mystique. Anthony Synnott contends that this dates back to ancient cultures and Christian traditions of beauty as connected to moral goodness and God – a person's appearance would reflect his/her soul and inner beauty. Conversely, evil would show as ugliness or grotesqueness, which is an idea much exploited in fiction (Synnott 1993: 78–79, 90–95). In a similar manner, the corporeal transformation of the undead merely makes the dehumanizing transformations of death visible.

In living dead films, transformative deaths of monsters-to-be are often followed in detail. The death scenes allow the viewer to witness the process, which starts from the contamination, unfolds with warning signs of forthcoming death and culminates in the transformative death, which makes the changes in body and personality irreversible. In *Bram Stoker's Dracula*, the transformative death of Lucy is described exhaustively. Her contamination by Dracula sets in motion her metamorphosis into a monster, and when her friends and family call for a doctor, he gets to hear Lucy's plea: 'Help me, Jack. I don't know what's happening to me. I'm changing. I can feel it.' Jack, the doctor, interprets the symptoms as a blood disease but cannot trace the primary cause of anaemia. When summoned, Van Helsing recognizes the telltale signs of a vampire: two bite marks on the neck, paleness, growing fangs, a violent reaction to garlic and changeable behaviour.

Although there is a recognizable moment of transformative death, it is the culmination of a longer process which further highlights the power of death. This transformative phase can be compared to the degenerative nature of death in modern societies, where most deaths are caused by long-term illnesses with slow changes in a person's body, self and social relations. In other words, Lucy's bodily changes only serve to accent the more important change of the death of a person as she was known. Her new, unknown or unrecognizable features render her dying process monstrous and alienating to others. In addition to physical and mental phenomena, transformation always includes social dimensions.

Davies (2002: 4–5) notes that death necessarily changes a person's identity because it changes his/her social status and relations to others. In transformative death, in fact, the monsters threaten the existing social and moral codes by virtue of their existence and behaviour. Because they are no longer recognized as persons, their actions are not limited by social norms. Zombies are an exemplary case of this. As Gregory A. Waller (1986: 276–78) and Mark Jancovich (1992: 91) argue, zombies act like animals, building their existence on instinctual behaviour, repressed desires or repressive control, instead of conscious decisions. And, yet, although they lack the rich mental life of vampires and mummies, even automated zombies perform some psychological and social continuance (see also Thompson 2006: 33; Greene & Mohammed 2006: xv; Webb & Byrnand 2008: 85–90, 95–96). Occasionally, as in *White Zombie, Resident Evil* and *The Return of the Living Dead*, zombies tend to recognize other people and might refuse, at least momentarily, to follow their violent instincts. Most mummies and vampires seem to be more conscious of the social and cultural norms, even if they, too, often choose to ignore them, acting on their instinctual drives. Vampires suck blood to the detriment of others' lives, and mummies use the bodies of the living for their own purposes. Thus, the living dead are often made to oppose social norms in a way that connects their psychological traits to the suppressed side of corporeal humanity.

Transformative death reveals how the actual event of death is an individual, physical and mental phenomenon with social reflections. It starts a liminal phase, during which the ritual subject (the dead person) is ambiguous because it has 'few or none of the attributes of the past or coming state', as Turner writes. He continues that, often, these liminal entities can be 'disguised as monsters to demonstrate that as liminal beings they have no status' (Turner 2008: 94–95). It is, therefore, their unfitness or the liminality between life and death that creates anxiety towards the living dead, who threaten the existing social order. In the process of liminality, the films also describe a social death, where transformative death has to be accepted by the bereaved. The term 'social death' refers to the end of a person's social identity and influence: a person may be physically dead and still exert social influence and vice versa (see, for example, Mulkay 1993: 32–34). Dying is, therefore, a long process, and transformative death has started this process in which a person has to be declared both socially and biologically dead – and in this very order in living dead films.

Social death constitutes the middle part of the filmic narration, where the effects of death are debated. And as Leffler (2000: 110–13) argues, in horror it is not the beginning or the end that is important, but the middle part that forces both the characters and the viewer to encounter otherness and the unknown. Living dead films mark otherness by death. Their narrations communicate the transformation process not only of the monsters but also of the victims' friends and family. The bereaved have to accept the death of their close ones to survive and to avoid becoming victims themselves, which makes the films harrowing and traumatic descriptions of mourning.

In *I Am Legend* (2007), Robert sits on the floor and pets his dog Sam after this lonely survivor's sole companion is infected by the undead. The falling hair sticks to Robert's fingers as the dog's symptoms aggravate. When the aggression becomes overwhelming and the dog tries to bite, Robert is forced to strangle him to prevent the transformation. During the powerful killing scene, the camera shows Robert's tearful face in a close-up, so that the addressing emphasizes not only his recognition of the transformation, but also the loss, grief and horror of that transformation. In this way, the dog's death scene also demands the viewer's emotional and corporeal response to dying. Indeed, unlike most American media presentations, which according to Charles and Donna Corr (2003: 43) often overlook grief and consequences of death, living dead films concentrate, beautifully and horrifyingly, on processes of loss and rejection.

As Norbert Elias has remarked, death is a problem to the living, not to the dead. The living have to find means to deal with death and loss, and with the anxiety they arouse (Elias 2001: 3). However, this is not always an easy task. Instead, as Carroll (1990: 128) maintains, it is typical of the horror genre that a monster's existence is not immediately accepted, even though it is recognized. While the characters and authorities fight the idea of the unnatural and the fantastic, the monster has time to enhance its power and influence. Victims are killed, and conflict will escalate until such a moment that the characters understand the nature of the monster, or accept the unknown death. For example, after the Count in *Dracula* (1931) has caused several deaths and some others to transform into vampires, Van Helsing starts to suspect vampirism. His peers first discard this as superstition, but the hypothesis is eventually proved, and support to kill Dracula gathers momentum.

The significance of acceptance has a bearing on the studying of death and the undead. An interesting comparison can be made, in fact, between the narration of death and Michel Foucault's theories of power, knowledge and social control, for he discusses the modernization process and the importance of knowledge in this process. For example, in *Discipline and Punish* (1975), Foucault argues that modernization shifted away from bodily processes towards control executed through knowledge. He also contends that knowledge produces power, and both power and knowledge are produced in complex relationships of multiple networks. This is how the borders of modern society and humanity are formed, defended and renegotiated in practices of knowledge and power (Foucault 1977). The living dead embody those parts of humanity which already seem under control in modern Western society – they represent death and corporeality that have been controlled through processes of medicalization and modernization. The undead, who defy the limits of death, also stand for the failure of societal self-control by refusing to be placed in accepted positions. Stories of the undead can, therefore, be viewed as struggles to restore and extend shared knowledge and control.

Furthermore, social death in living dead films is not just about accepting death and renegotiating with existing death systems, as processes of grief and mourning are an important part of these debates. This dimension of social death can be described with Julia Kristeva's concept of the abject, much used in horror and monster studies (Creed 1989; Creed 1995; King 2004; Shildrick 2002). Abjection is something that has been a part of a human being, but after separation from the subject it creates a threat to the identity and a source of chaos, contamination and fragility, which needs to be cut loose. Similarly, as a liminal phase is located between two stable states, the abject is located between object and subject. The experience of abjection is typically linked to bodily functions, such as vomiting, or a corpse. What was once part of humanity has become appalling (Kristeva 1982: 1–12). Jonathan Lake Crane further highlights the corpse's role as a source of abjection in horror. The corpse is a reminder of life and subject, both of which it ends up denying. As a source of mayhem, the corpse must be shut out, often with violence. Before such exclusion can take place, the protagonist and other characters need to accept the transformation of the diseased. They must negotiate between their memories and the abject (Crane 1994: 30–34).

If the characters are unable to deal with loss and grief, the survivors become easy victims for the newborn monster. For example, *Night of the Living Dead* starts by introducing a brother and sister. While Johnny is victimized by zombies, Barbra manages to run away. Later, once Barbra has barricaded herself, with the other survivors, into a small farmhouse, Johnny arrives at the scene as a zombie. Unable to accept the change in her brother, Barbra does not fight back but lets her brother tear her out of the house to be eaten by him and other zombies. This scene from 1968 is interestingly contrasted in *Resident Evil* (2002), where a zombified sister walks to her brother, one of the team members trying to escape zombies. Matthew calls her sister by name, hoping that she has survived, and for a short while it seems as if Lisa could connect with her brother, but she then attacks him. Matthew fights back, but is unable to do anything drastic. He is about to be zombified, just as Barbra was in *Night of the Living Dead*, but is saved by an intervention by Alice, the film's heroine. Indeed, if the characters are able, as Alice is, to accept the process that has started by the transformative death and accept the existence of the monster on its own terms rather than as someone it used to be, they will be given the keys and emotional capability to rid themselves of the monster.

Social death requires acceptance of death at two levels: comprehending death through knowledge and handling death emotionally through abjection. This difference is embodied in the different types of narrations of death. The transformative death of the main monster creates the tension of the story, but the dying processes of its victims are often more detailed. And whereas the main monster's social death is often about accepting its existence by gaining knowledge, the social death of the transformed loved ones highlights questions of mourning and acceptance of loss.

Although modern death systems seek to alienate death (through final death), the willingness of these films to pay attention to liminality and social death emphasizes the need to widen our understanding and scope of modern death. The failure of modern death systems that enables the birth of the monster critiques the limited understanding of death, whereas the requirement for abjection condemns the hastened grieving processes where the characters and viewers are not allowed to mourn for the loss of a person. The hastened process of grief resembles the role that grief has in modern American society. Although regarded as a natural and personal reaction to death, grief is ignored socially as much as possible. Grieving should not take too long or be too public. It should be discreet in order to disrupt social life as little as possible (Morgan 2003: 2; Corr & Corr 2003: 45–46). Social death in living dead films accentuates problems with existing modern death, such as grief and death having to be dealt with in private to keep from disturbing the running of society.

Although social death debates problematic encounters with death, final death (or the killing of the monster) puts both the monster and death back in their place. In this way, final death is about gaining control over a situation which has thrown the community off the track. Final death manages, finally, to restore death under social control, within the modern borders between life and death. The dramatization of death's exclusion also brings an end to the monster's existence and ensures that, this time, both the person and the body are positively dead, and no longer able to come back. Final death is an exclamation mark, showing that death needs to be barred from society, otherwise its continuing existence will decompose that society – as it does in the apocalyptical visions of zombie films.

In the narration of horror, as Carroll (1990: 102–03) describes, the story typically ends with the encounter with and the destruction of the monster. The use of death as closure 'tames' death, as Russell (1995: 2, 174) argues, because this death is expected and desired by the viewer. Final death, therefore, can be seen to produce catharsis, which many horror scholars consider a necessary emotional response to viewing a violent film. Catharsis explains how negative events and emotions can be used to serve 'moral' purposes by helping the viewer to process negative issues and to release emotional tension with a positive solution (Aristotle 1997: 69, 99–103; Grønstad 2003: 41). The killing of living dead creatures in the end may release anxiety, which may produce narrative catharsis, but it does not remove the moral question related to the killing of the monster. Indeed, as Stephen Prince (2000: 20–34) argues, catharsis is rather a cognitive term, and as such it does not explain away all the sensual dimensions of violent films: 'justified' solutions may provide pleasure for the viewer, but they still carry with them problematic dimensions of aggression. This becomes especially clear in films where the viewer is denied the final deaths of all undead and, instead, the presence of death becomes permanent.

The final death is an especially violent act, suggesting that conflicts can be solved with violence. The monster needs to be killed, as Edward Ingebretsen argues: 'the monster must be staked, burned, dismembered, or otherwise dispatched in the final reel'. Only through such extreme violence can the exclusion and death of a monster be secured, which then enables society to let go of the past and to restore balance (Ingebretsen 2001: 8, 11, 171, 173). The violent nature of the monster's death is highlighted by generic conventions, which decree that unnatural monsters cannot be killed naturally. The special methods required stem from the knowledge of a monster's weaknesses (Leffler 2000: 139–40). The mummy is an ancient creature who comes from both a different time and religion. This necessitates the use of knowledge of this ancient culture. A mummy cannot be killed with bullets, but rather through ancient spells, which it is forced to obey. Cinema has also adopted the age-old folk tradition where a vampire is pierced with a wooden stick or burned, or its head may be cut off. Zombies (excluding those from Haiti) will die if their brain is smashed – either by shooting them in the head or by cutting their heads off.

Final death has immediate effects. While transformative death is more like a process of dying, which slowly reveals the transformation of body and personality, final death destroys that which is monstrous and makes the body's connection to death explicit. Mummies and vampires, in particular, tend to undergo dramatic and sudden bodily changes, burning into ashes and turning into skeletons. In contrast, the most corporeal of the living dead monsters, zombies, who already have a corpse-like appearance, bypass such changes, but their corpses are disposed of by humans (often by fire). These extermination methods focus attention on an important difference between transformative and final deaths: the former are caused by an uncontrolled otherness, while the violence of the latter is a product of human control.

The narration of death breaks dying down into smaller phases, which punctuate both the narration and the addressed images of death. Moreover, this narration reverses the processes of dying, focusing on the personal, social and cultural aspects before physical death, which comes last in line. The physical existence of living dead characters forces the viewer to encounter all aspects of death, making death harder to marginalize and circumvent than is the ideal in modern medicalized understanding. Also, the actual death scenes add physical and violent elements essential to the dying process. As is obvious in some of the more recent films, the horror genre has become especially well known for spectacles of death events. However, at the narrative level, death events are mediated to the viewer by storytelling, either with or without explicit images of dying. In the classical films, explicit images of (violent) death were rare, whereas in the digital era excessive images of dying play an important part of the films. Whether each scene hides or reveals the images of death, the combination of storytelling and attraction elements allow living dead films to slow down the dying process, to draw attention to immediate experiences and concentrate on death scenes.

The death scenes are the 'numbers' of the living dead films. According to Cynthia Freeland, numbers are scenes that concentrate on the typical elements of each genre, such as violent acts in horror films. During these scenes, the spectacle overcomes the plot, although the spectacle can and often does connect to the narration and its aesthetic, emotional and cognitive goals and effects (Freeland 2000: 256–62). The numbers with death scenes are necessarily complex, because they are part of the narrative knowledge about death, integral to the narrative turning points of the story and components of horror films' emotional goals, but at the same time they are also aesthetic spectacles. For example, Catharine Russell and Asbjørn Grønstad explain that cinematic violence is typically used to give form to death, to capture and expose it. Violence extends the dying process and lends it movement, colour, sound and actors. Violent deaths can hence be described as performances and spectacles of the unseeable (Russell 1995: 175; Grønstad 2003: 9–10). Thus, the actual death scenes stall the physical processes of dying and provide spectacles of death.

Although death scenes lie at the core of living dead films, their narration is not straightforward. For example, Peter Verstraten (2009: 165) acknowledges that the horror experience typically and purposely blurs the distinction between story and discourse (or style), because tension is created by the limitations on the viewer's access to all of the elements of the story. The tension is often created by playing with the viewer's vision, by either showing too much or too little. As Carol J. Clover (1992: 166–67) argues, horror films can be considered projects where the viewer's own vision is constantly teased, threatened, confused and blocked. These films exploit the horror viewer's constant anticipation of something happening: they provide excessive information that makes the viewer fear for characters, or they withhold this information and force the viewer to experience horror with the characters (Tudor 1989: 107–09; Leffler 2000: 130–36; Carroll 1990: 128–44).

The showing of too much or too little takes place through two typical horror conventions: shock and suspense. David Scott Diffrient defines shock (or the shock cut) as a 'sudden, violent eruption or peak moment in a film narrative' which forces the viewer to react to the film with a startle. Moreover, he argues that the shock cut is especially important to the horror genre, because it explores 'the material of embodied presence' and generates 'technologies of fear'. In contrast to the shock's excess of images, suspense is rather based on empty images and increasing tension provided by other means (music, generic anticipation etc.). Also, horror's suspense and shock feed on each other: while neither works alone, they both use different relationships to images (Diffrient 2004: 52–63, 77–81).

The game of showing too much or too little also applies to death scenes. In addition to the emotional and aesthetic functions, this hiding and showing has been dictated by changing censorship demands and practices. In the classical era, in particular, there were strict rules about what could and could not be shown. The hiding and revealing of death was executed at the discursive level and through different narrative solutions, which as a manipulation of narrative events has potent emotional power, says Ralf Schneider (2005: 136). The play of hide and seek is thus part of the horror viewer's generic anticipation of being horrified by the horror film.

As in character engagement, then, the narrative structures of living dead films offer complex relationships to violent death events. First, narration can perform a spectacle or an act of violence. Second, it can authenticate the death events by concentrating on the consequences of these acts (corpses, funeral scenes etc.). Third, narration can confirm death by revealing the characters' affective reactions to the event. These three ways of mediating the death event to the viewer (act, consequences and reactions) can be used even within the same scene, all inviting different emotional, cognitive and physical reactions from the viewer. Essentially, the spectacles of violence heighten direct sensual reactions, while the consequences provide cognitive knowledge that the viewer can use in constructing the story and in giving causal meanings to death. Finally, the embodied reactions focus on an emotional engagement with the effects of death.

These different methods of mediating death events also highlight the medium-specificity of cinematic practices. It is not only what is shown (acts, consequences or reactions) or how they are shown (through which shots), but also the cinematic style that affects the spectacle of death. The viewer's attention is captured by camera movements, editing rhythms, duration and time, *mise-en-scène*, iconography, colour, sound, composition, movement, lighting and cinematographic techniques, such as focus, filters, lenses etc. (see also Powell 2005: 109–59). The use of varied cinematic techniques calls attention to the fabrication of death events, which renders these images technical, institutional, generic and medium-specific.

However, in addition to cinematic techniques, there are also contextual limitations and desires guiding death scenes. It is not only the changing cultural understandings of death, but also the changing censorship rules, development of special effects and changing cultural attitudes towards violence in mass media that have influenced the construction of an aesthetic and experiential relationship with death events in living dead films. Quite simply, death is brought under study differently in different Hollywood eras. The avoidance of actual images of violent death scenes is more typical in the classical era, whereas the death scenes of the post-classical and digital eras have become more detailed, sensual and accessible for the viewer. As my analysis of living dead films in subsequent chapters will show, the films have slowly shifted their emphasis from deaths at the story level (consequences and reactions), interpreted by the viewer, to the discursive level (acts) that the viewer witnesses and embraces as a bodily experience.

2.3. Symbolizing Death

'All films', in Leonard Quart's and Albert Auster's (2002: 4–5) words, 'can be considered political' because they, whether explicitly or implicitly, communicate with the audience and society, its values and problems. Correspondence with society does not imply that horror films screen or reflect 'real-world' events. Thus, the horror genre's images of death do not reflect the deaths of everyday life, but they nevertheless create a critique of their sociocultural background, not least because these films give visibility to death-related cultural tensions. The successful transgressions of boundaries at the films' discursive level have provided an opportunity for horror films to resemble, comment, challenge, interpret and influence public negotiations over death.

Instead of direct reflection of social issues, the correspondence or verisimilitude is filtered through the genre's discursive/textual forms and aesthetic conventions, as stressed by Neale, who adds that genre films can also have an impact on the 'real world' through this institutionalized relationship. Neale chooses to stress verisimilitude instead of direct social reflection for four reasons. First, generic verisimilitude can be based on, but also equally well ignore, societal and cultural systems. Second, different genres make use of sociocultural authenticity in different ways. Third, Hollywood's generic categorizations are widely known and they can thus inform public opinion. Fourth, both generic authenticity and cultural similitude can provide pleasure in equal measure (Neale 2000: 32–34, 213; Neale 1995: 160–62).

Genre films, and living dead films' generic understanding of death, too, adjust to changes in culture and society, not because they have to or because they conspire with a hidden agenda, but because their generic conventions and strategies make them an integral and dynamic part of that culture and society. As Thomas Schatz (1981: 31) writes, the 'success of any genre depends upon at least two factors: the thematic appeal and significance of the conflicts it repeatedly addresses and its flexibility in adjusting to the audience's and filmmaker's changing attitudes toward these conflicts'. In living dead films, the repeated conflicts relate to death and dying. Through the films' symbolic potential, living dead films may end up normalizing modern death-related practices or challenging them through fantasy and comment.

In living dead films, the central material is monstrosity and the corporeal nature of the undead. Thus, the monsters also embody the films' potential for social criticism. The etymological roots of the 'monster' in Latin – *monere* is to warn and *monstrare* points to something – refer to the monsters' symbolic tasks: they warn, teach, provide public shows and redefine boundaries (see, for example, Picart & Greek 2007: 12; Ingebretsen 2001: 4, 175). Through these social tasks, the living dead create narrative threats, function as scapegoats and allow the community to debate difficult social issues.

In fact, Wood (1984: 175–76) argues that in horror, 'monster threatens normality'. '[A]lthough so simple, the formula provides three variables: normality, the Monster, and, crucially, the relationship between the two', and Waller (1986: 340–55) emphasizes that the monsters represent the collapse and recreation of order in creating a feeling of civilization as both destroyed and preserved. In other words, every monster recreates and renews the idea of humanity and society. Without the reciprocal relationship, monster and normality reveal themselves as empty concepts. It is the negotiation process that takes place during the film-viewing which defines the concepts in relation to one another. Applied to living dead films, the definition could be formulated as follows: the undead threaten the living, or when the undead are understood as more general embodiments of death, death threatens life (social order). In this sense, the living dead represent death, which needs to be alienated from modern society but which refuses to do so. This is why the problematic relationship with the modern understanding of death starts the cinematically mediated negotiation in which death, the undead and the living become conceptualized, embodied and experienced.

The undead are employed to debate social boundaries and values, not only in relation to death, but through death as well. Indeed, death is always connected to life, and the undead can be used to comment not only cultural understandings of death, but also some of the social problems of being alive in contemporary society. For example, as it will be discussed in more detail later on, the classical zombie film *White Zombie* (1932) connects zombies to the issues of slavery, and by using the undead to embody slaves, this film also shows how slavery is made invisible and marginalized. This also brings forward another aspect of social death. Social death is not only about exclusion of dying or dead people from contemporary society, but also about loss of social identity in different cases of social history, such as slavery (Patterson 1982) or genocide (Card 2003). Similarly, in living dead films, often the very connection with death creates conflicts in the debated sociocultural issues. The bodies of the undead are important because corpses relate to both death and 'waste' (Creed 1995: 127–32, 146), and in this way death is used to mark issues that need to be abjected. By connecting different themes to the undead, living dead films discuss these themes' acceptable social expressions.

Davies has recognized three general responses to corpses: questions of impurity, fertility and fear. Impurity pertains to the corpse belonging to a different realm than the living, which leads to creating rituals of purifying the boundaries between life and death. By fertility, Davies refers to reactions where death reminds us of (and even celebrates) the importance of continuity of life. Lastly, fear connotes the anxieties triggered by death's ability to threaten this continuity of life (Davies 2002: 38–41). The three relationships can be compared to living dead characters in that mummies are connected to questions of impurity (death rituals), vampires to fertility (sexuality) and zombies to fear (destruction of society). Similar symbolism can be seen in the final deaths of these monsters: the mummies are killed by proper death rites, the vampires' weakness is their heart and the zombies' final death relates to the destruction of their brains.

First, ancient mummies in the modern world can be discussed in relation to accepted death rituals. Death rites, such as funeral and mourning rituals, are a society's way of controlling death, coping with corpses and assuring the continuity of society (Davies 2002: 1, 6–7; Bauman 1992, 24). For example, anthropologist Mary Douglas discusses how cultures are built on regulations, rules and categories. These rules give order and system to society, making filth, sickness and dead bodies, for example, abnormal because they create possible chaos. The conservation of categories through cleanliness becomes a sign of maintaining social order (Douglas 1996). In mummy films, questions of impurity and the socially accepted way of dealing with corpses are constantly repeated. Modern and Western death rituals are tested by the deviant traditions of ancient Egyptian mummies.

Ancient mummies belong to a rich death system which itself is part of a complex religious structure. In ancient Egypt, the preservation of the body was an important element of maintaining, not the body itself, but the human soul and spirit. Mummification did not seek to prevent the corpse from decaying, but rather aimed to create a resemblance of the deceased, because changes to the body's appearance would have jeopardized possibilities for afterlife. The body – which created a link between the different spiritual parts of a person – was, therefore, an integral part of the spiritual entity (Ikram 2003: 23–31; Barber 1988: 167–68).

However, when they were brought to Anglo-American fiction during the nineteenth century in the wake of increasing archaeological and scientific interest, mummies also came to be evaluated in relation to Western death systems. As part of Western fiction, mummies stopped reflecting ancient practices and instead started to project Western views on death, corpses and (ancient) Egypt. Similarly, Hollywood dismissed mummies as spiritual objects, and rather highlighted their bodies, which resist natural rotting and decay. In making mummies walk, film-makers also ignored the fact that the Egyptians had not expected their mummies to return to live in this world, but rather the next.

In *The Mummy* (1932), Imhotep both returns to life and becomes an undead. The archaeologists deduce that the mummy has been buried alive because he has committed a sin. Doctor Muller states that 'Imhotep was sentenced to death not only in this world, but in the next'. These notions compare to Western folklore where, according to Barber (1988: 29–38), the most common reasons for people to come back from the dead include predispositions (different, unpopular people or sinners), predestinations (people born in unfavourable conditions), events (things that they do or things that happen to them) and non-events (things that are left undone, for example, during funerary or burial practices). Three of the four categories also apply to the mummy. Imhotep has sinned in rebelling against the society's practices and boundaries. However, and more importantly, the people who punish the mummy are responsible for his resurrection because they condemn Imhotep to a liminal state and deny him the normal burial practices. Instead of embalming the corpse, they embalm the living body and open the possibility for the body, not only the spirit, to return back to life.

Thus, the Hollywood horror genre rendered the mummy a foreign, loathsome, primitive and pagan character, especially from the American perspective. The mummies' ancient corporeality challenges the practices of how death and dead people are managed in the United States. Crucially, it was the cultural and religious distance which helped to make the mummies and their death rituals threatening. In all religions, questions of death and afterlife are an important part of the doctrine. Mummy films bring together two different religious and death systems on a collision course. In the United States, questions of death and afterlife are dominated by Christianity, which centres on questions of resurrection: the disappearance of the body does not influence salvation of the soul (Segal 2004: 3–5, 17). When horror films linked the mummies' physicality to their resurrection in this life, these 'pagan' representatives of a different religion challenged prevailing Western values.

The ritual otherness of the mummies' feared resurrection potential is evident in the prominence given to ancient funerary and burial rituals. Both the classical *The Mummy* and its digital remake *The Mummy* include two different but comparable scenes with ancient death rituals – one from the past and another attempted in the modern world. The past ritual recounts a tainted love for the pharaoh's lover and an attempt to use impure death rites, while the modern ritual has the revived mummy attempt to resurrect his lost lover. The viewer is pushed to compare the two scenes in both films: the past rituals are mystified, making the mummy a victim of fate, whereas the modern ceremonies appear threatening. The rituals could, in fact, be accepted as part of a mystical past and primeval religion, but they become unacceptable in the modern world.

The classical *The Mummy* highlights the comparison between the ancient and the modern by framing the death rituals through one character, Helen. The mummy recognizes his lover Anck-es-en-Amon in her, and Helen's desire to know ancient Egypt almost comes true. The mummy reveals his past to Helen, and the ancient rituals are screened to the viewer as well with the mummy's voice-over narration. At first, Helen seems intrigued by the mystical rituals, but by the final reel, she comes to understand their impropriety in modern life. She appreciates that they belong to the past, which leads her to choose life today over ancient death.

The remake *The Mummy*, a product of digital spectacles, stresses the comparison between the past and the present through visual parallelism. The film opens with the ancient rituals and closes with the modern rites. The scenes where the mummy attempts to raise his lover from the dead are parallel: they happen in the same setting with the assistance of the same priests and in the same sequence. There are also important differences. The ancient version is mystified and even glorified, whereas the setting for the modern version (an ancient tomb) is that of decay, and the mummified priests have become grotesque skeletons. The opening ritual has turned into a rotting version of itself, illustrating how the modern world has no place for these ancient rituals.

In addition to the cultural, religious and temporal distance to the death rituals, the culturally different and strange preservation of dead bodies is similarly alienating. The denial of 'normal' (Western) death rites, as Davies (2002: 38–39) emphasizes, makes the foreign corpses ritually impure and poses a potential danger to society and its prevailing definitions of death. These films bypass the fact that, as Barber explains, mummification sought to ensure that the deceased could safely enter the realm of death. Still, the practice seems deviant, because the American practice is to dispose of bodies either by burial or cremation (Barber 1988: 166–68).

Although the embalming of bodies has been and still is a strong part of American funeral practices, the difference to mummification is the temporary and partial preparation process of the corpses (Davies 2005: 75–76). The open casket is seen to have a dual purpose, both quite suitable for a modern understanding of death. First, it locates the dead into a proper social category by making the corpse artificial with chemical and technical processes. Second, it denies the power of death with the life-like and humanized appearance of the corpse (Hallam, Hockey & Howarth 2001: 73–75). In comparison, the mummies' otherness relates to their strange preserved corpses, which become constant and visible reminders of death. Jasmin Day (2006: 106) maintains that from the Western perspective, these bodies which appear as if still in the process of dying seem to defy normal post-mortem processes. Modern Western societies expect death to be rejected, which the very existence of mummies conflicts with and links them with primitivism. Elias, for example, connects the rejection of death with a civilization process which has slowly repressed all signs of animality, including death, from culture and society. Death has, therefore, been marginalized from the centre of civilization and alienated from the public (Elias 2001: 17–19).

Thus, the insufficient primitive rituals leave mummies in an unclean and uncontrolled state. This liminality needs to be resolved. The mummy films narrate the Western need to re-control pagan and primitive death. Horror cinema, indeed, brings mummies back to life to correct their liminal state. The narration of death has its own importance here: the revival of the mummy makes its liminal state visible and open for study and acceptance. It is only after this that social death follows. Besides destroying the dead body, final death is also about exploring the superiority of modern and Western death and extending its power over ancient corpses. Mummy films expose, rebury and reject the mummies and death by Western standards, rather similarly as Day (2006: 35) reports that some mummies have, in fact, been reburied in accordance with Christian rituals in the assumption that these rites could be extended to pagan remains. Such narrations spotlight and negotiate Western attempts to control death and regulate relationships with dead bodies.

Second, vampire fiction tends to link the theme of death to sexual and gender tensions. Jonathan Dollimore (1998: xi–xx) argues that the link between sex and death is 'endemic to Western culture more generally', because they both connect to the corporeal and essential processes of life. This also clarifies what Davies (2002: 40) means by death's fertility: whereas life constantly reminds us of its inevitable resolution, death points out that life must go on. In this sense, vampire films suggest that the relationship with death is not only a negative but also a productive experience, which can bring meaning to life.

Perhaps one of the best-known conceptualizations of the link between sex and death has been formulated by Sigmund Freud in his concepts of *Eros* and *Thanatos* and through 'the pleasure principle' and 'the reality principle'. Both divisions are internal conflicts between mortality and the human need to sustain existence, culture and society immortally. *Eros*, the sex instinct, aims to the continuity of life and is closely tied to the pleasure principle: as humans, we seek pleasure. Disappointment in this desire starts to develop the reality principle, but we still wish to abandon the external pressure and disturbing forces that stand in pleasure's way. The last means is a desire to restore an earlier or original state of existence, that of death. This brings us to the death instinct, *Thanatos*. Although *Eros* and *Thanatos* pull in different directions – death is the ultimate reality principle and interruption of both the sex instinct and the pleasure principle – they are intimately connected (Freud 2011; Clack 2002: 61–68).

In the context of vampire films, Wood interprets the Freudian conflict in such a way that Dracula, who is potentially immortal, has won the reality principle and, therefore, represents the pleasure principle. As sexual norms are ideological constructs of a specific culture, the reality principle guides the socially accepted expressions of sexuality. However, Dracula is free from the conflicts of these principles and is able to reveal the repressed nature of sexuality (Wood 1996: 369–78). He employs the link between sex and death because his transformative death has liberated him from the reality principle. In other words, while transformative death is the death of a person, it also ends social, moral and other responsibilities. Vampires can thus openly challenge existing social norms, including those that regulate sexuality. Vampire figures typically seduce, violate the bodily boundaries of others and are overloaded with erotic imagery. Their bite, in particular, has become a metaphor for penetration or intercourse in uniting the victim and the vampire.

Andrew Tudor (1989: 165) writes that it is the human weaknesses of suppressed sexuality, desire for excitement and longing for immortality that give Dracula his powers. While Dracula may act out his sexual desires, his victims are still bound by social norms. For example, the prevailing Christian understandings where sex, sin and death connect, encourage expressions of sexuality in strictly regulated modes (marital heterosexuality), as Dollimore (1998: xxiii, 43–47) notes, continuing that such moralities burden women more than they do men. Indeed, stories of Dracula have often been seen to narrate threatening female sexuality. Elizabeth Signorotti (1996: 621–22), for example, sees that Dracula's kiss releases this threat and 'enables women to become sexual penetrators' who can enter men with their sharp teeth and 'reverse traditional gender roles and place men in the passive position customarily reserved for women'.

In Dracula's story, and many other vampire stories, the transformation makes women monstrous for men, because it liberates controlled sexuality, threatens the existing social order and changes the power relations between genders. From the male perspective, the transgressed sexuality which threatens normality needs to be re-tamed, a task typically carried out by the male vampire hunters. As Bruce McClelland (2006: 185) argues, the vampire hunters have played a crucial cultural role in helping 'a community bury the traces of injustice committed in the name of preserving things as they are'. Signorotti maintains that in Stoker's story, men 'cure' women and return them to their sexually passive positions. The most radical 'cure' takes place with Lucy, who is killed after her transformation and who is thus permanently cured from the horror that is female sexuality (Signorotti 1996: 622–23). In this interpretation, the final death of the victim restores the normality and normative sexuality, which is how the final death can be seen to link sex and death, not through liberation, as in the transformative death, but as a punishment.

However, transformative death can be seen from another perspective as well. For women, it can be empowering and liberating. From their perspective, films open possibilities for female sexuality. And even if the closures may punish sexual freedom and return women under male control, these films nevertheless open possibilities for alternative endings and viewing positions during the film, which can be seen as expressing feminist possibilities (Freeland 2003: 205; Zimmerman 1996: 386; Weiss 1992: 103–08). While final death is used as a punishment for female sexuality in several vampire films, transformative death also signifies empowerment and liberation as an escape from social restrictions. In this interpretation, death can be seen as liberation from restricting social norms, which in vampire films is often expressed through open and excessive sexual behaviour. Although in Dracula stories the sexual debates often concentrate on the limits of female sexuality, in many other vampire stories other forms of sexuality, such as gay, paedophilic or children's sexuality are also discussed. Through these socially and culturally controversial themes, vampire films explore whether death could also create the possibility of forming different kinds of social structures and norms by imagining behaviour outside the accepted cultural norms.

Third, zombies continue the discussion of the limits of existing social structures. Bauman argues that society finds death abnormal and dangerous, because death is an end to existence. In order to overcome this disruption, modern society has marked death as a personal dilemma, whereas the past, future and societal collectivity represent immortality. Societies – and nation states, in particular – provide stability as a counterforce to death's destructiveness (Bauman 1992: 24–26, 96–105, 114–27, 197–99). In zombie films, it is the animated dead that challenge the situation. By embracing society's fear of death, of the undead characters, the zombies represent death's destructive power in its most extreme form: they attack the structures of society. As Waller (1986: 280) says, they 'are the projection of our desire to destroy, to challenge the fundamental values of America, and to bring the institutions of our modern society to a halt'. Zombies are able to do this by their one-dimensionality, for their means of self-expression are limited to destruction and aggression. As Steven Shaviro (1993: 83–87) argues, irrational zombies represent a social process that takes place by its own force, at the same time criticizing and participating in society.

The mindless mass power of zombies is given an allegorical force denoting the might and control structures of society. In classical films, zombies were enslaved subjects following the orders of their master. Later on, the use of zombie masters have diminished, but the question of oppression has continued as the zombies have become enslaved by their instincts and needs. Still, even in the later films, zombies can be seen as allegories of mistreated people who turn against the society that failed to help them in time. For example, in *Resident Evil*, zombies are mistreated workers in the grips of a greedy corporation. In a broader sense, then, as Webb and Byrnand (2008: 85) emphasize, zombies are typically connected to questions of power and exploitation of power. Mimi Sheller (2003: 145) also argues that all zombies should be read as allegories, as they refer to the deprival of free will and physical control.

Zombie films challenge 'individual autonomy and rationalism', Badley (1995: 76) formulates, and are thus about 'fears about de-individuation', Punter (1996: 103) continues. The first-ever feature-length zombie film, *White Zombie*, already had an explicit power-related theme in conjuring up a potent slave allegory of the corpses working for their zombie master. Zombie films are also warning examples of alienation, for the zombies' connection to death makes them unknown, other and a threat to culture and society. In addition, zombies endanger personal identity because these embodiments of death highlight death's influence on autonomy. Similarly, as the zombies appear unable to impact the world around them, the deceased (or their loved ones) have no power over what is done to them in modern death where the corpses are handled by professionals. As a personal issue, the loss of a personal touch to death makes the alienated dying process incomprehensible and meaningless, reducing it to a mere biological phase. This is implied in the zombies' lack of consciousness, which makes the zombie-like state and social alienation frightening: it suggests that humans may not, after all, differ that much from other living things (animals, plants etc.).

However, it is the same social alienation that reveals, Webb and Byrnand (2008: 85) point out, the ceaseless destruction of society. Already in classical films, death threatens the existing social order. The theme is highlighted in later films where zombies become destructive social forces, because, in zombiedom, destruction can only go on. Thus, death can be understood as a revolutionary power which jeopardizes the existing but dysfunctional society. Endless annihilation is especially common in the films following *Night of the Living Dead*. These incorporate apocalyptic developments into the zombie tradition. While the *White Zombie's* zombie master is killed in the end and his servants follow him to his watery grave, in *Night of the Living Dead*, the zombies just keep coming. There are no consoling final deaths of the monsters. This underlines death's force of disintegration. The collapse of society is carried further in the following zombie films where zombie epidemics are enhanced and society is driven into chaos by the growing masses of enraged zombies. By the time of *Resident Evil*, killing the zombies no longer solves or criticizes anything. In these films, the existing social fractures open possibilities for zombie destruction. Thus, the death threatens the structures of society because it reveals the weaknesses in it and challenges society's capability to react to discontinuity or repressed issues.

From society's point of view, death threatens societal continuity. In fact, all societies have their 'death systems' – ways in which dying, death and grief are socially expected, encountered and controlled. In the United States, the death system includes predictions of life expectancy, preventing deaths, caring for the dying, disposing of the bodies (funeral practices), grieving modes and defence activities for violent deaths (social sanctions) (Morgan 2003: 1; Corr & Corr 2003: 41). Living dead films, with their undead characters, death events and death-related allegories, comment on these practices and throw the need for dealing with death back at the viewer. The films ask why undead monsters are created and should be popular in our culture in the first place, and why death depicted through them is often extremely violent. The films can, therefore, dare and reveal the viewer's ambivalent, and constantly changing, relationships with modern death and its representations.

Chapter 3

Classical Living Dead Films

The modernization of death, which seeks to hide death in everyday life through processes of professionalization and medicalization, was in the making before the first screenings of living dead films. In the early twentieth century, as modern medical science took over the controlling, ritualizing and hiding of death, death and dying were increasingly distanced from their traditional forms. Dying moved from the home to the hospital. At the same time, life expectancy started growing slowly. The average life expectancy was 59.7 years in 1930; by 1950 it was 68.2 years. The average life span had become almost ten years longer. The increase was mostly thanks to improved hygiene, living and working conditions, and the discovery of antibiotics and pain medications. For example, from 1900 to 1920, tuberculosis, influenza and pneumonia caused most of the American deaths. Death was a quick and frequent visitor. By 1930, the leading cause of death was major cardiovascular diseases, including heart failure. Compared with the numbers in 1900, only one-tenth died of infectious diseases in 1950. Death was quickly becoming medicalized, and dying signified medical failure. Medical science was expected to create cure instead of only relieving the suffering (Corr & Corr 2003; Information Please® Database 2011; NCHS Data 2009; Hoyert 2012).

Whereas sociocultural values and attitudes put their trust in science and medicalization, the inevitability of death both challenged the limits of modern beliefs and made the postponing of death one of the main goals of modern medicine. The cultural belief in science and distancing of death were also visible in the horror genre. Ideals of modern death were strongly present in the classical films where the professionals of death – doctors, in particular – study the role of the undead and tame monstrous death through their practices. Jason Colavito also argues that classical horror reacted to the changing scientific understanding of the world. In vampire films, for example, the scientists are the leading authorities to study vampires as phenomena, trying to understand their place in the world. The human understanding of the cosmos thus expands in the tight grip of science (Colavito 2008: 17, 211).

The golden age of Hollywood horror started with Universal Studios' *Dracula*, which opened in February 1931 with Béla Lugosi in the leading role. The success of *Dracula* elevated horror themes momentarily to feature production more generally, both at Universal and other studios. The wide production inevitably developed the narration and themes of horror cinema, and 1931–36 witnessed several horror productions within the classical Hollywood system, including *White Zombie* (1932) and *The Mummy* (1932). These classical living dead films tackled the themes of death, undeadness and anticipated feelings of terror in a rather formulaic manner. *Dracula* showed the way not only for the cinematic vampire characters but also fixed the motives, situations and the range of other characters for other living dead films. After *Dracula*, both *The Mummy* and *White Zombie* were mere rewritings of the same story. They all introduced the monster – vampire, mummy or zombie master – who starts to threaten the life (and purity) of a white woman. The young women get to represent transformative death in detail, as Mina and Helen both become affected by the undead, and Madeline transforms into an undead. However, later, the male heroes reveal the monster's true nature, save the women and, in the end, the monster is killed.

In the first films of each undead monster, death was part of both the narration and marketing. The interval texts of *Dracula*'s trailer declare: 'Back from the Grave. Back to Thrill and Chill You.' Similarly, the poster for *White Zombie* portrays the evil zombie master Béla Lugosi with the victim, a young woman in a white dress, captioned with: 'She was not alive nor dead. White Zombie. Performing his every desire.' And the narrator of the trailer of *The Mummy* asks: 'The Mummy. Is it dead or alive? Human or inhuman? You'll know, you'll see. You'll feel the awful, creeping, crawling terror that stands your hair on end and brings a scream to your lips.' As Clover (1992: 201) argues, all promotional material addresses the viewer directly, because it talks to 'you', as seen in the advertisements above, and builds up the viewer's expectations of a cinematic experience.

While death was made an anticipated theme of these stories, it was not any kind of death, but magical, horrifying and foreign. It was magical, because the embodiments of death challenged the scientific understanding of the world; horrifying because the undead became part of Hollywood's monster cavalcade; and foreign due to their exotic background. Vampires came from the backwoods of Eastern Europe, mummies were ancient Egyptians and zombies belonged to Haitian folklore. As a counterforce to magical, foreign and horrifying living dead, at the end of each film death was managed and controlled with Western scientific methods and by the authorities and professionals of death, such as Professor Van Helsing in *Dracula*. The films promise that death can be controlled and kept away from the public domain so that it ceases to threaten modern American civilization.

Death was kept away also from the cinematic audience, not only by alienating it through the embodied monstrousness at the level of the story, but also by excluding bodily violence and death scenes at the level of film discourse. The disposition to hide the death event from view is linked to the institutional and cultural contexts of classical Hollywood production. Violent contents were considered to be culturally controversial. In targeting itself to a large and homogenous audience, classical Hollywood was marketed as harmless entertainment suitable for all groups, including children. In such a context, horror appeared problematic, because most horror films were not received as innocent fun (Balio 1995: 3–4). There was huge social pressure for regulation of film contents, even more so if the contents were sexual and violent.

The production code (or Hays Code) which censored the violence, sex and otherwise inappropriate film content was introduced as early as the 1920s by the Motion Picture Producers and Distributors Association of America (MPAA) as a form of self-regulation in response to public pressure to control the morality of Hollywood. Although Hollywood's self-regulation started to gain wider influence only after the production of *Dracula, White*

Zombie and *The Mummy*, social demands for limiting the contents already existed, and several groups, such as American Catholics, publicly called for film censorship. Thus, although rules were not as strict yet, the shared social values somewhat restricted how violent death scenes could be filmed (Grønstad 2003: 125–27, 131; Prince 2003: 31–32; Doherty 1999: 1–10; Balio 1995: 4, 9, 303). However, as Prince (2003: 52–53, 85) argues, while they may look naïve or free from violence from our perspective, at the time these classical films were considered violent and were likely to raise anxiety and moral debates. They may have been discreet, but these films did not lack possibilities for mediating death and horrifying experiences.

In this chapter, I will approach the three major classical living dead films which have become the reference points for later films. On the one hand, I will analyse the ways in which death was mediated to the audiences in the classical films. On the other, I will discuss what these narrative solutions reveal from the death-related attitudes of the films. I will start with *Dracula*, the first living dead film with sound, and discuss how the narrative focus marks death and living dead as horrifying and unnatural, especially when compared with the morality of other characters. Second, I will study how *White Zombie* alienates death at both the levels of the story and discourse by playing with the viewer's vision to either reveal or hide death. After that, I will turn to *The Mummy*, which shows how the monster's background, appearance and gaze can be used to mark the character with primitive death, which is compared with the scientific methods of modern Western society.

3.1. *Dracula* – Horrifying and Unnatural Death

The cinematic horror transformed the existing traditions connected to the living dead into their own uses. In the case of vampires, there was a wide folklore and literature tradition to choose from. Western folklore presented vampires as decaying and barbaric corpses (Twitchell 1985: 105, 110, 112; Cole 2006: 183), but Hollywood built its vampires on Gothic fiction, which, from the early nineteenth century onwards, had been transforming vampires into civilized, erotic and attractive characters (Waller 1986: 54). Still, instead of leaning on the ambiguous and even romantic vampires of *The Vampyre* (1819) by John William Polidori and *Carmilla* (1872) by Joseph Sheridan Le Fanu, Hollywood went for Bram Stoker's novel *Dracula* (1897). Dracula, too, hinted at the seductive power of death, but for modern society it appropriately concentrated on questions of control, power and authority, not only in its own behaviour but also in relation to death. Benson Saler and Charles A. Ziegle add that Stoker's novel was conveniently structured as a monster-slaying story with cathartic possibilities. The openly monstrous figure of Dracula, therefore, fits easily into Hollywood horror and its understanding of monster stories (Saler and Ziegle 2003: 17–19).

Dracula created a Hollywood interpretation of Bram Stoker's novel to compete with the horror genre's international forefather, the German adaptation of *Nosferatu* (1922). In the silent German version, the emphasis is on the stylistic visual elements, whereas Hollywood not only adds sound to intensify the anticipating and terrifying effects of the story but it also concentrates on the causal relationships and character motivation of the story. The film also incorporated the aesthetic influences of German expressionism (cubistic environment, lighting techniques and strong shadows) into a frightening staging, make-up and special effects, which co-created a distinctive style of Hollywood horror (Balio 1995: 298–99; Tudor 1989: 27–29). *Dracula* was appreciated by critics and audience alike. '*The Film Daily* admitted that "there is no denying its dramatic power and thrills".' Gary Rhodes writes and continues that the horrifying dimension was also the key in the reception of the film: 'The manager of the Palace Theatre in Jacksonville, Florida, applauded Dracula's "good work" which was "mighty scary", while the manager of Houston's Majestic reported on how "seriously" his viewers took the film.' (Rhodes 2001: 122–23).

Dracula is a battle between two male characters, Dracula and Doctor Van Helsing, who dominate the narration and whose interaction creates the tension to the story. The vampire, a male personification of death, represents traditional and monstrous death, which threatens both the souls and bodies of his victims. In contrast, Van Helsing stands for the values of modern society and death, social control, knowledge and power. The bipolarity is visible also in the film's structure. The first part of the film concentrates on Dracula, whose monstrous powers are introduced for the viewer. During this part, the viewer is forced to recognize the monstrousness of this embodiment of death. The second part concentrates on Van Helsing, who defines vampirism and convinces other men to join his hunt to expose and kill the vampire. This part, therefore, emphasizes and justifies the alienation of death. In both parts, encounters with death or undeath guide the transitions from one narrative alignment position to another. In this film, which had a huge impact on later films and their narrative structures, all of the major alignment positions (heroes', victims' and monsters') are visible.

In the section where vampire as an embodiment of death is marked monstrous and unnatural, the first preferred alignment takes place with Renfield on his way to Transylvania, where he is expected to meet Count Dracula for a real-estate deal. The film opens with Renfield approaching Transylvania in a carriage. The narration focuses on his character, which represents Western rationality and the bourgeois world view familiar to the viewer. The locals and their irrational warnings about Dracula he dismisses as superstitious nonsense.

The viewer, however, is able to see Renfield's situation in a different light. Extra-textual knowledge of the story guides the viewer to take the locals' warnings and fears seriously, especially as the warnings are underlined by cutting to Dracula's castle, where the vampires rise from their coffins after darkness. Renfield, at this point, remains ignorant of the true state of events, but the viewer knows, which increases the tension to the narration. The information provided for the viewer by genre conventions and narrative clues is intended to make the viewer feel anxious for Renfield, who also becomes suspicious when he continues his lone journey towards Dracula's castle. He starts noticing strange things: a bat directing the horses, the decaying castle and his host's strange features. At this point, both the viewer and Renfield feel in awe of Dracula, who appears fascinating and horrifying at the same time.

When Renfield is attacked by Dracula, the shared fears come true. At the moment of the attack, the proposed alignment process shifts as well. From this point onwards, Renfield has been touched by death. And more often than not, the touch of death in itself creates marginalization and alienation of any character in living dead films. It shows how the idea of modern death as alienated from the public space influences the world of these films. In the case of Renfield, the distancing process is further emphasized by his reactions to encountering death. He becomes insane, and his incapability to deal with death puts him in a position where the viewer both pities him and is horrified by his transformation.

For a while after the viewer's alienation from Renfield, the narrative concentrates on Dracula. This alignment carries Dracula during his ocean journey and arrival in London, giving the viewer access to him approaching his victims aggressively or seductively. Dracula offers a position that is not available to the viewer in everyday life, presupposing negotiation over the offered violent encounters. The monstrous position can obviously become disturbing as well. For example, Cohen (2001: 252) holds that an occasional position of the monster, or understanding and sympathizing with an evil character, can also produce negative feelings and 'cause dissonance, guilt, or even fear'.

For instance, this is the case in a scene where Dracula kills a flower girl after his arrival in London. The viewer sees a girl trying to sell a flower to the vampire. Instead of taking the flower, Dracula leans towards the girl. When Dracula approaches the girl, the viewer is situated behind Dracula's back. This allows the viewer to witness the girl's expression change from welcoming to anxious. At this point, the viewer is shown a close-up of Dracula and his staring eyes, which cut back to the close-up of the flower girl. Her wide-open and trance-like eyes reveal how the victim reacts to this embodiment of death with amazement and anxiety. This dual positioning is, according to Wheeler Winston Dixon (1995: 7), a typical solution in the violent scenes, encouraging the viewer to try out different positions, those both of victim and tormentor.

Elizabeth Cowie argues that the very unpleasure can also contribute to the viewer's pleasure, as the horror film's dominant feature of aiming to horrify rests on the idea of unpleasure and traumatic events. The horror genre depends on the anxiety it stimulates in the viewer, and the understanding of the difference between reality and fiction stops cinematic trauma from turning into a real trauma. Unlike most theorists, Cowie does not try to explain how a negative emotion is turned into a positive experience, but considers the possibility that the viewer may enjoy these films because of their very unpleasantness (Cowie 2003: 27–34). By the same token, death may be a source of stress for a viewer, but it may also create excitement in the very encounter.

Moreover, Alison Landsberg notes that when a suggested position becomes uncomfortable for the viewer, they can distance themselves from that position. The uncomfortable position of the monster, for example, is not forced, even if it were to be cinematically stressed (Landsberg 2009: 222–28). In the flower girl scene, the narration of this classical film actually supports the viewer's distance from the death of the girl. After the shot where the threat is represented and countershot, which marks the horrific reaction, both the vampire and his victim disappear behind the corner. This hides the actual attack from the viewer. Still, during the empty shot, viewers can hear the girl screaming, and they can guess what is going on. This educated guess is later confirmed when the police find the girl's body on the street. The viewer is not forced to witness the actual death scene, although it is hinted at.

This scene proves, at the very least, the monstrous and deadly powers of the vampire. Thus, when new characters are introduced later on, the preferred alignment positions are also offered to the viewer. Dracula visits Doctor Seward and his company at the opera, and although the scene's dominating position is still Dracula's, the focus is shifted to Lucy, who finds Dracula's appearance bewitching. It is made obvious to the viewer that Lucy is dangerously affected by Dracula.

Lucy's transformative death becomes anticipated in a scene where Lucy and Mina are getting ready for the night after meeting Dracula at the opera. Lucy keeps singing Dracula's praises, deeply impressed by him. The cross-cutting camera reveals the silent character of Dracula standing in the darkness of the garden. When Lucy falls asleep, the viewer knows to expect the arrival of the vampire, who soon enough flies in from the open window as a bat and is transformed to his human form by the side of Lucy's bed. The vampire bends over, his teeth close to Lucy's white neck. At this point, the camera cuts away from the scene, the next shot showing Lucy's body in hospital and a voice pronouncing 'Another Dead'. The following conversation reveals that Lucy has died from blood loss despite several transfusions. There has apparently been a transformation phase, which is not shown. It is later suggested that Lucy has indeed become an undead, but this side plot is not further explored, as Lucy merely functions as proof of the vampire's powers. The implicit depiction of Lucy's transformative death is typical of classical films. Again, death has an alienating effect as the touch of death serves as a transformation in the narrative's perspective on characters.

However, Lucy's transformative death also introduces us to Van Helsing inspecting her body, after which he becomes the focus of the narration. He is trying to make sense of her death by investigating her blood cells: 'Gentlemen, we are dealing with the undead.' Van Helsing, in fact, proves to be the first Western character to understand the threat posed by a vampire, but unlike the superstitious locals of Transylvania, his approach is scientific. Struggling to expose Dracula's monstrousness, Van Helsing offers a sensible alignment position. He represents safety, knowledge and resistance of the vampire – or resistance of death. He is an embodiment of that authoritative and professional voice which modern society uses to repress and marginalize death. His understanding and approach invites the viewer to respect him after the 'true' nature of Count Dracula has been exposed. The film also makes clear the position of Dracula. The viewer can, still, choose to align with the vampire who threatens his victims and opposes his hunters, but the narration focuses on the more positive characters of the hunters and victims for the rest of the film.

In addition to Van Helsing, Mina, who becomes Dracula's next victim, plays an important role in the second part of the film. Whereas Lucy was used to create a culminating point for the vampire's powers, Mina becomes the means of either winning or losing this war between two strong and exceptional men. Van Helsing swears that he will 'protect those whom you would destroy', to which Dracula replies: 'You are too late. My blood now flows through her veins.' However, for her part, Mina stands for a dual relationship with death where it is both seductive and terrifying. She represents a problematic relationship with modern death in that she tries to maintain the ideal, but ultimately fails to do so.

In the classical living dead films, the relationship between (male) monsters and (female) victims was often eroticized and depicted as a love affair. Similarly, Mina's struggling with her pure love for John (life) and impure desire for Dracula (death) is emotional, although her resisting position to the vampire is the more desired one culturally. In these films, women hinted at a seductive relationship with death and they needed to be saved from their own desires by men. Such a patriarchal development is seen in other classical living dead films as well, which all have a seducing or possessing character (monster) who leaves his mark on women who need to be saved from both the monster and themselves. Bruce F. Kawin (1995: 311) argues that most classical horror films deal with a perverse or unsatisfactory love triangle: 'monster steals the girl, boy kills monster, girl kisses boy'. While this simple version can be seen in *Dracula*, it is similarly visible in *The Mummy* and *White Zombie*.

Although, at the end of these stories, normality returns through a monogamous, heterosexual relationship, when the women start an intimate relationship with something that should be alienated from modern society, both female sexuality and intimacy of death are given some thought. While the position of male fear of these issues is the preferred perspective, the viewer is provided with the option of a seductive relationship with otherness and death. Kawin recognizes this the horror film's necessity for 'some real emotional and ethical intercourse between monster and survivor, in the course of which both are changed'. For example, Kawin argues that the boy and the monster always represent 'two sides of the girl's own sexual desire (i.e. of her own sexual self-image)' (Kawin 1995: 311–12). In such a view, the boy speaks for the socially accepted form of sexuality, or monogamous, matrimonial sexuality (reality principle), whereas the monster represents open, deadly and free sexuality (pleasure principle).

The women of *Dracula*, and Mina in particular, can therefore be seen to fight with two conflicting sexualities. Mina is described as a virtuous woman who is respected and admired by men, especially by her fiancé, John. When Dracula enters Mina's room at midnight, she remembers the encounter as nightmarish the next day:

And when the dream came it seemed the whole room was filled with mist. It was so thick I could just see the lamp by the bed, a tiny spark in the fog. And then I saw two red eyes staring at me, and a white livid face came down out of the mist. It came closer … and closer. I felt its breath on my face … and then its lips.

While Mina is complaining that this dream has drained life out of her, Dracula walks into the room, and the whole situation changes. She forgets her previous complaints of feeling ill, announcing that she has never felt better in her life.

The scene illustrates how Mina is socially ashamed of her encounter with Dracula, but at being reminded of the available pleasures she is willing to explore the new path more closely. Next time, it is Mina who is the active party, walking to Dracula who is waiting for her in the garden. The following day she seems, once again, to be loyal to her virtuous self and asks Van Helsing to help save her soul at least, if not the sinful body, from the vampire. She denies herself from John as impure, guiding her fiancé: 'You mustn't touch me. And you mustn't kiss me – ever again.' However, she will later defend her new-found sexuality. She complains to John that other men are trying to lock her (her sexuality) in her room, even though the night is the only time she really feels alive.

Mina fights with her awakening sexuality and, according to Wood, it is the possibility of this awakening that constitutes the true horror of women's sexuality in *Dracula*. These women are consequently returned to the moral order and saved from their desires. It would be interesting to know, says Wood, what would happen if the women followed their desires, as sexuality is not only sexuality, but is connected to questions of power, action and energy (Wood 1996: 373). In *Dracula*, this alternative story is implied by Dracula's three wives back in Transylvania. They provide a first glimpse of the queer potential and potency of dealing with a different sexuality in vampire films. Harry M. Benshoff and Jean Griffin (2006: 76–77) maintain that horror films have proved important for queer audiences since the classical era: 'While horror films supposedly uphold heterosexuality as normative, they also present the sexually Other as fascinating and thrilling.' Queer and feminist readings of these films thus go hand in hand. The structure of the films reproduce matrimonial heterosexuality, but the possibilities to read alternative meanings inside the story provide emancipative positions for the viewer.

Although the process where Mina and Lucy struggle against their sexually oppressive social roles can also be read as emancipating, at the end of *Dracula*, the conventional norms prevail and the perspective of the hero is given preference: Dracula is killed. As Grant (2007: 48) and Rhonda Berenstein (1995: 231–35, 262) argue, horror films may allow fluid positions and pleasures, including monstrous positions, throughout the film narration, but most commonly, the end of these films restores the social order. The patriarchal composition of the story is explained by Richard Maltby as a crisis of patriarchal society during the Depression, which also impacted on a cultural crisis, leading to a rise in conservative attitudes. He argues that while women's sexuality was more daring in the films of the 1920s, the 1930s once again tried to isolate women's sexuality into monogamy and a state of innocence (Maltby 1995: 255–59).

Also, at the allegorical level of the story, the beginning of the living dead films forces death back into the public domain, challenging its marginalized role and studying it throughout the narration, but similar to the model created by *Dracula*, in the end, death is returned to its place in modern society and positioned firmly outside the legitimate social sphere. The final death of the main monster serves as closure in the classical films in particular, which respect the dramatic value of a distinct end. Vivian Sobchack continues that closure is important in solving major conflicts and ambiguities. In most cases, closure provides comforting security of death's final exclusion (Sobchack 1995: 105–06, 109, 112).

The moral dimension of the exclusion of death is foregrounded in the scene where Dracula is killed. At this point, Mina is under his power, as the vampire has kidnapped the girl and taken her to the ruins of the Abbey. Although the viewer fears for her innocence, the narration has distanced itself from her frame of reference because of her contamination by death. The focus is now on the heroes, on the perspectives of Van Helsing and John, who are trying to save Mina. Although Van Helsing's superior knowledge of vampires has earned him respect, the closing scene suggests that the viewer be aligned with John.

There are two important reasons for this shift. First, John models emotions and tensions for the viewer. Horrified at Mina's fate and desperate to rescue her, John's reaction to Mina's abduction is emotional – a position which the viewer can share. In contrast, Van Helsing is more interested in his own struggle with Dracula and wants to destroy the vampire and Mina, too, if she has already transformed. Second, then, John has a more moral relationship to violent death than does Van Helsing, who is prepared to violently kill the vampire(s) and takes it all in his stride. John, however, finds it hard to help him and has difficulties in witnessing the killing of a living being. John, therefore, becomes the ideal moral position for the viewer. He offers a clean and moral getaway from violent death.

The alienation from Van Helsing, and final death of Dracula, is further emphasized at the discursive level of the scene where the professor kills Dracula by piercing his heart. Instead of showing the act itself, the body of the vampire's victim, Mina, is used to communicate the action. Mina is in Dracula's power, and when Van Helsing prepares to strike the wooden stake through the vampire's heart, the camera cuts to Mina, who provides a reaction shot as she experiences every one of these blows to her body. In this way, the viewer is allowed to engage with Mina, who is saved. By replacing the act of violence with a reaction shot during the monster's final death, the demand for taking responsibility for violence is replaced with positive emotional alignment. Once Dracula is dead, Van Helsing is left alone in a decrepit castle, while John carries his beloved Mina (and the viewer) into the sunrise and a brighter future.

As *Dracula* shows, films may change character alignment, but they create hierarchies, too, between different character positions through allegiance. These hierarchies also mark the ideology or morality of the films and determine how the films mediate the relationships with death to the viewer. Carl Plantiga (1999: 253) claims that a film's emotional responses and engagement are 'fully integrated in the film's moral and ideological project'. In *Dracula*, for example, the discourse occasionally tells events from Dracula's point of view, but this position is made uncomfortable for the viewer. What is highlighted in contrast are the heroes' and victims' moral positions. And in the end, Mina's/John's emotional and innocent perspectives are morally and ethically more appreciated than Van Helsing's respectable, practical, but ultimately violent position. The idealization of responsibility is further stressed in the sequel *Dracula's Daughter* (1936), which starts with the police arresting Van Helsing for the murder of Dracula.

When evaluating the morality of characters in living dead films, the challenging question is how the justification of violence is carried out. The classical films tend to protect both their heroes and the viewers from the consequences of deadly violence. First, the question was circumvented by denying that there were problems with defensive violence in the first place. Similarly, as the viewer is distanced from Van Helsing at the moment of his violent act in *Dracula*, none of the main characters uses violence against the zombie master or his underlings in *White Zombie*. Instead, Charles Beaumont, the man who was responsible for Madeleine's zombification and who has been zombified himself, drags the zombie master to death with him as self-punishment and as an act of atonement. Furthermore, in *The Mummy*, there is no physical violence against the mummy whatsoever. Instead, an ancient ritual and intervention by an Egyptian god makes the mummy return to ashes. Second, the distance between the terrifying act and the viewer is highlighted: the spectator is not forced to witness the performance of death (see also Freeland 2000: 243).

3.2. *White Zombie* – Distancing and Alienating Death

Although death and dying were an important part of the classical films, the main tendency was to alienate these same phenomena at both the story level and discourse level. In *Dracula*, and also in *The Mummy*, the alienation is especially clear with the final deaths of the monsters, but in *White Zombie* alienation of the undead and images of death are underlined at the level of characters, events and symbolism. First, the zombies were alienated due to their cultural distance to the United States and their oppressed position as (monstrous) slave workers. Second, similarly as the viewer is denied any access to the zombies' perspective, the viewer is protected from the possible negative effects of confronting death at the levels of images and story.

In *White Zombie*, the references to magical death arise from zombies' roots in the Caribbean voodoo tradition where these non-personas are created by *Bokors* (priests) with voodoo magic. Once the *Bokor* traps the victim's soul and the victim dies, he/she keeps walking around with a catatonic face, without any memories and the ability to speak or recognize friends and loved ones. These features made their way into zombie films, where, most importantly, automated zombies were forced to obey their master in the absence of a free will of their own. This legend was introduced to American audiences in William Seabrook's book *The Magic Island* (1929), but into Western fiction more generally this legend was permanently assimilated through films (see also Bishop 2006: 197–98).

The mysterious nature of zombies, Haiti and voodoo cult associations were used in the marketing, as Rhodes notes. The film was first advertized as a mishmash of horror, thrill and love, and the varied themes also brought the film adverse reviews, but when the marketing concentrated on the film's unusual and mysterious elements, the film proved to be a relative success for its director Victor Halperin (Rhodes 2001: 124–35). By using horror formulas and themes, this film both exploited and exoticized the American moviegoers' awareness of Haiti and curiosity about voodoo practices (Fay 2008: 83).

White Zombie represents voodoo as a form of control and slavery. Indeed, in this film the true monster is Murder Legendre, the zombie master who uses his voodoo powers to intervene in the lives and autonomies of other people by turning them into zombies. In this film, zombies are not alienated because of what they do, but because their unnatural relationship with death and lack of autonomy are terrifying. It would be too simplifying to interpret the relationship between the zombie master and his subjects only as a metaphor of slavery in the Haitian and Caribbean context. Instead, *White Zombie's* perspective is undeniably American, with links to debates on the American occupation of Haiti (1915–34), which was nearing its end at the time of the film's release, as well as to questions of colonialism and postcolonialism. The American occupation has mainly fostered two emphases on the postcolonial interpretations of the film: the slave workers have inspired criticism of class, capitalism and labour, while possession based on ethnicity and womankind has stirred up an analysis of oppression built on race and gender. What is common to all earlier interpretations is that the zombies have created perfect allegories for oppression and submission (Fay 2008; Bishop 2008; Sheller 2003; Aizenberg 1999).

White Zombie's oppression stems from its undead characters. Legendre appears to have two kinds of zombie labour: servants and slave workers. First, the mill slaves are an exploitable and replaceable workforce. These zombies can be seen as an alienated workforce. They become a necessity for capitalism, which needs the legions of a workforce, and the most convenient workers are those who only work and ask for nothing else (Shaviro 2002: 281–85). Second, the servants are used not only as a workforce, but also as a strategic tool of control, which guarantees Legendre's power in the community. He admits that his zombie servants were once his enemies, including local authorities, whom he zombified in order to control them. The servant zombies function as warning examples for anyone who might step in Legendre's way. When seen as allegories of politics, the two zombie types stand for the two sides of the American occupation: the importance of economics and the presentation of power. The dual function is seen, for example, in Jennifer Fay's (2008: 82–83, 87–89) comment that the underlying reasons for this crusade for democracy were to gain control over strategic territory, win economic command and force economic dependency on the United States.

In addition to workers, the film introduces a new type of zombie and oppression. At the request of the jealous Beaumont, Legendre zombifies Madeline. *White Zombie's* narration first centres on Madeleine, who has come to the distant and exotic location of Haiti to get married. While the story begins through Madeleine's eyes, she is excluded from the narration when she is poisoned during her wedding. In her transformation into a zombie she gains horrific characteristics through death. She also loses her ability to speak and express herself, which, similarly to other silent zombies, highlights her exclusion. The voicelessness or inarticulateness is understood by Ingebretsen as a part of the monster's alienation process. When a monster is doomed to silence it is denied a common language and is excluded from being heard. The voicelessness of the monster becomes a way of removing sympathy (Ingebretsen 2001: 11, 37, 170). Similarly, only at the end of *White Zombie*, when Madeleine starts to fight her zombification, is her point of view restored to the narration. Saved from zombification (death), she regains her voice and position in society.

Her fate becomes central to the film. While the local zombies represent social problems, these remain marginal until they are encountered through a young, white woman (Aizenberg 1999: 462). Similarly, at an implicit level, death's disturbing power becomes problematic when it is met by a Western character and, in particular, by a white woman. Ellen Draper argues that men become enslaved to be used as workers, but Madeline is zombified because she is an object of male sexual desires. For Draper, the zombie women of the 1930s and 1940s films signify an allegory of women's oppressed position (both socially and economically) in a cultural situation where men have power and control over women (Draper 1988: 54). Edward Lowry and Richard deCordova summarize the male characters' relationship to Madeline as possessive. She is first possessed by Neil, her fiancé. After her burial and zombification, Beaumont owns Madeline as a zombie. After Beaumont regrets his possession, Legendre takes over, and finally, when both Legendre and Beaumont are destroyed, Neil regains possession of Madeline (Lowry & deCordova 1984: 351).

Still, while being zombified, Madeline manages momentarily to resist the possessing and controlling gaze of the zombie master. After Neil has followed Madeline to the castle, Legendre commands her to kill him. She obediently grabs a knife and approaches Neil. By his side, she raises the knife, but hesitates at the last moment and, for a short while, seems to recognize something. This short moment of consciousness and recognition is enough to save Neil's life, although Madeline still remains under Legendre's power. Her brief emotional reaction suggests the possibility of resistance. Even Legendre admits that if someday the zombies regained their consciousness, they would tear him apart. Legendre's comment refers to the awareness of the occupier (whether zombie master or another country) that oppressive actions cause hate and revengefulness. The risk and possibility of resistance is always there.

However, somewhat troublingly, resistance and oppression in *White Zombie* appear in a racial form where modern Westerners have the power and knowledge to resist the destructive force of death. When Madeline is threatened, the monster warns that it will contaminate the American realm of the world with death. As Bishop (2008: 141–50) notes, the major threat in *White Zombie* is hybridization and colonization of Western cultural purity by a primitive culture. Western ignorance of the fate of the local zombies shows that Western culture regards death as suitable for the more primitive societies. When death meets the realm and modernized West, the situation changes. In the end, when oppression is overcome by the Western characters, Western supremacy over death and the primitive is complete.

The rescue mission releases society from under Legendre's power. This is a moot question precisely because the release is carried out by Western characters – Neil and Burner the missionary. Ethnicity is further questioned through the ways in which the zombie characters are allowed to resist oppression. The local zombies remain unconscious the whole time, while the two Western zombies, Madeline and Beaumont, are given a chance to resist. Beaumont, in fact, starts to regret his actions after seeing the zombified Madeline playing piano with empty, lifeless and staring eyes. Beaumont sighs: 'I thought that beauty alone would satisfy. But the soul is gone. I can't bear those empty, staring eyes'. Legendre now turns against him and makes him one of his servants. Because Beaumont is the first man to comprehend the transformation process he is going through, Legendre accidentally prompts the possibility of zombie resistance. With his last remaining powers, Beaumont confronts his former ally and future zombie master and drags Legendre to death with him. Unlike in Madeline's case, Beaumont's resistance is based on rationality, which is necessary for resistance to be successful.

Thus, Beaumont comes to represent the zombie resistance that has so far been absent. As Bishop summarizes, the zombies had 'no voice, no opinions, no consciousness, and (most importantly) no ability to organize'. But Beaumont does this as a Westerner, while the Haitian slaves remain unconscious and follow their master to death. Bishop quite rightly argues that the colonial zombies remain as Others and without a place in the Western order. When the zombies are finally heard, it is rather recognition than true interaction: the marginalized are still in the margins, albeit in a different margin (Bishop 2008: 146–50). The ending is, indeed, slightly troubling, as it seems to hide problems with the American occupation by depicting Westerners as bringing civilization (also in the form of modern death), peace and democracy to society. As Fay maintains, the classical zombie films represent only the American side of the occupation trauma. The zombies are marked as monstrous, and their deadly jump into nothingness and Madeline's 'I dreamed' attitude erase all trace of the occupation, similar to having been erased from American memory (Fay 2008: 82–83, 93–94, 99). The closure also removes the zombies' threatening force of death from society, presenting white Western men, values and practices as modern saviours and as capable of opposing the destructive and primitive power of death.

Similarly, as the zombies are alienated from the story through oppression, they are also alienated at the level of film discourse. As embodiments of death, zombies are represented as horrifying characters, although they could also be read as mistreated ones. After all, *White Zombie* posed questions of unequal division of work, power and wealth, connecting not only with colonialism but also with the cultural trauma of the Great Depression when many audience members could sympathize with monsters as outsiders of society and victims of either bad luck or human wrongs (Skal 1993: 16, 114–15; Crane 1994: 72–74, 91–92; Wells 2002: 51; Carroll 1990: 208). Therefore, the marginalized position of the undead could be sympathized with, even if it also served to highlight their otherness.

Although, the automated zombies of *White Zombie* do not act monstrously on their own, from the beginning of the film discursive solutions are used to make them horrifying characters with whom intimate relationships should be avoided. Their monstrosity is created by different signals (sounds, visual cues, camera angles), *mise-en-scène* (setting, lighting, costumes and make-up, the monsters' outward appearances and figure expression), and relations on and off the screen. *White Zombie* introduces the monsters in the course of the first minutes of the film when Madeline and Neil (together with the viewer) encounter a group of zombies walking catatonically among the graves in the darkness. When shown on-screen for the first time, the zombies are shot from a low angle and through underlighting to stress the threat. Recognition of the undead takes place through their postures, iconographical symbols of graves and darkness, and the reaction of the couple's carriage driver – in shock, he starts driving madly towards the mansion. The white crosses looming in the darkness and the party's passing by several graves further amplifies the panicky getaway. When accused of almost getting them killed, the driver reacts: 'Worse than that, monsieur, we might have been caught', and explains their meeting with the clumsy and hollow-eyed men: 'They are not men, they are dead bodies – Zombies, living dead, corpses diggen from their graves.'

The viewer is given a number of cues to recognize generic conventions of horror and its monsters: character reactions and offered explanations, setting, sound, lighting, cutting, camera angles and the slow and catatonic movements of the living dead. However, when these are set aside, the zombies do not, in fact, appear very frightening, but rather emotionless and depressed. As Leffler notes, it is often the narration and narrative elements which tell the viewer that the monster should be feared. In the end, the viewer may find that the monster was not such a threat after all; it was the narration that transmitted fear and horror (Leffler 2001: 48, 180–82). Similarly, the horror genre typically narrates death as unnatural and disturbing without discussing whether death itself is horrifying.

This opening provides both recognition of the embodied death and an alignment through a horrified reaction. However, the opening says nothing about the zombies' monstrousness as such. By the mill scene, which shows the zombies working as slaves, it must be clear to the viewer that these creatures do not act monstrously unless they are ordered to. In this sense, they could be seen as tragic rather than terrifying, although the local people view them as monsters. The driver's reaction to the zombies is not stirred by anything that the zombies have done to him, but it stems from cultural beliefs and fears. The driver evaluates the zombies through their relationship to death, which he also offers to the viewer: the undead are unnatural, animated dead and, therefore, monstrous.

Whereas this film alienates death at the symbolical level of oppression and by marking the undead as monsters at the discursive level, death is alienated also at the level of images. In the classical living dead films, explicit death scenes were avoided and most death events take place off-screen. Although the actual act is rarely shown to the viewer at the discursive level, the event of death is still part of the narration. For example, the films reveal the events leading to death and the consequences of death, which follows the broader logic of causality in classical Hollywood narration (Bordwell, Staiger & Thompson 1996: 13). In other words, classical films often excluded bodily violence from their imagery, and acts of violent death are rarely shown to the viewer. Only the outcome is made clear, mostly through other characters' reactions, narrative consequences and only rarely through glimpses of actual corpses. This solution creates a rather different film/viewer relationship than do explicit death images, but the difference is not a question of effectiveness but rather of uses of cinematic strategies that create effectiveness through imagined witnessing. Indeed, consequences of death mediate, mostly at the cognitive level, the narrative turning points of the film, whereas reactions to hidden events mediate emotions and experiences related to death.

At the level of shots, in order to avoid showing the performances of death events, the classical films avoid objective shots which invite the viewer to be a silent witness of events, and characters' point-of-view shots which would reveal to the viewer what characters see. While preferring not to show the death scenes (acts), the classical films addressed the viewer with consequences and responses to death. In other words, classical films tend to use reaction shots when a character clearly sees something (a death event) that is not shown to the viewer, and the viewer is allowed to see only how the character reacts to what he or she sees. The film can also deny the viewer any kind of encounter with the event, as it can cut from the scene before the death event or use other means to narrate the event. (From how different shots are used to create on-screen and off-screen spaces, see, for example, Casetti 1998: 47–115).

At the level of film scenes and sequences, in order to avoid exploiting on-screen performances of violence, a typical aesthetic solution in classical living dead films was either to cut to the following scene before the act, or to show an empty image or any other part of the *mise-en-scène*. Furthermore, as images of violated bodies were a difficult topic, the lack of images was compensated with sound, which makes off-screen death scenes vivid and disturbing at the same time (see also Prince 2003: 207–45). The arrival of sound proved to be a most important invention for the horror genre and its conventions, as it made possible generic uses of anticipating sounds and special audio effects for shock and suspense. Regarding the death scenes, the main focus was on the sound-related consequences, including both dialogue and sound effects. As Giles (1984: 49) says, sound is a typical way of communicating frightful events while the gaze is restricted. Classical films, in fact, made good use of the newly found possibilities. Philip Hayward introduces a three-layered world of horror sounds: (1) music that creates tension and brings additional elements of anxiety to otherwise often empty images; (2) sound effects that, especially in classical films, use sounds of nature to create tension and a link to the wild (animal noises, thunder and storms etc.); and (3) voice performances where the dialogue creates dramatic acting and screaming, in particular, that accompanies horror stories with dramatic voices (Hayward 2009: 2, 6).

Not only did sound provide possibilities for sound effects, but also, as Nick Roddick stresses, it changed audience expectations and the narration. The advent of sound demanded more credibility from the dialogue, characters and stories (Roddick 1983: 10–11). This could be described as the last major shift from former cinematic attractions to classical Hollywood's realistic narration, seen in the classical living dead films' fascination with both sound effects and dialogue. However, Robert Spandoni argues that the arrival of sound impacted on the first horror sound films rather differently from most other genres. Sound did not add realism as such, but sound effects and dialogue were employed to stress the uncanny nature of horror and its monsters, to trigger sensations and feelings of strangeness (Spandoni 2007: 1–8, 121–27). Awkward pauses, unconnected lines and clichés about death became trademarks of living dead films. For example, just before her transformative death, Madeline in *White Zombie* mysteriously argues 'I see death'. Indeed, horror cinema adapted the coming of sound to its own uses, to focus on the spectacular nature of the genre.

With the help of these narrative solutions, classical horror films play with the viewer's expectations, promising but delaying the fulfilment of horrific events, often through restricting the viewer from seeing what is happening. Giles recognizes this as a fetishist structure, where the viewer is both afraid of looking and desires full vision. In such a structure, classical horror narration turns to defending the viewer from themself. While the narration provides the necessary psychological and culturally accepted defence mechanism, the viewer can enjoy the possibility of looking (Giles 1984: 45–48). This fetishist structure of hide-and-seek is made explicit in *White Zombie*'s depictions of violent death scenes, which emphasize the constant play with expectations and the revealing and hiding of death scenes. Violent death is imminent from the opening to the closure of the film, and whereas the first deaths are hidden from the discourse, the last ones are more detailed, with the narration slowly revealing the events of violent death to the viewer.

The film opens with a scene of death through a funeral: the corpse is buried in the middle of the road to be better guarded against the evil forces which might take advantage of the corpses. The enchanting music of the funeral wills the scene, even when the image does not concentrate on it. With the help of exotic music, the imagination of the viewer is thus triggered by a fascinating explanation of the dangers facing the dead, but any further knowledge is denied at this point. Interestingly, Giles argues that sometimes, '*not seeing* – the delayed, blocked or partial vision' is what provides a sense of horror and fear, and therefore the expected pleasure. Furthermore, he maintains that instead of an excess of images and emotions, the anticipatory vision is more interesting, because it implies the horrific event which it refuses to encounter. These restricted scenes promise, yet do not deliver (Giles 1984: 41–42).

The next death is already more than a suggestion, taking place at Legendre's mill, where the zombie slaves are working. First, the camera provides a long shot of the grinder, showing sugarcane being crushed by the blades. The image then cuts to the zombies carrying baskets full of sugarcane above the grinder. Suddenly, one of the zombies sways and silently falls over the edge. The fall or the moment when the body hits the blades is not shown, but the image cuts to the zombie slaves who continue to rotate the blades and mindlessly mince the body into pieces. This scene shows the viewer the preceding events and effects (or lack of them), but not the actual event of death. Also, what strikes the eye is the insensitivity of the other characters. No-one seems to notice or care about the death of a zombie, and even the sound world of the scene remains the same throughout. The viewer can only hear the screeching sound of the grinder, not even a single scream or climactic music indicating the accident, which remains hidden in a disturbing silence. When the image cuts to Beaumont, who has witnessed the scene and shows his astonishment at and confusion over the situation, the viewer is offered a position of experiencing discomfort with him.

The following death scene is the more closely observed transformative death of Madeline. The viewer is first allowed to watch Madeline being given a poisoned rose by Beaumont. Legendre then arrives and starts to create a voodoo doll for Madeline. The cuts between Madeline celebrating her wedding inside the house and Legendre starting the voodoo process behind the window create a cause/effect chain of Legendre becoming responsible for her death-like state. The actual event of her transformative death is shown through Neil, who holds Madeline in his arms. His subjective view exposes Madeline's stare with empty, dead eyes before the eyes finally close. The scene reveals her death to the viewer, yet it is not violent at the level of the image. It is rather like falling asleep, and as the film will go on to show, the poisoned rose has created a death-like state, not death itself. However, the revealing death scene opens up possibilities to depict the rest of the death events in more detail.

The next death takes place in Legendre's castle. Legendre has just poisoned Beaumont and laid bare his intentions of possessing both Madeline and Beaumont. Beaumont begs his servant to kill Legendre, but the master of the castle manages to prevent this. Suddenly, his zombies start to pile into the room, surrounding the servant, catching him and hauling him upstairs. However, the camera does not follow the zombies, but remains with Legendre and Beaumont, who is begging for mercy on behalf of his servant.

While the image lingers on these two men, a scream from upstairs implies a set of events to the viewer. The servant's scream enables the viewer to imagine the worst, but when the image suddenly cuts to the events upstairs, the zombies are still carrying the servant and nothing bad has yet happened. Similarly, Thomas Elsaesser argues that if the source of a sound is kept away from the frame, the viewer's imagination becomes more efficient in creating the source. The off-screen world of horror is in a central role, as it introduces a range of elements in order to surprise, shock or even mislead the viewer (Elsaesser 1998: 195–96). But the death scene is not over yet. While the servant has already seen the torrent that will be his end, the viewer is still in a non-seeing position. After a play of hide and reveal, the viewer sees the servant thrown into the torrent, where he desperately reaches out his hand. And once again, the actual scene of death is not revealed. Instead of focusing on the servant's death struggle, the camera follows the zombies leaving the scene.

The next scene of death depicts the death of the zombies in the final reel of the film. The zombies act under Legendre's command, but when Bruner, a missionary, knocks Legendre on the head, Legendre loses his hypnotic control over the zombies, who fall off the edge of the cliff one by one. The first of these falls is partly shown to the viewer: a zombie steps over the edge, while the following cut reveals the shadow of his falling body reflected on the face of the rock. However, before the body hits the awaiting rocks, the image is once again, and at the last moment, cut away. The event of death is unavoidable, but still not shown. Indeed, when an act or corpse is presented, the camera limits the viewer's gaze in one way or another. For example, shadows could be used to mediate the event. Or, if a corpse is shown to the viewer, the camera keeps its distance and limits the duration of the shot. There are no close-ups or lingering images of the corpses, not even of the monsters' final deaths. However, sometimes moments of death are shown if there is no explicit violence involved.

While the camera reveals more of the death scenes, there are still some restrictions which will be abolished by the time of the last death scene, that of Murder Legendre himself.

Regaining his consciousness after being hit on the head, Legendre realizes that he has lost his zombies and is fighting a losing battle. He tries to escape, but Beaumont catches up with him, forces him over the edge and jumps after him. The camera is not in the least interested in Beaumont's fall, but the fall of Legendre is followed in detail, although from a distance. The camera tracks Legendre's falling body, shows it hitting the rocks and lying there lifeless for a moment, before the sea washes the body away. The last death scene reveals everything and proves that the monstrous figure is dead, that the previous deaths and injuries caused by Legendre are avenged, and that the protagonists are free to continue their lives. The detailed death restores balance to the world at the same time as it fulfils the viewer's generic expectations. Still, while the closing scene concentrates on dying, the camera's objective gaze stays far from the falling body, keeping the viewer at a safe distance.

The restricted gaze emphasizes more the absence of an object of horror than excess of it. The absence has possibilities for creating horror, because the viewer may know what is going on although they are not allowed to witness it. What they can do instead is imagine these events. When the events are actually shown, it only reveals their artificial and constructed nature. Giles (1984: 48) argues that 'to look the horror in the face for very long robs it of its power'. This becomes evident in the closing scene of *White Zombie*, because the death of Legendre also means that he is deprived of his powers, the threat is dissolved and the viewer is allowed to master the image, and through image, master the image of death. The revealing and the controlling image of the final death of any monster is important in the creation of closure for classical films. Colin MacCabe (1986: 182–83) argues that seeing the actual image is considered to mediate the 'truth of events', whereas restricted views can also intentionally misinform the viewer. The revealing of the final death, therefore, proves that the monster is dead, which provides the classical necessity of returning the assaultive gaze back on itself, as Clover (1992: 208–09) formulates. Because the final deaths of the monsters provide closures, classical living dead films often describe them in more detail than the other deaths. By the end of *White Zombie*, the camera (and perhaps the viewer as well) has gained a controlling gaze over evil, the undead and even death – as in a truly modern world.

3.3. *The Mummy* and Scientific Death

Similarly, as in *Dracula* and *White Zombie*, the monstrous features of the undead and alienating narrative practices are highlighted in the classical mummy films. Hollywood took the spiritual curses related to protecting Egyptian tombs from grave robbers and other (by religious standards) impure people (Ikram 2003: 47–48, 195–200), and turned them into corporeal and deadly punishments on those who disturbed the mummy and made it rise from the dead. The first mummy films in the early 1930s were closely connected with Egyptomania, which was euphoric about the discovery of Tutankhamun's almost intact tomb in 1922. This find was especially intriguing to the horror genre because the crew had faced several misfortunes, leading the popular press to spread rumours of the mummy's curse (Lupton 2003: 31–32; Ikram 2003: 194; Craig & Smith 2003: 175). *The Mummy* (1932) exploits this euphoria. The beginning of the film introduces the mummy as an evil, undead and cursed being, of whom the writing on the casket buried with him warns: 'Death, eternal punishment, for anyone who opens this casket.'

Before Hollywood horror, the mummy figures had not necessarily been monstrous. Western literary tradition had rather emphasized the mummies' romantic nature: they appeared in preternatural love stories and embodied the nineteenth-century fascination with mystic ancient funeral and burial practices. This earlier tradition also presented mummies as victims, deployed as characters in romances where the mortal (men) fell in love with beautiful (female) mummies, or they were narrated through justified revenge when their peace had been disturbed. In contrast, the classical films abjected mummies, turning them into threatening monsters by drawing attention to their violent actions and perverse relationships with death and decay (see, for example, Ikram 2003: ix; Day 2006; Deane 2008: 385).

Hollywood burdened the mummies with evil and made them antagonists. In addition to the romance theme turned into a perversion, Day recognizes three other methods of this abjection process in the classical films. First, the undead status makes the mummy a liminal and impure character. Second, the films brand mummification as a pagan and barbaric ceremony which does not sanctify the dead bodies. And finally, the mummies become animal-like, especially in the classical sequels which make them unable to speak (Day 2006: 82–88). In other words, mummies started to represent occultism, past times and superstition – all the issues that conflict with the scientific ideals of the modern Western world.

At the time of the film's release, the Western attempt to deal with death-related topics scientifically refers to the idealization of modern death, which was starting to take a leading cultural role. In this process, mummies also came to represent traditional death that belongs to the past and could be studied and observed as part of the past, but which should not threaten modern life and its understanding of death. The central tension in the classical *The Mummy*, as in most classical living dead films, is created between modern Western and primitive foreign. In this film, ideals of scientification and professional management of death are contrasted with notions of traditional death, which, according to Walter (1994: 47), was quick and frequent, an open part of a community's life and was managed by priests and religious rituals. The mummy's (alias Imhotep alias Ardath Bey) representative role of traditional death is highlighted in his character: Imhotep was a priest in his own time and controlled the death rituals. Even his outer appearance where the skin still shows traces and prints of the shroud after his revival communicate his antiquity and link him with decay and the past.

The opening scene of *The Mummy* emphasizes the role of the mummy as an acceptable focus of archaeological studies, and his unacceptable role as an active figure in the modern world. The scene introduces Western scientists, archaeologist Sir Joseph Whemple, his assistant, and Doctor Muller, professor of occult sciences studying the ancient tomb findings and the mummy. Sir Joseph Whemple lectures on the importance of science: 'Our job is to increase the sum of human knowledge of the past, not to satisfy our own curiosity.' By focusing the viewer's attention on the three male characters studying the mummy, the scene suggests that it will be narrated from their perspective rather than that of the monster. It is their actions that become motivated and studied, while the mummy's motives remain unknown.

Where the older specialists aim to sift through the findings systematically, the young assistant is fascinated by the mummy, begging the others to focus on him, yearning to know who he was, why he deserved to be buried alive and what is in the mysterious box that was buried with him. When the older men finally agree to open the box, they find a casket with a curse on the cover. At this point, fascination merges with anxiety and doubt about the curse: should it be honoured or not? The scientific approach is further stressed in the response to Doctor Muller's plea for respect for the ancient curses. Whemple replies: 'In the interest of science, even if I believed in the curse, I'd go on with my work for the museum.' The older men take their debate on the curse's existence outside, leaving the assistant alone with the mummy. Although the narration occasionally cuts to the debating men during the rest of the scene, these cuts serve rather as intervals underlining the threat to the eager assistant when, turning a blind eye to the curse, he opens the casket and finds a scroll inside it.

It is through alignment with the assistant that the opening scene induces different emotions and reactions to the monster and to death in the space of a few minutes. During this one scene, fascination, anxiety and horror are addressed to the viewer. When the young man starts interpreting the scroll, the effects are brought home to the viewer at several levels, although mostly the discursive techniques concentrate and highlight the importance of the characters' figures, facial expressions and compositional relationships between characters through point-of-view shots (the viewer sees what a character sees from the character's perspective), reaction shots (the viewer sees how a character reacts to events) and close-ups (of faces, in particular) of both the assistant and the mummy. This scene crucially spotlights the mediating potential of the human face, although the whole posture of the body is used to communicate emotion as well. This is not surprising considering that the viewer tends to react to recognizable expressions and gestures, and even mimics these expressions rather automatically and involuntarily. Facial and bodily expressions are, therefore, forceful means of addressing emotions and experiences. Generating emotional responses, these cinematic expressions are also used to drag the viewer into the scene (Plantiga 1999: 240–43; Smith 1995: 96, 100–03).

The camera pans from the man to the mummy and back, revealing how the man's almost silent reading brings the mummy to life. First, the camera shoots the assistant unrolling the scroll and studying the signs, then pans to the mummy's corpse, which rests motionless and dead in its coffin, and finally pans back to the assistant. When the young man starts to read the spell, fascinated and unaware of the consequences of his actions, the camera cuts to a close-up of the mummy's face. The viewer witnesses the mummy slowly open his eyes, then move his arms and become animated. The assistant is still reading the scroll when the mummy extends his hand towards it. At this point, the camera returns to shoot the scroll in close-up. Suddenly, the mummy's hand appears, grabbing the scroll. The image pans backwards somewhat and shows the man finally raising his eyes from the text. His reaction is first amazement and disbelief, then fear. At this moment of recognition, film narration concentrates on the young man's face, expression and posture. The effect is further emphasized by the scream, which breaks the anticipating silence of the previous scene and turns into loud and hysterical laughter that seals the amazement, disbelief and horror into one continuing and affecting sound. From that moment on, once the man faces the animated mummy, the camera stays with him and mediates his emotional reactions to the viewer.

The man's face is first shot in close-up, followed by a shot of his frightened posture, which creates a combination of a reaction shot and a close-up. The reaction shot is effective, because it gives the viewer information about how the character reacts to what he sees and what emotions the event triggers – horror and shock. The close-up of the character's face provides intimate contact with the character and his emotions. Next, the point-of-view shot reveals that the assistant has been watching the mummy walk out of the tent. The camera pans to the floor, enabling the viewer to see the tail of the shroud being dragged through the door. The continuing point-of-view shot at the end of the scene gives the viewer access to the character's subjectivity and forces the viewer to align with his perspective. The hysterical laughter that surrounds this point-of-view image further accents the emotional shock as a reaction to a corpse that has been dead for more than 3,000 years being able to walk out of the door and disappear. When his scientist colleagues rush in on the scene, the only intelligible words the assistant is able to muster are: 'He went for a little walk. You should have seen his face.'

The opening scene shows how living dead films create different emotions in relation to death and undead monsters, and how these emotions provide interesting construction material for the viewer's experience. Indeed, in this one short scene, the relationship with death is at first filled with curiosity and exploration, but it also reveals the darker undertones of fear of the unknown. The initial fascination and anxiety is turned into horror by the resurrected mummy – and the reaction models the culturally acceptable response for the viewer as well.

The awakening of the mummy threatens the scientific procedures introduced in the opening and, later in the film, Doctor Muller, in particular, becomes a professional of death. As a professor of the occult, he is familiar with both modern Christianity and ancient paganism, which provides the necessary information needed to understand and control the past and its death rituals. He explains the existence of the mummy to the characters and the viewer alike, using his knowledge of the past to protect others. From this perspective, the mummy remains a religious relic from the past, and the ancient Egyptian funeral practices are studied and stripped of their powers by knowledge. The West uses its own scientific death system to control otherness.

The revived mummy and his primitive relationship to death become a threat to the modern world. Furthermore, Caroline Schroeder argues that in *The Mummy*, the modern and Judeo-Christian West discusses otherness through questions of religion and race. First, the dark mystery, primitiveness and superstition make ancient Egypt the Other, and second, modern Egypt is similarly distanced through Islam and the squalor of Cairo. These two are bound together by race so that Egyptian blood or non-whiteness is used as a 'visual codifier' that separates the superstitious people from the educated and cultural whiteness of the West (Schroeder 2003).

The colonial themes are visible at the level of narration, characters and images. Western characters take centre stage, while local people are absent or in subordinate positions – workers digging in the desert while Western archaeologists claim the credit or servants managing the households of Western people. Furthermore, Western superiority manifests in the chosen *mise-en-scène*. Most of the events take place at the excavation and museum run by Westerners and in the homes of Western authorities. The controlled locations reframe traditional death as a relic which can be studied but which does not influence the world outside museum institutions.

In the process, the film (like many archaeological films) becomes guilty of Orientalism: it remodels ancient Egypt as a demonic country that refuses to let go of its pagan magic (McGeough 2006: 182; Day 2006: 39, 60). This, as Schroeder (2003) argues, is to emphasize Western superiority, colonialism and imperialism, if not physically, then at least politically, economically and culturally. While the film highlights Western superiority on many levels, it still encounters traditional death, and the plot relies on the tension of the mummy's defying Western cultural and political colonialism. In these films, invasive and consuming death preys on Western practices, threatening American society's values and civilization. The fear of consumption was also related to the changing political and cultural power relations in the face of the Western world losing its colonial power.

At the time of *The Mummy*'s release, Egypt was slowly gaining independence from Britain and started to demand more self-government, also in relation to archaeological and cultural finds. Bradley Deane (2008: 406–07) maintains that this self-governance and occasional hostility towards the former colonial masters threatened the Western position and, symbolically, the mummies now turned into cursed competitors. Similarly, Day argues that the pre-classical mummy novels were an expression of guilt over Western colonialism and the seduction or rape of Egypt and its treasures. The new cultural context gave the mummy's revenge a new meaning: it threatened the autonomy of Western characters, in particular, and sought to exert its influence over what used to be a Western sphere (Day 2006: 38–66).

At the story level, Imhotep threatens to colonize at least part of the Western world by tempting Helen to join him in traditional death. Classical Hollywood chose not to communicate certain topical issues explicitly, but rather presented them through the individual's level, limiting the problems to the context of the main characters' lives. In a similar fashion, modern death has strived to limit the social and personal effects of dying and mourning at the level of the individual. The classical mummy, similarly, desires only to bring his lost lover back to life. Although he threatens Helen with a violent death and transformation, the threat of death is limited to one individual.

Helen is a hybrid character, half-British and half-Egyptian, and through her race, Schroeder (2003) argues, she becomes a symbol for the battle between West and East, and also for the battle over death-related practices. When Imhotep chooses her for the reincarnation of his ancient princess, Helen is caught between different worlds and times. Her role as a battlefield is underlined by a love triangle: she is torn between her desires for the Western Frank (modern saviour) and the Egyptian Ardath (traditional death), who are both in love with her. Part of her longs for an early grave and eternal love, whereas the other half wants a modern life freed from death. She begs Frank: 'There's death there for me. And life for something else inside me that isn't me. But it's alive too, and fighting for life. Save me from it, Frank.' This, indeed, can be seen as a symbolic reference to the suppressed death in modernity. Death desires to become noted, but it is constantly fought back. This ideological positioning invites the viewer to consider the Western ideals and practices as superior.

Ardath embodies traditional death seeking to fight its ground. As a representative of the colonizing power of an undead enemy, he threatens to consume Helen. This desire is visible in the scene where Ardath is allowed to express his desires and love for Helen. Although the mummy is abjected by multiple narrative choices, he is allowed to talk for himself and maintain at least some elements of the earlier romance stories and sympathetic characters. For example, Milly Williamson argues that positively addressed monsters' positions are available because they are offered in the text, too. These may be less obviously suggested positions in classical films, but even these monstrous positions are hybrid and thus open to multiple readings (Williamson 2005: 297–99). This particular sympathetic moment takes place in a sequence where Imhotep reveals his past to Helen through hypnosis. 'You shall not remember what I show you now and yet I shall awaken memories of love and crime and death.' The camera dives into the pool and into the mysterious past, which is framed by the mummy's voice-over narrating the death of an ancient princess and himself. The image then returns to the present, with Imhotep continuing his confession: 'My love has lasted longer than the temples of our gods. No man ever suffered as I did for you.'

This classical film has a whole sequence dedicated to the mummy's point of view, even if it takes place during hypnosis. It is not as if Helen would remember what has happened. Also, because of the hypnosis, the scene does not connect only to the romantic mummy, but also to his assaultive powers. In the classical living dead films, visually, one phenomenon catches the eye: the mediating role of staring eyes of both monsters and their victims. Carol Clover describes the repetitious gazes as assaultive (attacking) and reactive. Whereas the assaultive gaze is necessary to provide suspense and offence at the story level, horror narration stresses the reactive gaze of character (and viewer), which gives shelter and defence (Clover 1992: 191–200).

Although assaultive and reactive gazes have been widely used in horror narrations, classical living dead films were especially fascinated by their effects, not least because the gazes connected the films to the popular contemporary trend of hypnotization and mesmerism (Fay 2008: 83; Bishop 2008: 144). All classical undead monsters make use of their assaultive gaze to hypnotize or to seduce their victims and to control their enemies. The classical mummy, for example, resorts to the hypnotizing effect throughout the film. The very awakening of the mummy starts when he slowly opens his eyes, followed by repeated close-ups of the face, which stress the dark and mysterious eyes. His hypnotic powers are revealed when he arrives at Whemple's residence and meets the servant. The scene unfolds in low-key lighting, which highlights the mummy's impressive posture. During an intense and extreme close-up, the mummy's eyes grow bigger and lighter, contrasted by the dark background. The mummy does not kill the servant, only subordinates him, but the purpose of the scene is clear; in the next scene, when the mummy directs his hypnotic and assaultive gaze to his primary target, Helen, the viewer has already been warned of his powers.

The classical films made the assaultive (male) and reactive (female) gazes important means of addressing threat and tension to the viewer, who is, crucially, involved in this tension. The assaultive and reactive gazes are more often than not directed at the viewer as well (see also Clover 1992: 202–05; Lowry & deCordova 1984: 350–84). However, the camera not only reveals these assaultive and reactive gazes, but also often situates itself into either of these positions. Through the monster's point of view, the viewer is forced to take the perspective of the possessor. Uncomfortably enough, the monster does not only possess the victims, but also often possesses the images of the film as well. From time to time, the mummy's gaze is directed to the camera, and it is during these shots that the viewer, too, becomes possessed by his gaze. The viewer is invited into the position of the possessor and the possessed at the same time, suddenly becoming conscious and sometimes even horrified of his/her own possessive or assaultive gaze of violence, horror and death.

As these different gazes show, a violent positioning is possible even if the classical living dead films were expected to hide the actual death events. This is exactly Lowry's and deCordova's (1984: 349) point: when the camera situates the viewer in a sadistic position, the viewer is expected to participate in the violent death, although the actual viewers have potential to distance themselves from or reject the image.

The growing tension between the mummy's hypnotic gaze and Helen's adaptable gaze suggests an important feature in the use of assaultive and reactive gazes in the classical living dead films, that of gender. Clover stresses that the horror film's assaultive gaze is usually male, while the feminine aspect is found in the reactive. This reflects horror's tendency to simplify gender roles in that monsters and heroes are usually men, and women are made into victims (Clover 1992: 12, 211–12). Similarly, classical living dead films use women to authenticate the monstrous threat, and the struggle for and against violent deaths is likewise experienced, culminated and solved through women.

This penchant for placing women in a reactive role and men in the assaultive role, directing the monster's assaultive gaze towards women and the hero's assaultive gaze to the monster, can be compared to the cultural gender roles of death systems. According to Walter, when death was modernized it was also masculinized: the death industry of doctors, funeral directors, police officers, soldiers etc. came to be controlled by men, whereas women have historically carried the responsibility for mourning and reacting to death (Walter 1994: 13, 18). Similarly, in classical living dead films, men can be seen to produce death in violent ways and to act against death, to exclude death from society and control it by struggling and abjecting the undead monsters. In contrast to the dual role of men, women are made to represent emotional struggle, to be overwhelmed with encounters of death or undead monsters and to create emotional responses to these embodiments of death. For example, in *The Mummy's Hand* (1940), Marta is an active character at the beginning of the film. She proves her skills with a shooting scene and demands to be kept informed about archaeological diggings. However, after the mummy is revived she turns into a helpless, screaming and fainting figure. Whereas the men of the film actively engage with the dead, Marta's role is to reflect the anxiety.

In *The Mummy*, however, it is not Frank who destroys the mummy. Instead, once Helen realizes that Imhotep plans to mummify her as part of the transformation rites, she begs,

I'm alive! I'm young. I won't die. I loved you once, but now you belong with the dead. I am Anck-es-en-Amon, but I … I'm somebody else too. I want to live, even in a strange new world.

In the end, what she chooses is modern death and the modern world. Invoking the help of the ancient goddess Isis, she turns the ancient spells (with a bolt of lightning) against Imhotep. Thus, the mummy is not defeated by Western methods, but by the laws of his own religion to which he is bound. Based on this ending, Carol Siri Johnson argues that *The Mummy* should be read as an anti-colonialist film. The mummy proves stronger than Westerners or their science, and his hypnotic exoticism and sexuality is a challenge to white male supremacy. This challenge is highlighted when he is beaten by a half-foreign woman (Johnson 1991/1992: 106, 114). Furthermore, Day (2006: 69) points out that it is often the scientists who are made fools in the classical films for their denial of the magical world. In comparison, Helen, who recognizes both worlds, does not deny the possibility of traditional practices, even if her choice gives superiority to modernity.

This interpretation shows how the film does not oversimplify the superiority of the Western modern world, although the Western characters believe in the supremacy of modern science. Also, the film does not end with an ancient killing scene, but in a setting where Muller advises Frank to call back Helen's soul, now captivated in ancient Egypt. At the final moment, then, not only do the modern practices appear as a better choice, but also the Western men are convinced that they can summon the return of the modern order. Despite the challenges, modern, 'civilized' and scientific death overcomes traditional, religious and pagan death. *The Mummy* acknowledges the existence of traditional death, but makes it an outmoded and monstrous choice in comparison with modern practices.

3.4. Idealization of Modern Death

In these three classical films, *Dracula*, *White Zombie* and *The Mummy*, which also function as starting points for later living dead films, death was represented as a monstrous event, and as something that should be abjected and distanced from the modern world. The social climate of the 1930s did not encourage embracing images of or ideas about death that would radically challenge attitudes towards modern death. Instead, the desire to exclude death is visible at the levels of both discourse and story in these films.

While death was an important part of narration, it was mediated in other ways than through direct witnessing. Death was encountered in alienated, controlled and protected ways. Violent acts were rarely shown to the viewer, yet consequences provided the narrative turning points and the characters' reactions addressed the emotionality of these events. This kind of construction of death as an alienated off-screen event correlates with ideas about modern death, which is controlled, hidden and excluded from the public sphere. Similarly, viewers were protected from violent images of death and were, instead, offered a positive relationship with a moral character to experience death with.

The very hiding of death was visible also in the ways that the living dead's threat was limited to the private sphere. Each of the monsters threatened individuals, not whole societies or a world at the same time. Also, this threat was most often directed to women, who in the classical films were often separated from the public domain and isolated in private spaces. Thus, death never became a public problem, but remained limited. A socially circumscribed death of this kind could be defeated, controlled and solved by other individuals with the help of experts and modern science.

The alienation of death was further highlighted by representing those characters fighting death as moral citizens, with death and its embodiments seen as an immoral disturbance. Indeed, in the classical films, the use of immoral, evil and distanced monster positions were highlighted. One ideologically embedded way to do this was to highlight the undead monsters' foreignness. Classical films used ancient settings, romantic lands and mysterious monsters that were alien to the United States (Wood 1984: 171–72, 183; Jones 1997: 152). Cultural distance made these monsters seem exotic, but in its otherness it also protected American society from being contaminated by them or being exposed to the spectre of death that they were made to represent. This was also highlighted by making the undead represent traditional death – remains from the past who defy the practices of modern death.

In contrast, the heroes of the stories were often related to science and knowledge – take Professor Van Helsing in *Dracula*, for example. These doctors, archaeologists and missionaries signified Western supremacy over primitive, pagan and non-American death in modern society. At the symbolic level, these professionals were even able to protect other people from death: Mina in *Dracula*, Helen in *The Mummy* and Madeline in *White Zombie* are rescued from the embodiments of a traditional death. In these stories, science is able to re-control and tame death. The narration of these films starts with the introduction of magical, traditional, unnatural and horrifying death, which is encountered and studied throughout the story and, finally, made harmless, which is also evidenced in the classical films' moral closure of the main monster's final death. This highlights the denouement of the films as a means to control death, idealize modern death and alienate the sources of discomfort. The final deaths of the monsters also followed the wider tendency of classical

Hollywood where closure and happy endings were common practice. In classical narration, closure unifies the viewer's experience, and reinforces both causality and the meaning of the story (Bordwell, Staiger & Thompson 1996: 47).

Yet, the fantasizing middle section of these films rendered the controlled image of death flawed, as death was still mediated to the viewer via the narration. For example, the mere existence of the living dead and the centrality of death as a theme can be seen to challenge the borders of modern sanitized and insulated death. In these films, the love stories between the undead and women show how the openness in encountering death-related issues makes it possible to grasp the seductive and liberating role of death as well. That death is seductive can be seen in its desire to return to an intimate and close relationship, although the authoritative voices of the film keep distancing it.

Indeed, even if the main alignment remained with the other characters, there was a real possibility of the viewer having some sympathy for the monsters in these classical films. However, when the production code started to gain influence, possible alignments were limited because any sympathy shown towards evil characters was considered a threat to the prevailing moral standards (Doherty 1999: 347–60). Thus, when Kharis the mummy returned to the screen in the 1940s, he was unable to speak because his tongue was cut out in the embalming process. Without a voice, he becomes less likeable than Imhotep and more of a walking dead. Thus, in the mummy sequels of the 1940s, such as *The Mummy's Hand* (1940), the charismatic Imhotep was replaced with a simpler, less likeable and action-oriented mummy, who remained in his shrouds, moved clumsily and, unlike the independent character of Imhotep, Kharis was controlled by a high priest, his master.

Living dead films and their sequels, therefore, started to change as early as the 1940s, although (or perhaps because) they were lacking new ideas and mostly circulated storylines and characters from the first round of living dead films. On the one hand, these 1940s films propped up the idea that (embodied) death needed to be excluded and marginalized. The production code, which was fully implemented after 1934, further limited the use of violence and sex, among other issues. The institutions of marriage and home had to be respected, and brutality was not allowed to be shown in detail. This made the use of violent death and erotically seductive monsters problematic. Furthermore, the films could no longer show sympathy for the monsters (Doherty 1999: 347–60).

The change in the sympathy shown towards the monsters is visible in the *Dracula* sequels of *Dracula's Daughter* (1936) and *Son of Dracula* (1943). They both narrate a rather similar story where the relative of Count Dracula continues the family's vampire threat. In *Dracula's Daughter*, a female vampire seeks help from a doctor to rid her curse: 'I need you to save my soul.' However, she is incapable of controlling her bloodlust and, in the end, she is killed. In this film, the vampire is presented as capable of love and guilt. Only a few years later, in *Son of Dracula*, it is almost impossible to feel for the vampire, Count Alucard, whose aggression and violence isolates his new bride from the rest of her family. The count has come to the United States to enjoy the 'young and virile race', and he seeks power and new hunting grounds more than he seeks the bride. It later transpires that the count is unlovable, as the bride has also used the count in her desire to gain immortality. There is no true love or sympathy. The power-lust monsters deserve to be excluded through final death.

On the other hand, some changes challenge modern death in ways that the films of 1930s did not. The cultural otherness of death is questioned when the undead start to colonize the United States, as is the case in *Son of Dracula*. In a similar manner, the sequels to *The Mummy's Hand* brought Kharis to the United States. The high priest and Kharis head for the United States in *The Mummy's Tomb* (1942), *The Mummy's Ghost* (1944) and *The Mummy's Curse* (1944) in order to bring back the lost princess and take revenge on those who stole her. Here, too, the threat of death remains alien, although it is brought onto American soil.

Another small crack in the image of modern death was produced by the zombie films, where the theme of taking advantage of the undead state became popular, as is evident in the zombification and deprivation of free will in the heritage frauds portrayed in *The Living Ghost* (1942) and *The Ghost Breakers* (1940). In addition, a number of films accuse doctors of zombification. For example, in *The Return of Doctor X* (1939), zombification is part of Doctor Flegg's experimental repertoire with synthetic blood, while Doctor Sangre in *King of Zombies* (1941) uses zombification not only to enslave his workers, but also to gain war intelligence from American military personnel, and in *Voodoo Man* (1944) Doctor Marlowe transfers the life essence of young girls into his dead wife. These doctors misuse their powers to control death, while it is typically a more ethical doctor or other authority who manages to intervene and return balance to the society. As Colavito (2008: 225–26) concludes, science had become an institutionalized part of society by the 1940s, but the Second World War and experiments with the atomic bomb slowly started to cast longer shadows over science's triumphant role. In the living dead films, the gradual increase in the questioning of both medicalized and scientific death became more visible during the transitional era.

Chapter 4

Undead of the Transitional Era

Classical Hollywood held its own until the 1950s. When change came, it was not about abandoning classical values, but rather readjusting to a changing world. This entailed changes to filmic production, marketing, narration, imagery and themes. Since the early 1950s, television challenged Hollywood's role as the leading (family) entertainment form in the United States. Not only was movie attendance declining, but also the myth of a homogenous audience had reached its end. Hollywood was forced to change its production modes to meet the needs of a changing audience composition. During the transition years, moviegoers grew younger and more segmented. Also, the old censorship model became outdated, as both international movies and television were showing more graphic and sexual scenes than Hollywood was allowed to. Although the old studios recognized the changes and the new audience segments, they struggled to adjust and found that the power positions changed accordingly. Independent productions and new narrative strategies, including horror narrations such as *Night of the Living Dead*, now gained popularity (see Doherty 2002; Gomery 1998: 247–49; Bordwell, Staiger & Thompson 1996: 9–10, 331–32; Smith 1998: 6–7, 14–16; Maltby 1998: 34).

When Hollywood started to rebrand itself during the 1950s, the production values had shifted, which allowed a more direct addressing of death events. However, more importantly, the sociocultural climate had changed as well. The role that death played in culture was rather different to that of the 1930s when the ideals of modern death were settling in. By the 1950s, death was taking place in institutions and dying people were handled by health-care professionals instead of family members. Life expectancy kept increasing, although not as dramatically as at the beginning of the century (Corr & Corr 2003; Information Please® Database 2011; NCHS Data 2009; Hoyert 2012). 'Natural' death remained hidden away for most of the transition era, but violent death forced its way into American consciousness in a new way. Indeed, in the aftermath of the Second World War, atomic bombs and concentration camps, and at the beginning of the atomic age, armament and the Cold War, the American imagination had been penetrated by 'unnatural' and violent death. The disturbing power of mass-scale violent death heightened its influence and recognition. At the deeper lever of cultural attitudes and values, these pervasive mass threats changed the way in which terror and the evil potential of man was understood: there was growing awareness of man's potential for depravity, cruelty, mass destruction and loss of values to an extraordinary extent (see also Wells 2002: 56–58; Skal 1993: 229; Tudor 1989: 39–47; Goldberg 1998: 50).

In the post-war United States, science fiction films and horror films, in particular, found new possibilities in the apocalyptic tone. For example, *Invisible Invaders* (1959) combines the science fiction themes of aliens with the horror film's idea of living dead characters, when aliens arrive in the wake of the world's new atomic age. Because the human characters have reached a certain level of progress, they now need to be placed under the aliens' universal dictatorship. Invisible to the human eye, the aliens use the bodies of the dead for communication and killing the living. The film clearly narrates the fears of the consequences of the atomic age, but in the end, when the aliens are defeated, the nations have also learned to work together instead of against each other. Many critics see such films as metaphors for social resistance and as questioning the social order and personal, cultural and national identities in the post-war United States (Crane 1994: 105–09; Wells 2002: 58).

The changing cultural context of the living dead films can be detected in the increasingly inclusive images of death as well, as in the more frequent use of death scenes and a more critical relationship to death. In the transition era, deaths materialize on-screen, and although in many cases death events are still narrated through characters, their subjective views are now brought to complement the reaction shots. In the aftermath of the Second World War, the cultural recognition of the role of (violent) death started to change, and at the same time, the limitations of classical horror films' use of violence became outdated and naïve. The production code still existed, but it was slowly losing its grip. In *The Return of Dracula* (1958) and *Curse of the Faceless Man* (1958), the death scenes both follow and renew the classical rules of not showing any acts of violence. By *Night of the Living Dead* (1968), the production code was abandoned and new explicit images of death and dying were visible on screen.

In this chapter, I will address the increasing consciousness of violent death and increasing use of explicit images of death during the transitional era. I will also discuss the need to recognize the American responsibility over violent death – visible in the characters and locations of the story. For example, *The Return of Dracula* brought the vampire to the United States. Furthermore, I will study the conflicting roles of science in the transitional living dead films. The scientific explanations held influence in terms of defining and managing natural death – as the case of the naturally mummified body in *Curse of the Faceless Man* shows. However, in the wake of the atomic bomb and other weapons of mass destruction, science also created threatening images, where it was used, to produce depictions of megadeaths, as the mass phenomena of zombies in *Night of the Living Dead* brings to the fore. In sum, this chapter shows how the transition films used the public consciousness of violent death, if not to challenge, at the very least to expose the limits of the ideals of modern death.

4.1. Familial and Americanized Vampires

In the aftermath of the Second World War, mass-scale and mass-mediated violent death penetrated the American consciousness and forced the American public to face their social responsibilities. Symbolically, in the opening scene of *The Return of Dracula* (1958), the viewer observes Dracula's abandoned coffin in a European graveyard, framed with a voice-over:

> It is a known fact that there existed in Central Europe a Count Dracula. Though human in appearance and cultured in manner, he was, in truth, a thing undead. A force of evil. A vampire. Feeding on the blood of innocent people, he turned them into his own kind, thus spreading his evil dominion ever wider. The attempts to find and destroy this evil were never proven completely successful. And so, the search continues to this very day.

In the next scene, the viewer sees Dracula on his way to the United States. In this opening, Dracula is disconnected from the old continent, brought instead to the 1950s United States with all his might. Whereas the living dead had crossed this frontier already during the 1940s, this time the undead character is accepted into the American family as well. In fact, when Dracula gets off the train, he is mistaken for a missing relative whom Dracula has killed. He even explains his arrival to his new (stolen) family: 'I feel quite excited. I only hope your family will understand certain things about me. See, my life has been confined, that's why I have come here, for freedom. I must have it'. The chosen term 'freedom' also highlights the changing role of death as part of American culture, which no longer frowns on violent death.

The opening of the film redirects the responsibility for violent death to the United States, stressing that, on the surface, society may be civilized, but it has dark undertones of violence and death. As Robin Wood notes, horror started to become both American and familial. Where the 1930s monster was foreign, the 1950s brought horror closer to home, if not onto American soil, then at least into the characters. Horror and death also started to emerge from American families (Wood 1984: 183–85). Rather similarly, a year earlier, *The Vampire* (1957) had combined scientific experiments and the Americanization of familiar horror monsters into the same film. Here, scientific experimentation with vampire bats leads to the vampirization of the local doctor, a single parent of a young girl. Devastating consequences tear the family apart. This Hollywood horror's tendency to enhance the role of a familiar threat became formulated as a convention in Alfred Hitchcock's *Psycho* (1961). Soon after, television also made the most of the vampires' familial possibilities, when the characters were introduced to different genres. Such situation comedies as *The Munsters* (1964–66) and *The Addams Family* (1964–66) depicted the monsters' home lives with mothers who could be construed as vampires, although this was left to the viewer's imagination. A few years later, the vampire character of Barnabas soon became a (romantic) superstar in the daily soap opera *Dark Shadows* (1966–71) as a Collins family member.

In *The Return of Dracula*, new contexts are also searched by addressing the new audience. Thomas Doherty argues that because the old studios were inflexible to react to cultural changes, the more marginalized horror genre became something of a pioneer in adapting to the new viewer group and emerging youth culture. In the horror genre, the change in the viewer base was significant: the young became the main audience group with almost three-quarters of the viewers being under 25 years old (Doherty 1995: 298–303; for changing audience structure, see also Medovoi 2005: 135–38). Horror 'flicks', with teenagers cast in the leading roles, were the studios' answer to the changing audience structures of the 1950s. When teenagers were introduced as the horror film's main characters during the transition period, several scholars have since interpreted horror films as portraying adolescents' sexual anxieties. For example, Walter Evans holds that the stories with transforming monsters – including vampire films – compare to the troubled teenagers with changing bodies and uncontrollable feelings. Similar physical and psychological changes can be found in transgressing monstrousness, emerging adolescent sexuality and sexual experimentation (Evans 1984: 54–56, 61).

Also, *The Return of Dracula* discusses borders of the teenage body and sexuality, but it does so in close relationship to questions about age and authority, and imagines teenage sexuality as being socioculturally threatening. Henry A. Giroux argues that cinematic youth representations are ambivalent because they represent simultaneously the future and the end of society. The young are in a transitional space in their expression of 'individual freedom, social power, and critical agency'. This is also why they pose a threat to society, for the potential of transgressive teenage sexuality calls for repression and control, not acceptance (Giroux 2002: 171–78).

In *The Return of Dracula*, teenagers have to find their own sexualities, while adults, who know the process, are unable to make it any easier for the teenagers, but yet the adults assume that the teenagers will follow the socially accepted rules. While the film is not a direct remake of Bram Stoker's novel, the characters are comparable to those of the original story, yet rearranged in relation to questions of age. Dracula retains his role as a sexually seductive monster, whereas a teenage character, Rachel, is made to play Mina's role, and Rachel's blind friend Jennie is Lucy. Tim, the boy next door and Rachel's boyfriend, is a reflection of John Harker, and Van Helsing is replaced by a European vampire hunter who tracks Dracula down to the United States. The roles are rearranged because the adults fail to protect Rachel and Jennie. Rachel's mother constantly leaves her two children alone at home, unaware of the influence Dracula is gaining on her daughter. Similarly disconnected and distant from teenage life are the authorities, that is, the European vampire hunters, the local police and the doctor. They trace the vampire, but they are never in the right place at the right time to protect the teenagers.

As Giroux argues, youth representations in the transition films remain contradictory. The young are given a voice, but from an adult perspective (Giroux 2002: 170, 177; see also Medovoi 2005: 140–65). Indeed, the adult characters still expect the teenagers to make the right decisions. If not, the teenagers get punished by death when they engage in pre-marital sex. This was especially common in the 1970s and 1980s horror series of teenage slashers, including *Halloween* and *Friday the 13th*, where the teens' sexual activities resulted in sudden death. The killer had the power to punish young people for their immoral actions. In *The Return of Dracula*, death's punishing power is related to the teenage girls Jennie and Rachel. For them, Dracula becomes a dark temptation of unleashed and unacceptable sexuality. We get a hint of the girls' curiosity about sexuality when we see them reading an erotically charged novel together.

Jennie becomes the vampire's first victim. Dracula enters her bedroom at night and seduces her with promises of freedom and experiences a blind girl would not otherwise get: 'I can take you from the blackness into a light.' Even though Jennie is afraid, she allows Dracula to give her the kiss of transformative death. In this film, the transformative, social and final deaths of Jennie are explored in more detail than Lucy's implied fate in the classical film. The exploration of Jennie's transformative death seeds from her exposure to Dracula. The following morning, a doctor calls Jennie's friend, Rachel, who rushes to her friend's death bed. Before her first death, Jennie tries to warn Rachel, giving her a crucifix for protection. She says that even if she does not know how the story they had been reading continues past the kiss, she has experienced it herself and has been punished for her curiosity. The viewer is able to see how the encounter with Dracula has weakened and changed the sick girl, leading Jennie to die of blood loss. The fascination with Jennie's death does not end there. The viewer goes on to participate in her funeral with other characters, and after the funeral, the viewer, in fact, joins Dracula in visiting Jennie's grave and reviving her by demanding her to 'come, we have work to do'.

Later, vampire hunters find Jennie's coffin empty, and when she returns to her resting place, the viewer attends her punishment for transgressive sexuality, or final death, in a killing scene which is given a specific role in the film. The inspiration for this scene can be sought from the influential British Hammer productions of the mid-1950s, which recreated the images of known monsters, including the living dead, through more graphic and colourful styles. Hammer films such as *Horror of Dracula* (1957) and *The Mummy* (1959) welcomed young American viewers with colourful scenes of sex, violence and nudity (see also Soren 1997: 144–51; Wells 2002: 63–64; Twitchell 1985: 60; Jancovich 1992: 75–76). The success of such images made Hollywood exploitation film-makers follow suit, leading to such productions as *The Return of Dracula* (see also Doherty 2002: 123). Seeking to tempt the newly emerged teenage audiences, this film updated its story through beautiful girls and the shock effects of horror. More importantly, these transitions spoke of a changing world where the new generation considered violent death part of their world view and reality, and thus part of their cinematic expression as well.

Similarly, the final death of Jennie is a rather direct copy of Lucy's death scene in the Hammer film *Horror of Dracula*. Both films combine Lucy's overly red blood and transformation from an agonized creature to a character at peace. *The Return of Dracula* uses the idea of montage to suggest a violent death without actually showing the violent act objectively. The montage connects the image of a spear-hammering man, the blood running and a picture of Jennie's face when she transforms to a motionless state and closes her eyes. Although the viewer cannot see her speared, the spear is being hammered revealingly enough. Some access to excessive death is provided also by the only coloured images of the otherwise black-and-white film: the red blood running from Jennie's now dead body is telling enough. In connecting individual images which do not contain excessive violence as such but which imply a violent process, the film invites the viewer to experience violence through imagination.

As Prince argues, montage became one important means of extending violent cinematic contents, because the combining of different images through editing allowed violent scenes more space, although the death event itself lasted no longer than in the classical films. It was just given more screen-time, which has grown to be an increasingly popular tactic since the classical films (Prince 2003: 35–36). Similarly, by using such editing techniques, *The Return of Dracula* exploits violent references without actually showing the graphic acts. The film thus manages to stay true to the code while pushing its limits.

Jennie follows Dracula because of her curiosity and desire for sexual experiences. Rachel, too, is about to enter this adult world. The film makes frequent allegations to Rachel and her boyfriend Tim's experimentation with sex. They are in danger of being led astray before formalizing their relationship through marriage. Toying with sexuality has opened a door for Rachel to feel curious about Dracula as well, and as with Jennie, Dracula comes to symbolize illicit sexual forces. However, his illicitness is a product of the adult perspective addressed in the film. Dracula's horrifying sexuality thus warns teenagers of what will happen if the accepted limits of society are crossed.

Although the moral burden of sexual behaviour is aimed at girls, the film also shows some cultural change in relation to gender. In comparison with the classical version's Lucy or Mina, at the end of the film it is Rachel who is mostly responsible for the destruction of Dracula. The closing scene takes place in a cave where Rachel encounters Dracula. His seductive power is momentarily disturbed, and at this moment Rachel realizes the danger she is in. Trying to escape, Rachel runs into Tim, and together they face the vampire and resist his seductive power. They work as a couple and together they survive. However, Rachel and Tim are not strong enough to fight back at the vampire (or destructive sexuality) by themselves. They get strength, not only from each other, but from Christianity. The final scene suggests that the desired teenage life without impure pre-marital sexual relationships is possible through self-control and with the help of God. Rachel and Tim have been tempted, tested and they have successfully faced their demons. Having internalized the socially accepted norms regulating sexuality, they escape deadly punishment. Instead, with a crucifix, they force Dracula to back down and he falls into an open well.

When Dracula dies by falling down a mineshaft, the camera does not shun from the moment of violent death. Viewers are not allowed to see the exact instant that Dracula is impaled on the poles at the bottom of the shaft, but they are permitted to observe the death and Dracula's transformation in the final death through an objective camera shot. The film also welcomes viewers to witness the event of death by slowly bringing them closer to Dracula's death struggle: the image is reframed from long shot to close-up. Also, the consequences are exploited: when the image is filled with blood, the pierced body starts to transform into a skeleton. The picture series is carried out with a sequence of dissolving images, until only a skeleton remains. Interestingly, the images zoom in as close to the decaying body as a close-up of the deadly wound. The viewer is distanced from the image only after Dracula's transformation has ended and he is dead beyond question. In confirming the death of the monster, the scene provides closure, but at the same time it is also disturbing in forcing the viewer close to death. It does not spare the viewer from the violent effect of these images.

4.2. Mummy – Scientific Control of Natural Death

By the 1950s, modern death had become a cultural norm. Like death, which had moved from the private (the home) to the public (the hospital) sphere and into specialist hands, mummies were controllable and their monstrousness detectable. Following Universal's 1940s sequels, the mummies of the 1950s appeared wrapped in bandages, moved slowly and they were unable to speak. As Day (2006: 89) argues, violence became their only way of self-expression. Indeed, these clumsy corpses' only advantage appeared to be their supernatural strength and people's fear of embodied death. Furthermore, during the transition era, the mummy legend was suffering from a dearth of ideas. For example, *Pharaoh's Curse* (1957) created the typical imagery of the revenge on the tomb-openers. The only addition was the theme of internal horror, as the mummy does not resurrect as such, but uses soul transference to transform one of the intruders into a blood-sucking monster who turns against his own team.

Interestingly, mummies were absent from the relatively popular reconstructions of ancient Egypt, when Hollywood was trying to compete with television in such spectacles as *The Egyptian* (1954) or *Land of the Pharaohs* (1955), although even in these films, the Egyptian gods were depicted as powerless (Serafy 2003: 77, 85). Similarly, when the famous comedy duo Bud Abbott and Lou Costello made their mummy comedy *Abbott and Costello Meet the Mummy* (1955), a key element of their parody built on the bad make-up of the wrapped mummies and on the animal-like grunting figure one could easily escape. In a way, ancient death had become powerless when modern science could produce more death in seconds than any deadly creature of yore.

The belief in the ability of science to handle natural death continued strong in living dead films – to a certain extent. *Curse of the Faceless Man*, a United Artists film directed by Edward L. Cahn, is a case in point. This 1958 film tries to renew the mummy legend by taking the story to Pompeii and naturally mummified bodies which have been created by the erupting volcano and which are then examined with modern medical methods. Interestingly, in this film, the faceless man is not intentionally mummified or mystical as such, but a victim of a natural process of mummification. As natural death could still be handled with the help of science, he becomes a source of interest for understanding the processes of death. In this way, this film represents what Colavito calls modernist horror with positivism and the idea that 'science is the only way to understand the world', including death. Yet, the film contrasts to the otherwise typical theme of transitional age, or era of psycho-atomic horror as Colavito calls it, when the saving graces of science tend to be negated by science's capability to destroy the world (Colavito 2008: 225–31).

Curse of the Faceless Man departed from the earlier mummy films by relocating the events in Italy. Still, a connection to primitive religion is retained: the mummy character, aka Quintillus Aurelius, hails from an Etruscan background and also carries a magical medallion with a curse:

The house on the fourth hill of Pompeii shall fall. Its people shall perish, and whatsoever stands between me and what is mine shall perish. I visit the curse upon them until eternity … the fires of the Earth shall consume them. I am the son of Etruscan gods. I will live when the Roman is no more. Quintillus Aurelius.

Whereas the mummy is unable to tell his story, the story is recreated by the archaeologists who study his body and the myths of Pompeii. An American artist, Tina, a mediating character between Quintillus and the scientists, becomes a key to this study. Tina, staying in the cursed house, resembles an aristocratic woman who died when Vesuvius erupted. This is how she becomes connected with the mummy at an unconscious level and starts to channel his desires and needs. When the scientists notice this, they use hypnotism to reveal Quintillus' secrets. In hypnosis, Tina relives the last day of Pompeii. She narrates how the aristocratic woman dismisses the love of the Etruscan slave as improper and how the slave then curses her, the house she lives in and the whole city of Pompeii. In a way, this scene turns the classical mummy's hypnotic power against the monster and transforms the hypnotism from magical power to a scientific practice.

In the first half of the twentieth century, the scientific interest and the new technologies of X-rays and chemical tests had opened up the process of Egyptian mummification (Aufderheide 2003: 15–17). The spiritual and traditional death could now be understood and controlled. In *Curse of the Faceless Man*, the mummy is brought to the museum to be subjected to X-ray and chemical testing, which replace the manifesting of ancient spells. These methods are accompanied by historical research, thus highlighting the museum as a place for research or knowledge, and as a place to store the relics and tame the past through categorizing. The myths and superstition belong to the past. As Dr Romano demonstrates: 'What we believe is not important; what can be proved is'. When mysterious incidents nevertheless keep occurring, Dr Romano continues to put his trust in science, because the unknown phenomena are those which science has not yet explained. The mummy's revival is not a threat to this belief, but a source of excitement: 'Here we are so close of solving the mystery of life and death'. At the end of the film, the scientists settle with the explanation that the radioactive radiation to which the body has been exposed in X-ray testing is the reason for the revivals.

However, the use of multiple narrating voices enables the viewer to interpret the events in a mystical way. When the scientists evaluate the body of the mummy, they keep to the facts. In contrast, the narrator's voice-over, which the film uses throughout, addresses their inner doubts (or the narrator's interpretation of these doubts). For example, the narrator interprets Dr Paul Mallon's thoughts: 'for he was wondering now if the faceless aborigine she had painted was an impossibility'. Thus, the narrator represents the horror genre's openness for mystery and the unknown, whereas the dialogue of the characters advocates the scientific approach. This contradiction also represents the cultural contradiction between a spiritual and scientific understanding of the world. The scientific understanding of modern society is played out by the characters, and even if they have doubts of its explanatory power, they keep these doubts to themselves, as part of the hidden and private, similarly to the role of death at the time.

Throughout, the film's main approach is that of observation. The scientists realize that the mummy does not intentionally seek to colonize the modern world – he lives in the past and does not even apprehend that he has been revived in the modern world. Instead, he recaptures the last day of Pompeii and hopes to find protection from the erupting Vesuvius. At the same time, the scientists observe and do not intervene. They do not even need to kill the mummy, as the sea destroys his body. When the ashes of Vesuvius covered the slave's body, a dry and hard cast that naturally mummified the body was created. The chemical reaction with seawater destroys this cast, and the mummy's body disappears in the waves. In this film, then, traditional death is the object of historical and scientific research rather than an actual threat to the modern world. Among the undead films, *Curse of the Faceless Man* plays an extreme role in its idealization of modern death.

Curse of the Faceless Man even respects the tradition of hiding the act of killing. The film's first death events, in particular, borrow their structure from *The Mummy* of the 1930s. The first death event occurs in the cross-cutting sequence where the scientists discuss the discovery at the museum at the same time as a driver is delivering that body. A close-up of the driver allows the viewer to see the animated body behind him, and following the opening of the classical mummy film, the driver registers the threat when he sees a hand reaching for him. He screams in horror when the hand grasps his neck. The fading cut returns to the museum where the phone rings bringing news of the car crash. At the scene of the accident, the driver is lifted into the ambulance in a body bag. The next death scene follows the death of the museum guard. This time the death is not mediated with an empty image of the wall as it was in the classical film where a museum guard was also killed by the mummy. Instead, the viewer is allowed to see how the mummy raises his hand to hit the guard. The movement is visible, yet the moment of contact is partially obscured by the mummified body. An objective camera shot also shows the guard falling to the ground before the scene returns to follow the classical solution where a glimpse of the corpse lying on the floor is mediated before the camera concentrates on the scientists' interpretation of the events.

In the final scene, violence becomes more explicit, pushing the limits of the code. Two policemen are trying to save a girl when the mummy hits them on the head. Again, the actual contact is only partially visible as the image concentrates on the movement, but the consequences are explicit as the camera focuses in on a medium close-up of the body hitting the rocks and a bloody wound which covers half of the head. These final images show that even if in *Curse of the Faceless Man* death is still alienated, violent images were slowly gaining ground. In general, the transition era increased the use of partially blocked images of death at the expense of empty images and how the camera started to frame death events closer to the bodies. The changes become evident in *Night of the Living Dead* where both zombies and death scenes start avoiding the modern desire for control.

4.3. Getting Out of Control – Zombies, Violence and Death

In the transition era, zombie films found ways of renewal. Characters started to distance themselves from their Haitian background, growing more closely connected to reanimated and infectious corpses. Interestingly, *The Plague of Zombies* (1966) brings the old and new themes together: a doctor travels to a Cornish village after hearing of a strange epidemic. He finds that not only are the young village people fatally infected, but they also come back after their death. It later turns out that a factory owner, who has returned from Haiti, poisons and revives the young people with the help of voodoo rituals to gain free labour for his factory. The familiar theme of slaved zombies thus meets the new motif of infection.

A couple of years later, the theme of infection was mainstreamed in George Romero's *Night of the Living Dead* (1968). The protagonists – hysteric Barbra, African-American Ben, a young couple and the father, mother and injured daughter of the Cooper family – are trying to survive in a country house surrounded by reanimated, unburied and cannibalistic corpses. In many ways, this low-budget and black-and-white film can be seen as a culmination of the transition period. It was not only an independent production, but it also ignored some of the key rules of classical Hollywood, including the production code, which had survived until 1967.

In addition to changing production practices, the film discussed changing cultural practices. *Night of the Living Dead* was among the apocalyptic visions that set in motion a nihilistic vogue in Hollywood films of the late 1960s and the 1970s (Quart & Auster 2002: 10; Russell 1995: 174–208). Romero's film casts an endlessly growing number of zombies to make their mass threat overpowering and the deadly fate of the survivors seemingly unavoidable. Also, the film exaggerated violence, made deaths more inventive and recreated the zombie tradition with cannibalism. This change in the tradition continued to debate issues of mindless death, but it further highlighted the zombies' corporeality; the visual awkwardness, trance-like walking and physicality remained and were even further stressed with an added element of obsessive and consuming cannibalism.

The film has been connected to the American cultural trauma of the late 1960s. Romero had previously directed rather positive hippie films, but the optimism of youth movements (and hippies, in particular) was fading. Optimism gave way to nihilistic themes in the face of an escalating war in Vietnam, growing violence between authorities and countercultures, an emerging sense of social chaos, race and gender questions, and distrust between different groups. American society was about to self-destruct, and this film became a cynical political allegory of the United States (see also Phillips 2005: 86–100; Becker 2006: 45–47; Shaviro 1993: 82).

The allegorical power of the zombies is highlighted right from the opening frames of the film, with a camera shot of a solitary car being driven down an empty country road. The opening credits rolling, the camera follows the car to the local cemetery. Just before the car is parked, we see the American flag flying in the cemetery, interpreted by Grant (2007: 54) as 'a clear attack on American society', because in the midst of the escalating war in Vietnam it shows the connection between death and American society. Furthermore, when Barbra and John are attacked under the flag, the zombie creates an allegory for social revolution. This time, there is no zombie master to blame – instead, only military and scientific experiments are offered as the one likely cause of zombification. These experiments have released radiation, which subsequently renders the unburied corpses reanimated and cannibalistic.

In this sense, it is the existing social order, the silent acceptance of events and, most of all, the desire to make modern warfare even more effective and deadly that have caused the problem. Here, modern science creates more death than it manages to explain.

Furthermore, Romero's film brings the military's responsibility for death out in the open rather than hiding it on foreign battlefields, away from the American consciousness. Traditionally, as Davies (2005: 75–76) argues, the sacrifice of the soldiers' lives has been loaded with positive meaning, because these deaths maintain the existing nation and highlight social continuance. Here, the reanimated dead, however, deny such sacrificial power, reminding us instead of death's power to disrupt society. They refuse to suppress society's capability of and responsibility for bringing death on its members. In the process, their aggressive behaviour destroys the material structures of a nation, including such social institutions as hospitals, shopping malls, churches, laboratories, prisons, army barracks and private families. As such, these pathetic creatures can be interpreted as culture and its values in decay.

Moreover, the phenomenon that brings the dead back to life is now a mass occurrence. This, Grant (2007: 52–53) notes, makes zombies into allegories not only of revolution, but also 'of modern crowd behaviour'. As a metaphor for mass culture, the zombies act as mindless creatures rather than active beings. Instead of producing, they only consume. Furthermore, their cannibalism is the ultimate form of consumption. Similarly, Wood (1984: 189) argues that cannibalism represents the ultimate possession, and Hoberman (2003: 261) sees it as a symbolic reflection of how the United States self-destructs. The zombies become political scapegoats for instability, threat and death. Society fails to recognize that, deep down, outer threats are born in the relationship to existing society, also failing to see that internal issues can prove to be more pervasive than external perils. Indeed, the zombies actively attack the society that created them, and therefore become revolutionary figures – unlike their classical relatives – by not accepting their fate in marginalized silence. The zombies force society to encounter a problematic and violent relationship to death.

In this film, death lost its power to resolve issues – an increasing tendency in the 1960s, when television mediated violent images to the American audiences. While the Cold War and a global nuclear arsenal created an enduring public atmosphere of death, mediated images of the Vietnam War, in particular, changed cultural practices when the war brought images of death and dying in war onto television screens for the first time. These images, along with the assassinations of John F. and Robert Kennedy and Martin Luther King Jr, 'brought the reality of death and dying into America's living rooms', as Christina Staudt argues (Staudt 2009: 8; see also Grønstad 2003: 169–77; Sobchack 2000: 112–14). For example, when President Kennedy was shot in 1963, the pictures of the assassination and Kennedy's transition from life to death were more publicly and directly violent than any film violence ever before. In turn, these televised images of detailed and graphic death rendered the cinematic limitations of the production code hypocritical and outdated.

In early 1968, then, the production code was replaced by an age classification system. While classical horror films had gained their power by what they did not show, horror was now both able and allowed to do more than just suggest. The era of modern cinematic violence had begun (see also Prince 2003: 30; Doherty 1999: 345). Of the living dead films, *The Fearless Vampire Killers* (1967) by Roman Polanski renewed the erotic imagery, whereas Romero's *Night of the Living Dead* was the first to reveal, if not detailed acts of violence, then at least elaborate images of graphic corpses. The contrast to classical films is, nevertheless, explicit. The camera's distance is abolished in the construction of the death scenes in *Night of the Living Dead*, where close-ups force death into the viewer's gaze, and detailed images of dying or dead people compel the viewer to follow the process and ugliness of violence. This ability to place the viewer close to the horrific events was partly generated, as Katherine Zimmer states, by the new camera technology of the 1950s and 1960s. New portable and lighter cameras encouraged both closeness and unstable images, shifting the focus from continuity to disjuncture (Zimmer 2004: 39–42).

The impression that the camera is participating in the events rather than observing them from a safe position is confirmed with the first zombie attack in the graveyard. When a strange man suddenly grasps Barbra, her brother Johnny intervenes, putting up a fight. For the entire sequence, the camera stays close to the fighting couple, and both the close proximity and hand-held shooting heighten the viewer's feeling of being involved. The very proximity makes it hard to get a clear picture of what is happening, because the men occasionally drift out of the picture or get too close to the camera. Furthermore, when Johnny has lost the battle and the zombie has chased Barbra to their car, the camera is situated next to Barbra on the passenger seat inside the car, where it follows the zombie's attempts to get in through the window. With such a positioning of the gaze, the viewer is shut into this same claustrophobic space, without any apparent getaway from the situation or the image.

The opening makes clear that this film has discarded restrictions on violent scenes in creating tension, preferring to compose a sense of closeness to produce an atmosphere of shocking participation in the events. It does not mean, however, that the camera would reveal everything at once. Instead, it stays with the characters, first with Barbra and when more characters appear, with them as well. The narration stays so close to the characters, in fact, that the film ends up using a more uncommon narrative solution than was the case with classical living dead films. In *Night of the Living Dead*, the viewer learns about the monster together with the other characters instead of being shown a monster whose nature is immediately revealed to the viewer, although not necessarily to the characters (see, for example, Carroll 1990: 127–28). The film thus takes all control away from the viewer.

This is also how the film's first graphic image of a corpse is executed. Barbra has escaped to a farm house and realizes that the house is surrounded by zombies trying to get in. She starts to search the house, with the camera positioned at the top of the stairs and revealing Barbra walking up the steps slowly and cautiously. The image cuts to a close-up of her face and frightened look. The narration does not end with the reaction shot, however, but a subjective shot is offered as well, when the image cuts to her point-of-view shot. This is a close-up of a violated corpse's face where the flesh has been removed, the eyes are open and the mouth appears to be fixed in a scream. The following reaction shot reveals that Barbra has covered her eyes with her hands before running back down. The scene can be viewed as an interesting parallel to the horror film's changing relation to violent images. Barbra covers her eyes at this first encounter with a violated corpse, just as the earlier horror films used to hide images of violent death from the viewer's gaze.

The scene is repeated not long after, now with Ben, who comes to see what frightened Barbra. The camera is fixed in the same position at the top of the stairs, where as the viewer knows by now, the body is. Ben, too, takes the steps slowly. And once again the image cuts to the close-up of the corpse's face and returns to capture the reaction of Ben, who does not scream as Barbra did, but is still clearly freaked out and almost falls down the stairs. In a symbolic shift, Ben does not cover his eyes, which makes the relationship with violent death more openly addressed – from this point on, the film shifts from shunning death, turning to study it in greater and greater detail.

Such closeness, provided by character-centred narration, is evident throughout the film. However, this closeness is also ambiguous, due to the breaking down of the moral hierarchy between heroes and monsters. Here, monsters are rather starting points for the characters' violent behaviour, which tests the morality of human nature. As Matt Becker (2006: 42–43) and Kendall R. Phillips (2005: 98–99) claim, this film redefined the use of main characters in horror films: these characters are conflicted and disturbingly ordinary in their egoistic motivations and violent reactions in a desperate situation. In this film, normality becomes monstrosity at both the levels of zombification and main characterization.

We can recognize four different groups of people in *Night of the Living Dead*: Ben and Barbra; the young couple Tom and Judy; the Cooper family with father, mother and infected child; and zombie-killing officials. First, the main tension is created between Ben and Mr Cooper who both see themselves as leaders of the group, arguing whether they should defend themselves against the zombies in the house or hide in the cellar. Their argument culminates in a fight over a gun, which is when Cooper is injured. Second, Tom and Judy become mediators in this conflict and are later killed in an attempted getaway. Third, the Cooper family holds together behind a façade of happy family life, until the daughter, ironically, eats her parents. Finally, Ben and Barbra, the protagonists, also face their end. Barbra is hunted down by her zombified brother, and Ben is killed by the officials pursuing the zombies. Thus, ultimately, the film denies the viewer any kind of moral resolution.

As Jancovich (1992: 90) observes, 'the zombies outside are responsible for hardly any of the main characters' deaths'. Most of the deaths occur because the survivors cannot agree among themselves. In what follows, the viewer is expected to become frustrated and confused with the offered positions. None of the main characters is innocent; each appears to have more weaknesses than positive characteristics. With all the characters making mistakes and coming to false conclusions, the hierarchy of moral characters becomes harder to detect. The survivors are unable to work together and become their own worst enemies. Although the killing of the zombies is easy in theory, it fails in practice, because the very existence of the zombies has already shown that the core problem of American society lies in increasing diversities and distrust.

Romero's other zombie films, too, deal with similar issues of distrust and internal conflicts that lead to destruction. The people in these films are unable to work together, forming smaller groups, instead, which end up fighting, not the zombies, but one another. In *Dawn of the Dead* (1978), we have the survivors inside the shopping mall and a biker gang outside it, and while the two cannot get along, the zombies are able to destroy both. In *Day of the Dead* (1985), the competitive groups are the scientists and the army; and in *Land of the Dead* (2005), different social classes. Waller maintained in 1986 that each one of Romero's films recreates images of violence and regenerates its causes, aims and justifications. The living characters hold potential for monstrosity, as most of them are already corrupted: if they become undead, the change is not that drastic. Even those who are not corrupted face turning into the living dead (Waller 1986: 340–55).

In Romero's films, and in several subsequent zombie apocalypses, it is human beings who are cruel to one another in the midst of crisis. These films are extreme examples of how horror films can present humans as more monstrous than the monster figures themselves. While the zombies follow their basic instincts, the human characters draw on conscious decisions and, therefore, ought to be responsible for their actions. The emphasis has changed in such a way that highlights the artificiality of justification, which questions the role of the living, especially when they are aggressive towards both the monsters and other characters. This violent conflict between the living and the living dead only serves to demonstrate that there is no 'natural' difference between these groups. Interestingly, the zombies could also be construed as a positive social force whose revolutionary power could awaken humans to change their society and to avoid conflicts that lead to increasingly violent deaths, although the film also recognizes the failure of modern society to live up to these expectations. Ever since the classical era, as Crane and Skal argue, horror films have revelled in destroying relationships between individuals and society at large. By the time of post-classical horror, if not before, the stories dwell on a dystopian world where the people have no chance of survival. The destiny of the world, therefore, is out of their hands (Crane 1994: 6–16, 137–40; Skal 1993: 379).

One of the most influential scenes of destruction and consumption in the film takes place within the Cooper family, who are made to represent (dysfunctional) American family values. This scene also exemplifies the changing aesthetic practices regarding death acts in the living dead films. Previously in the story, Ben has shot Cooper, who staggers down the stairs to the basement, where he dies next to his sick daughter. A little later, Helen, the mother, escapes the invading zombies to the basement as well, only to find her beloved daughter, Karen, eating the ripped-off arm of her father. The viewer knows from previous experience that Karen has been zombified and that Helen is now in danger. The mother, however, finds this hard to accept, which is why she does not fight back, although she does try to escape.

The failure of accepting loss, and abjecting the corpse, is highlighted by Karen's killing of her mother in a prolonged sequence, which also becomes the film's ultimate image of violent death, at both the levels of experience and constructed image. The scene is so brutal, graphic and detailed that its aesthetic features are singularly foregrounded, even while the film still respects some moral codes from the classical era. The zombie film's director, George Romero, would later recall that while

> there was no MPAA censor's office or local censor board any more, you didn't have that panel of experts that were issuing dictates and reviewing films, saying, You can leave this in, but you have to take that out. But there was this unwritten law which said you had to be polite and just show the shadow and not show the knife entering flesh.
>
> (Vieira 2003: 242–43)

As Romero points out, the scene never shows the flesh being attacked, but rather builds the sequence through empty images and, most notably, through carefully framed point-of-view shots. The scene, nevertheless, unveils the potential of revealed images and the power of forcing the viewer to be arrested by the image and, in turn, to be impressed by its ghastly contents.

The scene is executed by paralleling point-of-view shots of mother and daughter. When Helen, the mother, enters the basement, the camera chooses her subjective point-of-view shot, as she witnesses Karen eating her father. As viewers, we also get to see Helen through the daughter's eyes and are able to feel some of the mother's reactions: she cannot believe what is happening. The image then returns to Helen's perspective, and the viewer witnesses Karen holding out her arms, as if to hug her mother. From this point forward, the camera shifts between the subjective views of these two characters. Through Karen's eyes, the viewer sees the mother run away from her and fall on the ground. Through Helen's eyes, we see Karen grip a hoe and slowly approach her mother with the hoe raised above her head.

When Karen is so close to her mother that her own shadow covers the image of Helen's face and a close-up of Helen's screaming face fills the image, the hoe strikes for the first time. The point-of-view shots now shift between Helen's view of the raised hands bringing the hoe down repeatedly and Karen's view of Helen's tormented face, which is slowly being covered with bloodstains. The death struggle is detailed through Helen's facial expressions and the bloody hoe that continues its deadly work. When Helen dies, and her face transforms from animate to inanimate without losing its horrified expression, the camera cuts away to a shot of the basement wall, where the shadow of Karen makes it clear that her work continues, with bloodstains now covering the walls as well.

Like the final death of Jennie in *The Return of Dracula*, this matricide sequence uses montage to create a series of shots where none of the used images contains violence as such, but where the consequences of images – raised hoe, screaming face of the victim, lowered hoe, bloodstains on the wall – suggest that the viewer is left to decode the scene in detail. The suggestion is especially poignant because the scene is accompanied by an intense screeching sound, reminding the viewer of the shower scene in *Psycho*, which further emphasizes the slashing nature of the murder. However, what differentiates *Night of the Living Dead* from *The Return of Dracula*, for example, is the frequency of edited cuts: the changes between point-of-view shots are so fast that the increasing tempo makes the scene so much more aggressive. Indeed, whereas in the classical era an average shot length was 8–11 seconds, in the mid-1960s the cutting tempo accelerated so that average length decreased to 6–8 seconds, and since then the pace has increased even more (Bordwell 2006: 121–22).

In this case, the scene follows the classical code that guides the film-maker to cut away from violence. However, the aesthetic solutions are used in such an excessive way that rather mocks the code. This, according to Prince (2003: 220), becomes a typical resolution in post-classical and digital films, which can choose to adapt the classical codes of violence for their own purposes, not hiding graphic violence, but rather highlighting it. The use of images lacking in violence is compensated with aggressive and fast montage. The distanced and stable camera is replaced with close-ups and a non-static camera, and the narration effectively employs the use of shadow to reveal the death event as a partially blocked image. Most importantly, although the characters are still in the focus of the camera's gaze, the reaction shots are now accompanied with subjective views. In other words, the viewer is allowed to react to the event with the character, not only through the character.

In its overemphasized sensual effects, this scene produces a sublime result. The background of the concept is found in aesthetic theories, such as the writings of Edmund Burke and Immanuel Kant. Whereas Burke (1990: 36, 51–53, 119–21, 145) connects the sublime directly to fascinating and painful experiences of horror and suspense, Kant (1965: 54–55) links it to the aesthetics of artworks and representations. Both of them, however, see the sublime exceeding physical limits, moral essence and human sense. According to James Donald, horror films combine these two traditional views on the sublime. Horror themes arouse powerful emotions but the genre still remains a representation and fictitious (Donald 1989: 241).

Accordingly, the sublime can be defined as an aesthetic sensation and experience that is created when the viewer encounters something that exceeds human senses and comprehension. With a sublime experience, the viewer may enjoy something disturbing, because the concept brings together feelings of pain and pleasure, and sensations of horror and excitement (Leffler 2000: 74–77; Freeland 2000: 236–37; Freeland 1999: 66). The scene where Karen kills her mother is one such sublime scene: a child brutally murdering her mother is obscene and terrifying, but the scene is aesthetically constructed with details, built to fascinate the viewer. In this scene, the transition from the classical films' lack of dying to the excess of dying is complete.

As this scene from *Night of the Living Dead* illustrates, the sublime gazing and its excess of images allows the viewer to enjoy how dying is created and how the aesthetic representation of extreme feelings is unified. A sublime experience allows the viewer to be fascinated by such horrifying aesthetics of death, which both magnifies and slows down the scenes to create physical and emotional reactions in the viewer. However, the sublime is not only about feasting on images. Despite its demand for extreme and disturbing emotional experiences, its sociocultural and generic contexts invite the viewer to create meanings as well, Freeland argues. She continues that through this cognition, the sublime also provides understanding and thoughts. Accordingly, Freeland maintains that the sublime experience consists of four main features: emotional conflict between horror and pleasure, greatness of image, painfulness of image and a reflection of these, including a moral perspective to the story (Freeland 1999: 68, 82). In general, not only in this scene, the narration of *Night of the Living Dead* focuses on diminishing the borders between the living and the undead, between the morality of different characters and also between the viewer and images. Whereas death is getting out of the control of modern society, the viewer is allowed to have less possibilities to distance him/herself from the discourse and the story.

Only in two cases the film actually distances itself from the intimate character-based viewing. The first takes place shortly after an attempted escape scene where a young couple, Tony and Judy, have been blown up in the car, and Ben and Cooper have fought each other in a desperate situation. Suddenly, the image cuts from inside the house to outside where zombies are approaching the car with the charred bodies inside. For a while, the camera lingers with close-ups of the zombies who tear the flesh out of the body parts with their teeth and then eat these parts. The scene is there for the shock and attraction of violent images, and also to remind the viewer that the real threat should be the deadly figures, not the people inside the house. The scene is soon repeated, but now from the familiar character-based location and through a subjective shot of Ben staring out the window at the zombies.

The second scene where the camera distances itself from the surrounded people in the farmhouse comes towards the end. The camera reveals its objective position by focusing on the rescue team, which is cleaning up and killing the zombies. The change is purposeful because it contrasts the perspective of Ben as the last survivor and that of the rescue team. When Ben hears the approaching sounds of dogs and gun shots, he comes out from his shelter in the basement and goes to the window, prepared to shoot any zombies if he has to. At the same time, the rescue team is nearing the house, more than prepared to shoot the zombies, as has already been shown. When they see movement by the window, then, they interpret this as a threat and shoot Ben. The change of positions is important in highlighting the narration's cynicism – at the end of the film, death does not relieve, but instead causes anxiety.

Especially when the role of violence as a moral solution is denied, as it is in this ending, the previous deaths in the film appear more violent and irrational. Grønstad (2003: 283), too, maintains that when violence fails to provide narrative closure, it turns into a spectacle, which underlines and makes visible the role of violence. The final scene of *Night of the Living Dead* not only cements the film's cynical attitude, but also broadcasts a broader development of increasing irrationality and violence which had started to dominate horror films in the late 1960s. In fact, as Kevin Heffernan (2002: 59, 66) writes, the release of *Night of the Living Dead* caused public outrage for its 'pornography of violence' or use of graphic violence, cynical world view and nihilistic ending. Indeed, the apocalyptic images insist that death cannot be alienated from society. The argument is that if people run away from death, try to barricade or hide it, it will sooner or later consume them.

4.4. Challenging the Ideals of Modern Death

Whereas in the classical era, cinematic death used to be something that the camera did not concentrate on, in the course of the transitional era, death became addressed more openly, slowly unveiling violent images. The living dead films started to oppose the hiding of death events and shifted their narrative emphasis from the causality to the actual events of death. The clever use of montage, in particular, shows how even the use of impossible objective images can result in denying the alienation of death imagery. By refusing to marginalize encounters with death events, these films forced death back on the public agenda – at least in terms of a debate on American responsibility for violent deaths.

In the wake of the Second World War, the introduction of weapons of mass destruction and the war in Vietnam, violent death forced itself into the public consciousness. Similarly, in the transition era, living dead films began to refuse to limit and isolate death and dying. Revealingly, the threat of death grows throughout *Night of the Living Dead*. From a single zombie in the graveyard, the film soon introduces several zombies surrounding the house. Television broadcasts claim that this is not an isolated incident; similar events are occurring elsewhere as well. The sequels all irrevocably show that the living have no refuge against death in the guise of zombies – an outbreak which has reached pandemic proportions. Death events, similarly, were not only (partly) revealed to the viewer, but the number of deaths also kept growing. In the process, the final deaths of monsters also lost its power to resolve issues. In this way, the transition era's films started to challenge the possibility of distancing the United States and its citizens from death and dying.

Living dead films also brought the living dead to the United States, which they have not left since. By bringing Dracula to the United States in *The Return of Dracula* and by making the zombies represent ordinary Americans in *Night of the Living Dead*, the transition films concluded that death could not be ousted from public consciousness. They also demanded American society to acknowledge its own violent nature. In this way, the living dead phenomenon became demystified, and violent death came to be articulated publicly as an internal threat to American society. Although the undead monsters were still evil, the other characters' positive role was slowly being questioned. Could the authorities be trusted, and were the other characters able to make rational decisions and stay in control when encountering death?

Indeed, in *Night of the Living Dead*, it is not death as such which needs to be alienated. True deadliness is found in human nature. The film lays bare the hypocrisy of denying death, because it is the violent nature of humans that produces more and more death every day. This cynical world view with a desperate cry for responsibility over violent death has become more visible in the post-classical and digital eras. As Murray Smith, Deborah Knight and George McKnight argue, morally positive characters are harder to discern in later films than in the classical films. Horror films may lack morally positive or ideal characters altogether (Knight & McKnight 2003: 218–19; Smith 1995: 222).

As a counter effect to the decline in the morality of human characters, the monster's perspective became central to the films' narrative. This perspective is more clearly visible in the post-classical films; however, this nascent sympathetic alignment was already present in transitional films. For example, the transition film *Curse of the Faceless Man* does not yet allow its mummy to have a voice, but other people make an effort to understand his motives by creating a tragic love story. Following this film, mummies began to be given a voice. For example, in *The Cat Creature* (1973), the mummy priestess justifies her murders by death's painfulness: 'You don't know what it is like, to be buried away alone in the darkness, century upon century of blackness, paralyzed, unable to move or breathe. You are conscious of every crawling moment.'

With vampires, television took to softening their image with comedic or romantic elements – the new vampire of horror cinema gave all vampires equal rights of evil and devastation. For example, in the 1960s and 1970s, European films featured openly erotic vampire stories of lesbian vampires, in particular. This development, say Bonnie Zimmerman and Andrea Weiss, is related to the rising feminist movement. Lesbian vampires could be seen as a counteraction to Dracula, for they replaced male possession of women with female possession of women with lovers who were equally violent and deadly (Zimmerman 1996: 382; Weiss 1992: 87–88, 90–93, 103). Also influential in the United States was the civil rights movement, which impacted on Hollywood through such Blaxploitation films as *Blacula* (1972), the story of a black and evil vampire in the contemporary United States. In a way, by the end of the transition era, everyone, regardless of their race, gender or profession, or even regardless of their narrative positions as heroes or monsters, had the right to be deadly.

Chapter 5

Post-Classical Undead

Hollywood horror had differentiated itself from the classical mode of narration by the mid-1970s (Tudor 1989: 150–51; Smith 1998: 11), but the classical era has maintained its position as a significant reference point. According to Peter Kramer (1998: 289), 'post-classicism' stresses that despite changes in style, narration and institutions, there are several continuities as well, bringing the two main eras, classical and post-classical, closely together. Compared with the classical period's well-structured production mode, the post-classical era employs more self-conscious, intertextual and nostalgic processes and techniques of presentation. Post-classical Hollywood is known for its blockbuster movies with high-profile effects and substantial marketing budgets. These films also use increasingly episodic structures at the expense of causal storytelling, more open endings instead of closures and more self-reflective generic narration instead of a clear plot (Smith 1998: 11; Buckland 1998: 167–75; Cook 1998: 230–31; Carroll 1990: 210–13; Tudor 1989: 179–80). Similarly, in the living dead films, continuing commentary on horror genre conventions takes place, and the final deaths of monsters become rare, leaving stories more open to the continuing presence of death.

If the transition era was filled with fear of nuclear war, the latter half of the twentieth century was marked by the comeback of ordinary death – visible in the questions of the decaying body and lengthened dying processes, treatment of dead bodies and personalization of dying and death. After the publication of such influential books on death and dying as Jessica Mitford's *The American Way of Death* (1963) and Elisabeth Kübler-Ross's *On Death and Dying* (1969), ordinary death resurfaced as a topic for public discussion. These, and other publications, revealed the limitations of institutionalized, medicalized and mechanical death by paying attention to a dignified death and processes of grief. Mitford, for example, showed how the tabooing of death had both emotional and financial costs. When communal practices had been replaced with professionalism and the families of the deceased were denied access to the details and practices of handling a corpse, the death industry (funeral parlours, mortuaries, funeral homes, funeral directors etc.) gained the authoritative role of defining the disposal of the dead. And, as part of the industrialization of the death process, modest and ordinary procedures soon gave way to commercialized products. The cost of dying and funerals multiplied, when the funeral industry sold its services on the basis that love and the significance of the dead could be calculated by the money spent on funerals (Mitford 1963: 20–21, 65, 92). Thus, the consequences of alienation of death started to raise public concern in the United States.

In the late twentieth century, medicalization has increased life expectancy further, which now stands between 70 and 80 years in the United States (Hoyert 2012). People grow up assuming that they will grow to be old. The death of aged people has made death less disturbing to the social dimensions of public life, as the social contribution of the dying has usually been limited before their actual passing. However, when death comes in old age, people's relationships are longer than they used to be, and this, according to some critics, can emphasize death and dying as a private experience and increase the emotional stress of parting (Morgan 2003: 1–2; Walter 1994: 23). Death has turned into an increasingly intimate experience and, as such, people have started to seek personal solutions of self-help (coffin-building courses, support groups, etc.) and commercialized practices. Along with personalized death, says Walter, death has become a consumer choice – a private, intimate and emotional issue. In this sense, death underwent a revival. Talk of death and even public images of death have increased to such an extent that we can now speak about a society obsessed with death (Walter 1994: 1–39). Similarly, in the living dead films, encounters with death have become part of individualized projects of survival and commercialized experiences.

In addition to death in old age, the processes of dying are now longer, as most deaths are caused by degenerative diseases or isolated long-term illnesses (Hoyert 2012). The lengthened processes demand special attention for the quality of the last years of each person's life. This has caused a boom in hospices and the palliative care movement, with the view that medical care is not enough on its own but that end-of-life care should also look after the psychological, spiritual and emotional needs of the dying and their families. The modern hospice movement spread from London to the United States in the late 1960s. The first American hospice home, New Haven Hospice, opened in 1974, and in 1979 the hospice movement started to get public financial support (Bennahum 2003: 3–7).

This movement is related to a wider cultural and social movement of death awareness which focuses on end-of-life issues and bereavement. It gains its power from a loosely connected network of academic scholars, educators, self-help groups and several institutions, such as the National Hospice and Palliative Care Organization. The movement has gained success in the latter part of the twentieth century, and many of its roots can be traced to the late 1960s and early 1970s when academic studies on death and dying gained popularity, the first death education courses emerged and hospice and palliative care practices started to form. By the late 1970s, the process of dying had become the subject of several radio, television and print media debates in the United States. Since then the movement has become more and more institutionalized in its desire to increase the individualization of end-of-life experiences (Doka 2003: 50–55; Staudt 2009: 15–17).

When the death awareness movement, including hospice and palliative care movements, gained more publicity, living dead films were also influenced by the general demand for better care and respect for the dying and dead. This is evident in the 1973 zombie film *Children Shouldn't Play with Dead Things*, which demanded more respect for the dead. The film portrays a group of actors reviving the buried dead as part of their performance.

To them, burial is a joke while the dead are the losers of society. In mocking the rituals, they disturb the cemetery and get their just deserts by being eaten away.

In addition to a growing awareness of lengthened dying processes, the post-classical era also related to the new ways of dying. The latter half of the twentieth century was marked by different types of death-related threats in an age when Americans were beginning to live longer and die of progressive diseases linked with such lifestyle factors as eating, drinking, using drugs, smoking or sexual behaviour. For example, a number of vampire films bring to mind contemporary themes of AIDS or drug addiction. *Vampire's Kiss* (1988) is a trip to the mind of a mentally ill man who imagines being bitten by a vampire. *Innocent Blood* (1992) is a story about a sex-addicted young woman vampire, and *The Addiction* (1995) creates a tale of a young woman's increasing addiction to vampirism. This film makes references to drugs more than obvious, as the young woman does not drink directly from the bodies, but prefers injecting the blood into her veins. All these films deal with mortal threats, and by connecting the threat to the undead, they create a warning image of premature death. In a way, drug use is also a theme of Wes Craven's zombie film *The Serpent and the Rainbow* (1988), which returns to the zombies' Haitian home ground and themes of voodoo. Through mystified rituals, drugs and illusions, the film creates a nightmarish journey of death and being buried alive.

The prevailing role of degenerative diseases also created fears and questions related directly to the bodily processes of dying. Post-classical living dead films eagerly address these body-related fears. Several theorists contend that the performative and fragmented nature of constructed bodily identities emphasizes bodies as personal projects. The bodies and other dimensions of identity are individualized, constructed, transformed, challenged and modified, which clearly shows in the horror film industry's increased interest in bodies (Csabai & Erós 2003: 206–07; Klesse 2000: 19; Skal 1993: 311, 323). The growing emphasis on the body reveals an important change in the narration of the living dead films. The protective narration of the classical films processed death primarily at the story level and as either a psychological or ontological experience. In comparison, the post-classical films frame detailed images of death, which are excessive and open in a way that highlights the physical experience instead. As Barbara Creed argues, post-classical horror films 'address the viewer directly' through embodied experiences. These films aim at realism – on the level of experience – in their destruction of bodies and in attacking the viewer's body as well. Such attacks cross the boundaries between the symbolic and the real (Creed 1995: 156–57). Thus, the films address the viewer's embodied fears related to decaying bodies.

The increasing use of bodily violence was especially visible in the post-classical films. The films include graphic scenes of bodies being ripped apart and fantastical images of mutilated and bloody corpses. However, the horror genre was not unique in its relation to violence, as violence increased in other genres as well (Prince 2000: 6–19). There was no direct censorship, but the rating system guided and limited the contents of Hollywood films. The rating system has undergone several adjustments, but its main function is to limit the access to films with adult-themed contents from younger audiences. The horror genre identifies itself as dubious genre, and therefore most films belong to either R-category (only for those over 17 years old) or PG-13 category (material inappropriate for under 13 years old). During the post-classical era, the most common, R-rated, category contained almost half of all Hollywood films. With a couple of non-rated exceptions, most of the living dead films from 1975 to 1995 were produced within this category, which allows adult themes, mild sex scenes and intense or persistent violence (MPAA; Sandler 2007: 48–64; De Vany 2004: 101–02; Maltby 2003: 598–600).

In this chapter, I will discuss how the living dead films of the post-classical era discuss the public issues related to normal death and increasing death awareness, such as fear of bodily changes, mistreatment of dying people, and demands for individualized choices and the creation of an intimate relationship with death. First, by using *Dawn of the Mummy* (1981) as an example of violent body horror, I will discuss the possibilities to experience the limits of the human body and individualized fears of managing approaching death. Second, an analysis of *Return of the Living Dead* (1985) will discuss the fears of malpractice related to dying and the dead. These fears tend to be directed towards impersonal funeral industries. Third, I will look into the case of self-expressive vampires, such as Dracula in *Bram Stoker's Dracula* (1992), and how they can be read as symbols of death awareness and a desire to re-establish a more intimate and personal relationship with death. In all of these films, ordinary death appears to be making a comeback because it is no longer dealt with by professionals but rather by ordinary people. However, as professionalization has diminished the readiness to handle death-related practices, a return to ordinary death becomes ambiguous, causing both anxiety and desire for intimacy.

5.1. Mummies and Body Horror

Dawn of the Mummy (1981) is part of the horror genre's video revolution during the early 1980s when VCR had made its way to American homes. Several horror films were released straight to video. These low-budget films had their own audiences and they, intentionally, as Linda Badley argues, exaggerated the horror conventions and challenged mainstream ideas of good taste. These videos included extremely violent films, and in their own time, they caused moral panic over uncontrollable and purposefully shocking video content. However, their rebellious attitude also addressed the eager audiences which gave these videos cult repetition and helped the horror to reinvent itself (Badley 2010, 46–59).

By intentionally challenging mainstream values and ideas, the video horror also has progressive potential to address culturally sensitive issues. Although *Dawn of the Mummy* is in many ways a repetitious and non-inventive low-budget film, its unleashed attitude towards bodily mutilation and an uncontrollable force of death manages to foreground the topical fears of degeneration and loss of control over a dying body (and mind). The film is rather conventionally situated in Egypt, but after the mummy is accidentally revived, the main mummy and his army of mummies hunt their victims to eat their internal organs. In this way, this mummy film draws its inspiration from apocalyptic zombie films, and the mummies have more similarities with Romero's zombies than with earlier mummy traditions. All in all, the film is a rip-off of Romero's zombie film *Dawn of the Dead* (1978), where the zombie apocalypse cannot be controlled anymore, and zombies symbolize endless and aimless consumption.

In *Dawn of the Mummy*, archaeologists are replaced by tomb raiders, and scientific excavation methods make way for a race of who is going to dig fastest and sell the finds at the highest price, without regard for what relics might be destroyed during the process. Besides the tomb raiders, an American fashion team use the tomb as a setting and sell the fashion by using images and myths of death. For these two groups, ancient (or traditional) death is something that can be sold, not something to be studied. Their commercialized use of the mummy also comments on the commercialized practices of American modern death. Whereas in modern society the management of death is outsourced to professionals, the professional funeral industry has become the most influential definer of cultural death-related attitudes and practices in the United States. They define the proper places and times for emotional mourning, such as wakes, viewings and funerals. In addition, other institutions provide countless informal and formal programmes of death-related activities, such as counselling, therapy, peer groups and imaginative funeral services (Davies 2002: 36–38; McIlwain 2005: 241; Corr & Corr 2003: 49–50). Thus, death has become something that can be sold to the dying and those in mourning, just as it is sold to the eager audiences of horror films, for instance.

Another aspect of the professionalization of death is visible in *Dawn of the Mummy*: the ordinary people have no means to manage death on their own. In the film, at first the characters see pagan death as profitable, not threatening, but things change when the fashion team accidentally awakens the mummy. When the ensuing apocalypse proves that death cannot be rejected or tamed, the characters realize that they have no skills to encounter death. They perish in front of it. The film illustrates that the professionalization and commercialization of death may have negative cultural consequences. Instead of scientifically controlling death rites and mummies, the film imagines the negative consequences of alienating death, when an ancient mummy and death are not encountered by professionals, but by random people, tomb raiders, fashion people and local villagers who have no expertise in dealing with it.

The earlier mummy films had carefully studied and re-controlled the undead nature and foreign rituals, but the post-classical *Dawn of the Mummy* cannot re-control its monster. The non-professional people show, in fact, that the outsourced professionalism of death does not always give the sought-after protection. The characters do not fight the mummy with knowledge but with violence, and rather hopelessly they fail time after time. As their final attempt they lure the main mummy into a warehouse filled with dynamite. After the explosion the characters are content, but the closing image reveals that the mummy has survived. Without professionals, archaeologists or doctors, the random people who are left to deal with unexpected encounters with corpses are helpless. The film shows what can happen if people's skills of managing death are impoverished.

Mummies, it seems, similar to apocalyptic zombies before them, have now become out of control. This is highlighted in the unlimited threat of the post-classical (and digital) mummies. Where the previous films had limited the mummies' threat to individuals (lost lover or people disturbing the sanctity of their tomb), this time the mummy yearns to 'rise and kill'. In its previous life, the mummy was a violent tyrant sentenced to undeath. In this life, he and his army return to wreak havoc. The mummies' overwhelming, grotesque and violent presence in the modern world makes death a spectacle.

Dawn of the Mummy is also drastically more violent and graphic than previous mummy films. The differentiation with earlier mummy films is highlighted in the early embalming scene where the viewer is invited to witness how the stomach of the body is slashed open and the bloody internal organs are placed into Canopic jars. The focus on the mummification scene is turned from a spiritual ritual into a dismembering of the dead body. By concentrating on the frailty of the human body, the film draws inspiration more from cannibalistic zombie films than from other mummy characters. So, when the mummy and his army are accidentally brought to life, they start a violent campaign to hunt the living, eating their entrails, which the viewer is shown directly.

The film's explicit bodily violence follows a wider cultural tendency. Lisa Badley argues that modern culture had become obsessed with bodies by the 1980s. The biomedicalization and secularization had dented both the supernatural beliefs and spirituality related to death. Instead, the materiality of death, such as decomposition, became the new horror. This cultural relocation from psyche to body is visible in the narration and images of film (Badley 1995: 24–29). No wonder that Colavito calls this era a time of body horror: horror films clearly became obsessed with 'ritual mutilation of the human body'. Similarly, he argues that the medical and biotechnological possibilities, including the readiness to keep the dead alive with medical technology, have turned the body into a source of horror (Colavito 2008: 18).

The mummy films, too, renewed their imagery by featuring detailed body horror. Since the classical films, the mummy remained wrapped for the following decades, hiding the details of the preserved body, but some of these secrets are revealed in the post-classical films. Even *Time Walker* (1982), which introduces an alien mummy who just wants to establish contact with its own planet and go home (like E.T.), highlights the poisonous body of the undead, whose touch burns and destroys the bodies of the living. Furthermore, in *Dawn of the Mummy*, shroud pieces hang on the monstrous body, but otherwise the body is preserved, yet decaying at the same time. When the mummy is brought back to life – the photo shoot casting a piercing spotlight – we see what appears to be burnt flesh on his skeletal body. Here, historical accuracies are abandoned for the sake of grotesque bodies, special effects and experiences through shock values.

The graphic images of *Dawn of the Mummy* sought influence from the gore or splatter films. Gore (excessive use of blood) and splatter (dismembering of bodies and excess of entrails) refer to bloody violence within any horror subgenre. In such films, the body becomes flesh, blood flows, skin peels off and bodies are decapitated (Freeland 2000: 241–42; Jancovich 1992: 113). In one of the scenes, one of the fashion models encounters the awakened mummies. She tries to run away, but one of the mummies catches her ankle. After being captured, the mummies consume her body, similarly to Romero's zombies. In this scene, her body marks the source of horror. In comparison with the classical films – in which the monsters' and characters' gazes marked death – the marking is now done by the monsters' attacking and characters' reactive bodies. Post-classical horror is, indeed, marked by a dual relationship to the body: while an attacking body is both threatening and exciting at the same time, the attacked body is an important metaphor in the post-classical period. As Grønstad (2003: 161, 191) maintains, classical violence has changed from 'a narration about the body' to a post-classical version of 'a narration by the body', or from the 'euphemistic portrayals of the violated and wounded body' to 'the vulnerability of the flesh'.

Dawn of the Mummy employs a graphic style to produce exaggeration. Later in the film, when the awakened and aggressive mummies invade an Egyptian town, the death scenes get plenty and detailed: so many are now happening at once that the camera starts focusing on the numbers of deaths along with the vulnerabilities of the bodies. Open access to fantasized images of dying brings home the unrealistic nature of film violence. Freeland (2000: 190, 271) compares these graphic images that show more pain, blood and screaming than is realistic or even believable to pornographic sex acts that make sex 'better' than in reality. Similarly, Grønstad argues that post-classical films proclaim that 'violence may be this, but at least nothing more'. This use of exaggerated violent spectacles compares with classical films where, in avoiding the use of explicit violence, films made the bodily consequences of violence invisible and abstract (Grønstad 2003: 140, 282).

The aesthetics of *Dawn of the Mummy* are not about avoiding the detailed physical violence, but addressing death as a fantastical spectacle. One especially powerful scene presents the viewer with a butcher happily doing his job before suddenly stopping in his tracks, amazed. A subjective shot reveals a monstrous undead body before the camera cuts to a partly blocked image. The camera is placed behind the mummy in a way that the viewer is allowed to see its raised hand and the butcher's shocked reaction. In many ways, the cutting of the scene is reminiscent of *Night of the Living Dead*'s mother/daughter scene, as in the next cut the gaze returns to the mummy and his raised weapon. Unlike in Romero's film, the next cut to the attacked person does not frame the actual act of violence out of the image. This close-cut concentrates on the face and expressions of the dying person, but as the mummy plunges the knife deep into the butcher's head, the knife piercing the body is also shown. Although the image takes advantage of the fantastical body of the mummy, the main attention is on the mutilation of a living body.

The direct images of this death scene both emphasize and reveal death's aestheticized nature. Although the characters and their relation to death events remain an important part of the story, the showing of actual death events is given more space and prominence in the narration. In this scene, the butcher is a mere side character with no special relationship with the main character. Indeed, not all death scenes have characters that a viewer can align or ally with; instead, emotions and experiences are invited through the framing of images, sounds and effects. Thus, post-classical films have adopted cinematic techniques which underscore the visuality of death, such as prolonged on-screen death scenes, use of montage, slow motion, extreme close-ups and graphic effects (Prince 2003: 17, 35–36; Sobchack 2000: 118). All give form to and extend the process where the body transforms from being to another kind of being or non-being. Similarly, the rest of the butcher scene centres on the close-up of a mutilated and bloody head. The expression on the face is surprised, and the eyes stare, dead. This slowed-down moment of death is what Russell calls a ballet, or 'danse macabre' of cinematic violent death. He argues that violent death scenes sometimes narrate and present death in slow motion, broken into individual scenes, and both the death and the affected body become deconstructed in a most concrete way (Russell 1995: 186–87).

Moreover, Shaviro recognizes that the constructive nature of the images creates an affective reality through perception, which is further enhanced by the cinema's power to draw on 'technology for intensifying and renewing experiences'. This makes the experiences produced by images, sounds and movements both personally encountered and socially shared (Shaviro 1993: 37–40, 64, 258, 263). In other words, death in the post-classical living dead films is primarily an embodied phenomenon, which creates shared experiences of death and dying for the viewer. The distinction from earlier films can be formulated in different character-mediated experiences. In classical films, the characters see death on behalf of the viewer who is socially excluded from a seeing position, while the characters of the post-classical films embody death for the viewer who is not yet experiencing the actual physical death experience.

These experiences do not try to imitate everyday life experiences as such, but they do comment on everyday life's relations to death. According to Altman, the norms and values of everyday life are often conflicted in generic films, but rather than a negative conflict, this is a place where a cultural work can critically study the very values and norms. The pleasure of genre cinema can arise from such conflicts and differences, because genres offer a countercultural pleasure (Altman 1999: 147–52). The ways in which post-classical films encounter death through (re)constructed death imageries and deconstructed dying processes can supply us with emotional, cognitive and aesthetic pleasure exactly because these images replace the modern idea of clinical death with embodied experiences.

5.2. Mistreatment of Dead – Zombies and Death Industries

The post-classical era saw the viewer's knowledge of the genre conventions and mythologies gain a bigger role (Elsaesser 1998: 195). This is also visible in the success of Dan O'Bannon's *The Return of the Living Dead* (1985), which self-consciously and ironically compares itself to *Night of the Living Dead*. The film is based on John Russo's eponymous novel. Russo worked together with Romero in *Night of the Living Dead* and kept the rights to the title 'Living Dead'. Despite the connections between the films, the atmospheres are quite different. *Night of the Living Dead* is dark and serious, whereas *The Return of the Living Dead* is comical and youth-oriented in its use of rebellion, nudity and punk culture. In the beginning, the medical warehouse worker reveals to a new staff member that the events in *Night of the Living Dead* were true and that those reanimated bodies were stored in their warehouse. The contamination restarts when evidence of zombified bodies is being exhibited.

The film continues the familiar cynical and apocalyptic tendencies of Romero's film. Also, Romero continued his saga with two post-classical era films, *Dawn of the Dead* (1978) and *Day of the Dead* (1985). These sequels continued the political commentary in a nihilistic and cynical spirit. However, Bishop argues that *Day of the Dead* failed at the box office, because the young horror audience wanted entertaining films instead of politics. He claims that *The Return of the Living Dead* does not aim at serious social criticism, but instead creates a comic monster tale with close connections to youth cultures (Bishop 2010: 15, 158, 183). However, this is a rather limited view of the film's social potential. After all, the film manages to create a rather interesting image of the American public's doubts about the practices of death-related industries, such as medical care, the funeral industry and American military.

This film is obsessed with death in more ways than one. The locations (cemetery, funeral home and medical warehouse), professions (mortician, medical staff etc.), iconography (tombs, skeletons, corpses, crematorium) and dialogue all concentrate on death. For example, at the funeral home, the mortician describes in detail the bodily effects of death and the burning of the corpse. Moreover, the young protagonists who rebel against the social norms are especially intrigued by death – one of the key taboos in society. They constantly talk about death. For example, one of the characters, Trash, asks her friends: 'Do you ever wonder about all the different ways of dying? You know, violently? And wonder, like, what would be the most horrible way to die?' Spider's answer – 'I try not to think about dying too much'– seems to follow the ideals of modern death, whereas many other characters have a more curious attitude towards death.

Death is also visible at the level of images, as *The Return of the Living Dead* depends on bodily reactions to dead bodies. Interestingly, this film also emphasizes the connection between embodiments of death and death-related experiences in being filled with images of corpses in different forms. Even before the mass resurrection of the dead, the viewer is introduced to stored skeletons and preserved and stuffed bodies of both animals and humans. Later, after the revival of the dead, corpses in different states of decay take the scene, and even dismembered body parts keep on living. The body horror is executed also through detailed bodily violence. When one half-melted body attacks one of the characters (ironically named Suicide), the viewer is allowed to see the attacking, grotesque body through the victim's subjective view. The image then cuts to an objective view of the monster's opening mouth before jumping to an extreme close-up of his teeth penetrating the skull. The camera then backs away and shows how the body collapses on the floor.

This excess of death, however, is more than superficial curiosity or an attempt to shock the audience. Instead, the film touches upon the growing awareness of death-related issues. One growing public discussion was concerned with how dying people were treated in institutions. Quite soon after the release of *The Return of the Living Dead*, hospice benefits were made permanent in the United States in 1986, and so the hospice and palliative care movements became recognized by the American Congress. The legislation on adequate care for the dying and funeral practices placed death more firmly on the public agenda (Staudt 2009: 15–17; Bennahum 2003: 6–7). This general awareness also raised concerns about how the dying and dead were being treated.

The Return of the Living Dead explores the fears about how, after our death (or in some cases even before it), we are reduced to mere corpses and, therefore, open to possible mistreatment. In this film, the dead are still in pain, but no one in the death industry or society understands this. Although the zombies consume the living cannibalistically, the film makes them victims of misunderstanding and mistreatment. The revived dead act monstrously because of their physical pain, not because they are evil as such. The viewer's potential for sympathizing with the monsters is also increased by giving the zombies the capability to talk and think – a rather unique narrative device to the zombie film tradition. For example, a female zombie is able to justify her actions when she is asked why she eats people. She does it because of 'the pain of being dead', as 'I can feel myself rot'. Indeed, rising from their graves, the dead appear conscious of the dying and decaying processes their bodies are going through. Only the eating of brains of others makes the physical pain of being dead go away. Although, the convention of silent zombies has maintained its dominant position, this film follows the wider trend of the post-classical era, when the perspective of the undead started to open up (visible in vampire films, in particular).

By questioning the prevailing understanding of death, the film also debates the changing definitions of death. Until 1981, death had been defined as the absence of cardinal signs (heartbeat and breathing), but the President's Commission Report deemed that brain death would be a more appropriate definition (Kellehear 2009: 135). In the film, paramedics examine two infected men and declare that 'you have no pulse, your blood pressure's zero-over-zero, you have no pupillary response, no reflexes and your temperature is 70 degrees', adding that 'technically, you're not alive. Except you're conscious, so we don't know what it means'. The listed symptoms fit the previous definition of death, but not the new one. If the zombies appear dead, but are conscious, can they be dead? And if they are not dead, is it then right to treat them like corpses?

This film gives the viewer an imagined glimpse of being dead. It is not a peaceful image. In the sequels – *Return of the Living Dead Part II* (1988), *Return of the Living Dead III* (1993), *Return of the Living Dead: Necropolis* (2005) and *Return of the Living Dead: Rave to the Grave* (2005) – the question of being dead is further debated. For example, *Return of the Living Dead III* narrates its story from inside Julie's – the main character – head. Speculating what it is like to be dead, Julie concludes after becoming zombified that death is both physically painful and causes personal anxiety and loneliness. When the dead attack the living, it is partly because of their pain and partly because their rights and feelings are ignored by society.

In this sense, the zombies of *The Return of the Living Dead* have revolutionary potential, especially in relation to criticism levelled at the production and consumerism of the death industry. The events of the film concentrate on three main locations – the cemetery, the funerary home and the warehouse supplying medical material. Because these are the places where the dead are peripheralized in society, they are also the places from which they make their return. During their reanimation, they destroy not only the property of these institutions, but also the people working within them and other local authorities, such as paramedics and police officers, who often deal with the dead in society. Several scenes contrast the authoritative voices of death and the voices of the dead experiencing death. The authorities approach to the topic is a medicalized one when they describe the process of dying and degeneration. The zombies describe their personal encounters. As Bishop (2010: 185) argues, the distance between the two voices speaks of a cynical image of the American 'realities of death' and death industry. For example, Mitford (1963) exposed several malpractices taking place within the death industry in that the dead were being carelessly handled and disposed of – their connection with humanity forgotten. Talk of possible malpractices continued in the 1980s; for example, in the 1982 Congressional Hearing into the practices of the funeral industry.

In addition to *The Return of the Living Dead*, there is a line of post-classical zombie films that address public fears of what the death industry, either the medical staff or funeral doctors, does with dead people. The funeral director of *Phantasm* (1979) turns dead people into his slaves, and *Re-Animator* (1985) discusses brain death by introducing a crazy scientist who brings dead people back to life to study them. Also, *Dead and Buried* (1981) challenges the practices of funeral directors and embalming: a small-town funeral director orders his zombified dead to kill the living visitors of the city for him to be able to embalm and make the bodies more beautiful than they were. He then brings them back to life and makes them his servants. The film's unethical and inhuman handling of the dead extends to cover the sphere of the living as well. Most of the zombies in *Dead and Buried* do not rebel against their maker; however, in *The Return of the Living Dead* the zombies rise against the existing system and demand recognition for the rights of the dying and the dead.

Furthermore, following the older zombie tradition, *The Return of the Living Dead* discusses one more institution – the American military. The reanimation of the dead is once again connected to military experiments, but this time the military is prepared to own up – in its own way. The film ends with the protagonists' reporting the events to the military, whose response is to bomb the whole area and all those in it, both the dead and the living. Its solution betrays the people's trust and only causes more violent death. However, it is suggested that the dead are not returned to their graves for good, but they will soon rise again and avenge their mistreatment. In *The Return of the Living Dead*, modern society cannot rid itself of death and its place in public conflicts. The possibility of a bad death, in particular, exposes fractures in the modern institutions' death-related practices.

5.3. Desire for Self-Expressive Vampires

Vampires, especially in literary traditions, have had dual roots. On the one hand, we have Stoker's depiction of Dracula as a sexual predator in love with death and (sexual) possession. The archetype of evil predator dominated the earlier part of the twentieth century – coinciding with the beginning of a cinematic tradition. On the other hand, there is an earlier romantic vampire fiction with romantic and tragic lovers, with an emphasis on sexual intimacy and empowerment (Auerbach 1995: 1, 13, 95–98, 191; Williamson 2005: 292–93; Williamson 2003: 101–02). For a long time, Hollywood was occupied with evil vampires, but since the post-classical era both of these two different vampire traditions have competed for their on-screen time.

The death-related corporeality and amazing monstrosity have increased in several post-classical and digital living dead films, including vampire films. For example, in *Fright Night* (1985), which renewed the teenage interest in vampires through inventive violence and a nostalgic relationship to the old vampire tradition, a dying vampire turns first into a slimy and disgusting bat before starting to burn into an animal-like skeleton. Similarly, the vampires of *From Dusk till Dawn* (1996) are bloodsucking and flesh-eating monstrous bodies that exude slime and other suspect substances.

However, at the same time, the sympathetic features of some television vampires were borrowed by horror films. Dan Curtis' 1973 television film *Bram Stoker's Dracula* and John Badham's *Dracula* (1979) introduced the love plots. For example, Badham's count was charming and well-liked among women. He embarks on a romance with Lucy, who finds that the men who feel threatened by the vampire are wrong: 'Tormenting him who is the saddest, the kindest of all.' In the end, the men fail to kill Dracula, who escapes in the form of a bat, leaving the tearful Lucy to smile knowingly.

The family theme, too, was strengthened in vampire films. In such teenage films as *Near Dark* (1987) and *The Lost Boys* (1987), the vampires create an alternative family (gang) where teenagers can have a sense of belonging and acceptance at the same time as they are able to rebel against societal norms and rules. In both films, the main characters are saved when they find a connection with some sort of normal family. For example, in *Near Dark*, Caleb is saved from the vampire gang by his father, who cures him with a blood transfusion. In the end, his vampire girlfriend is also saved to make his family whole. These films connect the horror genre's tendency to choose 'moral' solutions to unwanted teenager behaviour in the guise of gangs. Yet, these films addressed the desire to belong, even from the vampires' perspective and, since the 1990s, this tendency has become overwhelming in the cinematic tradition.

The theme of belonging had already been featured in literature with the self-searching vampire type who became famous in Anne Rice's first novel *Interview with a Vampire* (1976) – the first in the series of *Vampire Chronicles*. Rice's figure had transformed into a secularized character who was communal rather than solitary, and a reluctant and self-doubting killer rather than a cruel and intentional predator (Punter & Byron 2004: 271; Tomc 1997: 96; Zanger 1997: 17–21). Also, in the film version of Rice's novel, *Interview with the Vampire: The Vampire Chronicles* (1994), Louis becomes the archetype of cinematic self-searching vampires. The film is a flashback of Louis' life as he recounts it to a journalist. In this self-narration, he evaluates his choices, lifestyle and emotions. He concludes the narration with: 'I go on, night after night. I feed on those who cross my path. But all my passion went with her golden hair. I'm a spirit of preternatural flesh. Detached. Unchangeable. Empty.'

Perhaps because of the duality of their tradition, it is the vampire films which have most clearly exhibited the changing perspective and the increasing use of the monster's voice in living dead films. What has decreased, in particular, is the differentiation between monstrous and other positions. Post-classical living dead films, in particular, more readily offer the viewer the positions, voice and tragedy of the monster. While the monsters have been more or less tragic since the first living dead films, the change is executed at the discursive level of the narrative viewpoint and the preferred character engagements: the post-classical living dead films emphasize and explain the perspective of the undead much more than the classical films. William Hughes (2000: 151, 155) argues that as the post-classical films have become more tolerant of the monster's perspective, some of the vampires, such as Louis, have become prisoners of their own self-interpretation and the pointlessness of their lifestyle. Indeed, for Louis, being a vampire is a burden: 'there was a hell, and no matter where we moved to I was in it.'

The access to the tragedy of the embodiments of death discusses with the rise of the death awareness movement in the United States, which gained visible public power in the 1980s. This movement gave the dying and their families a voice as a contrast to the authority of those in the death industry. Similarly, in living dead films, viewpoints started to change so that the undead were not only defined by others, but also the monster's perspective and self-definition were allowed. Vampire films, similarly, highlight how the embodiments of death feel and narrate death.

The changing traditions are visible even in the Dracula legacy when Francis Ford Coppola directed a reinterpretation of the original novel with a sympathetic, self-conscious and tragic vampire in *Bram Stoker's Dracula* (1992). Because of these changes in monster image, some, such as Tomasz Warchol (2003: 7–8), have claimed that Coppola has destroyed Dracula as the most pervasive vampire, because he changed its spirit and turned the vampire into a human. However, the renewal of genre conventions is not destruction as such, but a differentiation to the formula and its themes. In this film, the competing monster interpretations create the main tendency for the film – both Dracula and his victims represent conflicting attitudes towards death. On the one hand, death is still something that is feared, monstrous and abjected. On the other, death can be embraced and seen as part of life and identity, not exterior to it.

In the film, a lot of attention is directed to the transforming identity of Dracula. It opens with a scene from the fifteenth century, introducing Prince Vlad the Impaler who is both a violent and ruthless warrior, as well as a devoted and loving husband. After one victorious battle, he finds out that his wife has committed suicide after receiving false news of her husband's death. Devastated and revengeful, he feels betrayed by God and curses not only the Church, but also himself. He becomes undead, causing his own transformation into a monster. However, his motivation lies not only in the lust for deadly revenge, but also in lost love.

Later on, the post-classical discourse frames Dracula as a lonely man, resentful of his prolonged and unfortunate life on earth. With tears in his eyes, Dracula tells Jonathan Harker, who has arrived at his castle to complete a real-estate deal, about his life after the death of his wife: 'My life at its best is a misery.' During this sequence, Dracula accidentally sees Mina's picture, which gives him hope. He recognizes his dead beloved in the picture, which both upsets him and gives him a prospect of regaining that love. 'Do you believe in destiny? That even the powers of time can be altered for a single purpose? That the luckiest man who walks on this earth is the one who finds ... true love?' Because the viewer has witnessed his unfortunate but apparently lasting love, the vampire's worldview becomes more accessible and understandable. Indeed, the post-classical vampire desires personal attachment and meanings to be attached to the return of death. He does not force death back on the public, as happened in the classical films; rather, he seduces the viewer to desire its return.

The change in tradition is visible at the level of dialogue. The 1930s Dracula was forced into the position of a stranger unable to communicate his desire for love, whereas the Dracula of the 1990s openly discusses his desire and inability to love. Béla Lugosi's classical Dracula was able to speak, but was restricted to explaining himself in quoted poems or short sentences, such as 'I am Dracula', 'I never drink wine' and 'I dislike mirrors, Van Helsing will explain'. These are statements rather than explanations or self-expressions, and the ultimate power of definition is given to others. In fact, Hughes (2000: 149) argues that because others speak for him and, more importantly, because his antagonists speak for him, Dracula was made both physiologically and morally the 'other'. Furthermore, in this case, the other characters and the viewer are supposed to trust an authority's definitions, whereas the viewpoints of the deceased are not considered valuable. The contradiction with Coppola's post-classical *Bram Stoker's Dracula* is enormous. His Dracula is given more room for self-expression, even self-loathing: 'I am nothing. Lifeless. Soulless. Hated and feared. I am dead to all the world. Hear me. I am the monster that breathing men would kill. I am Dracula.' This scene takes the famous statement of the earlier film and expands it to contain more expressive power than the short statement of the 1930s – 'I am Dracula' – ever did. Interestingly, the self-expression has not only revealed the sympathetic side of monstrosity, but the tragedy of it, too.

Although *Bram Stoker's Dracula* begins by offering affective alignment with Dracula in the same way as some films introduce their protagonists, the position of Dracula is still marked with ambivalence from the start. The generic knowledge of Dracula's wickedness and evil deeds ensures that the viewer is aware of the monstrousness of his position. This is why Smith claims that even if our alignment with the monster seems perverse at first glance, these affectively positioned monsters are often only partially evil: although amoral and vicious, the characters are given some attractive qualities. It is, therefore, not their evil actions or traits that cue alignment, but rather the viewer may engage with the monster in spite of these actions (Smith 1999: 220–25). When this discussion is returned to the idea of modern death, it appears that although death is a disturbing or even frightening event, such ambivalent positions of embodied death suggest that it is still possible to create a more familiar and meaningful, yet ambiguous, relationship with it.

Also, the monstrousness appears to be a question of perspective. From Jonathan's position, the vampire appears monstrous and threatening. Interestingly, both of these contradictory perspectives are offered to the viewer, and the viewer is, in fact, provided with two competing alignments at the same time. For example, Jonathan's horror becomes evident from a point-of-view shot which shows him witness the nature of Dracula's prey, a human baby. A reaction shot unmasks his shock and disgust. In contrast, the position of Dracula, created through the combination of a close-up and a reaction shot, when he is accused of not being capable of loving, demonstrates the distress of this lonely man who desires nothing more than to love again. Dracula's deeds may be monstrous, but by changing the addressed alignment in the middle of the scene, it raises the question of whether he is monstrous by his nature. Or, if death is a disturbing event, is it monstrous in itself?

The same ambivalence between humanity and monstrosity is present in Dracula's constantly shifting form. Not only is he capable of transforming himself into a bat, a werewolf, a swarm of rats or beautiful mist, but his human embodiment is transforming, too. Depending on the amount of blood he has had, his human form changes from a decrepit old man to a handsome young man. Dracula also exploits these different forms to his advantage. In order to seduce, he appears as a young man; in order to intimidate his enemies, he takes on the form of a monstrous werewolf, which foregrounds the grotesqueness of his occasionally conventional beauty. Warchol argues that this particular Dracula not only uses transformation between different forms but also he is imprisoned by it. Different forms represent his two sides – human and monster. His inner ambivalence is made visible in the changing physical appearance (Warchol 2003: 7–8).

The ambivalence is also related to the common theme of vampire films, that of sexuality. Christopher McGunnigle claims that Dracula's sexuality was deconstructed by the loss of his wife Elisabeta and his self-transformation into a monster. From this point onwards, McGunnigle insists, Dracula uses his now queered sexuality as punishment. Mina offers him a way to restore his heterosexual identity and relieve him of queerness. In the end, however, he is killed, but his death, too, can be seen as a restoration of traditional sexual norms which demand that transgressing sexuality be punished with death (McGunnigle 2005: 176–83). Although punishable queer sexuality is a common theme in vampire films, especially during the early 1990s when sex, death and homosexuality were closely linked through AIDS (see, for example, Nixon 1997), McGunnigle fails to see the possibilities of a queer reading which gives space to alternative sexualities. This brings us to an important dimension of *Bram Stoker's Dracula*. The main thing is not whether Dracula chooses victims on the basis of gender. What counts is desire, and not only his desire to engage with the living, but his victims' desires to create a relationship with death as well.

George E. Haggerty points out that horror narratives are not so much about heterosexuality or queerness as about desire itself. He continues that desire is related to power, the exercise or resistance of power, or powerlessness (Haggerty 2006: 2). In this sense, desire should not be seen as lack, as something that is missing and needs to be fulfilled, which is what McGunnigle appears to do. Dracula makes clear that even if he possessed Mina, his monstrous nature would not change; it would just gain new elements. A more suitable desire model can be found in the Deleuzian tradition of interpretation where desire is a productive experience, not a negation of something else (Powell 2005: 20–21, 93). Elspeth Probyn has taken the Deleuzian idea of desire further. Desire is always in relation to something, rearranging its position and relationships. It is social and productive, longing to become something other. Such an understanding of desire makes it a positive social force, which can rework different social relations in society, including gender relations (Probyn 1996: 13, 42–62).

Similarly, in *Bram Stoker's Dracula*, desire – sexual desire, in particular – can be understood as a social force and part of the power relations, symbolized in Dracula's four main victims: two men, Renfield and Harker; and two women, Lucy and Mina. These four create two comparable couples in that Renfield and Lucy are the willing victims, whereas Harker and Mina are more resistant to the seductive power. The two couples come to represent desire's emancipative potency and the film's unbalanced gender roles. The women's desire for a vampire life and death liberates them, whereas the men's desire for vampiric life shows their inability to accept the power of desire and to allow death to change them. The women are thus made to represent a positive relationship with death, whereas the men are afraid of the becoming power of dying.

The contradiction between empowerment and deprivation of power is first of all seen in the film's whore figures, Renfield and Lucy, who both seem eager victims of Dracula. Lisa Nyström maintains that Lucy is a 'threat to the patriarchal values', for she appears independent and sexual even before Dracula's arrival. She creates anxiety in men because she represents an 'attempt to regain control of her own sexual and biological power' (Nyström 2009: 69, 72–73). When Dracula comes along, Lucy does not think twice. For her, the vampire offers an alternative way of exploring sexuality.

Bram Stoker's Dracula invites the viewer to participate in Lucy's seduction, contamination and transformation. The seduction is a violent but aesthetic scene: we see Lucy standing in her bedroom, wearing a blood-red nightgown as a reference to sexuality and sinfulness. There is a sudden change in atmosphere. Lucy senses a vampire's call in the now stormy night. She opens the doors to the garden, letting in the strong wind. Her dress becomes entangled around her like a bridal trail. Her appearance is all the more pronounced when she is contrasted with Mina, who sees Lucy disappear into the gardens. Mina is dressed in a pure white gown, marking both her innocence and her so far secure position in the story. When Lucy walks into the stormy night, the scenery is toned blue in the thunderstorm which lights up the garden and fills the scene with a rumble. Moreover, the hue renders the scenery a mystical, even mythical air. We are no longer in a secure and welcoming garden. Entranced, Lucy walks towards the centre of the garden labyrinth to meet the vampire who has assumed the form of a werewolf. The viewer is summoned to witness the beast ravage Lucy in a sex act that makes her contamination appear more fantastic than realistic.

The embodied scene, which is filled with aesthetic detail, is further dramatized as Lucy's contamination becomes confirmed through a transformation phase. This time, the physicality of the transformation also stands out, with visible signs of what is occurring. She grows paler, her fangs start to grow and she starts to reject garlic and other anti-vampiric symbols. The changes do not appear subtly, either: she is clearly in agony and pain throughout the transformation. Her change to the undead state is drastic, because the changes have become irreversible and all of her lively colours have been drained from her. Lucy's detailed bodily changes and physical encounter with Dracula show how the attacking and reactive gazes of the classical films have been replaced by bodies and embodiments. In her seduction scene, it is the threatening male body that possesses the woman, and as the transformative phase shows, it is the female body that becomes a means of mediating the power, physicality and embodiments of death and violence of the living dead films.

During her transformation phase, Lucy is still conscious of the immorality of her actions. For example, she asks Mina not to tell anyone that she has been attacked by the vampire. While Leah Wyman and George Dionisopoulos (1999: 37) interpret the request as Lucy's embarrassment about what has happened, it would be equally warranted to suggest that the request stresses Lucy's desire to keep her sex affair as a secret, because she wants to avoid being moralized and re-tamed by others. After her transformative death, not only are her desires liberated, but she also enters into a perverse marriage with a vampire where, instead of having children, she feasts on them. What finalizes her transformation is the outcome of a monstrous mother figure, leaving her to fulfil her desires in an abusive way, especially from the viewer's perspective, who is still bound by the social norms.

While Lucy finds a new identity in seduction and transformative death, Renfield's fate is different. The actual seduction scene between Renfield and Dracula is kept from the viewer, but it is clear that the seduction does not lead to a final transformation. Rather, Renfield is made Dracula's obedient servant. His transformation has started: in his lust for blood, he eats insects and little animals. At the same time, however, he stills holds on to his former identity and is, therefore, denied the becoming, or empowering, power of desire. The internal conflict with a desire he cannot follow drives him crazy, turning him into an impotent character who has lost his autonomy and identity. The difference between Lucy and Renfield is also evident in their attitude towards death. Lucy embraces death, whereas Renfield avoids it and thus prolongs the painful transformation process.

Unlike Renfield and Lucy, Harker and Mina do not wish to become vampires. They are engaged and their sexual fulfilment is waiting to happen within the moral limits of society, but Dracula then interferes. Harker travels to his castle, is taken prisoner and gets attacked by Dracula's concubines. He manages to escape, leaving three lustful lovers behind, which we could interpret as Harker having resisted the socially unaccepted desire. However, he later confesses to Van Helsing that 'I was impotent with fear'. Carol C. Corbin and Robert A. Campbell (1999: 47) hold that Harker is a typical modern man who cannot rationally understand the supernatural events he is witnessing. The scene can also be read in relation to sexuality, to which the word 'impotent' refers. In this light, the scene suggests that Harker could not act on desire when he saw it, but became afraid and escaped instead of embracing the opportunity and becoming something else. He is not a hero in the traditional sense of being brave; rather, he is undressed from his position of power.

The position of power is given to Mina instead. Dracula sees his dead wife in Mina, who chooses to give herself to Dracula in the end. Unlike in Harker's case, this is Mina's active decision. The vampire could easily possess her, but before the deadly kiss, Dracula reveals his true identity and both the positive – 'I give you life eternal, everlasting love, the power of the storm and the beasts of the earth' – and the negative effects of vampirism – 'You will be cursed to walk in the shadow of death for all eternity'. He almost regrets his actions by stating: 'I love you too much to condemn you.' However, Mina has made up her mind. She sees the possibilities open to her if she dies from the restrictions and rules of this world and is born in the other world of freedom and unbarred sexuality. She demands to be taken 'away from all this death' and drinks the blood of Dracula. As with Lucy, such a choice highlights the liberating elements of undeadness.

In *Bram Stoker's Dracula*, the traditional understanding of an active and passive gender is challenged, for the women are willing to give in to desire and change, while the men are forced to lose their power, too impotent to encounter desire. This is further emphasized by the women's active roles. In the end, it is Mina who kills the vampire in a prolonged moment of death. The viewer is allowed to see how the monstrous body changes into the body of the man he used to be. The injured Dracula retreats to his chapel and falls on the floor. Mina helps him to die as she pushes the stake deep into his heart. An extreme close-up then lingers on his face, enabling the viewer to encounter the moment of Dracula's final death. His face slowly turns immobile, bringing a countenance of peace. Here, Dracula is allowed to die as a human, not as a monster. After his death, and after kissing the dead body, Mina, with tears on her face, makes sure that he can rest in peace and cuts his head off with a sword. Mina has the power to kill Dracula out of pity and love, whereas in the classical *Dracula* the vampire is killed by vengeful, jealous and insecure men. Such a change in gender roles challenges traditional identities, argues Hilary Neroni. She claims that the women in post-classical films increasingly started to employ on-screen violence, which defies men's active masculinity and distances women from passive femininity (Neroni 2005: ix, 32–46, 160).

Death, therefore, has a potentially liberating role in this film. Choosing a deadly fate is not a punishment but a reward for breaking the social norms that limit the encounters with one's own life and identity. However, this potential is utilized differently by the genders. Death is liberating for women, but as the rules make more sense to men, they fail to see the need for change. Therefore, in the encounter with desire, they lose their power position and become trapped in an old-fashioned understanding of the gendered world. At the implicit level, the film symbolizes the change in death's role as well. The women who in fiction represent the reactive roles to death are more open to allow death back into the public realm, whereas the men as controllers of death in modern society have difficulties negotiating changes in the modern understanding of death.

5.4. Ambiguous Return of Ordinary Death

At the same time that modernization has privatized death, the living dead films have provided more open access to the processes and phases of dying, at both the levels of undead characters and images of death. The post-classical films continued the irrational and violent tendency that had started to take shape during the transition era. Since the 1970s, the increasing cultural acceptance of violent images and the rise of body horror, which concentrates on bodily transformations and disintegration, has further emphasized the excessive imagery of death. However, whereas in the transition era these violent images were used to comment on the tensions after the Second World War and during the Cold War era, in the post-classical era, the violent images began to reflect individuals and their personal, embodied fears.

In particular, dying in old age has made degenerating bodies a significant fear. The post-classical films grasp this fear by featuring both grotesque undead monsters and spectacular bodily violence. The viewer is made graphically aware of the consequences of death – whether in the form of decaying bodies or in the vulnerability of flesh. These films rely on excessive death imagery, focusing on heightened and sensational bodily experiences. Such changes call increasing attention to the viewer's responsibility for the cinematic death experience. When the narration does not protect the viewer from death or keep it at a safe distance, they are required to have other means of encountering death. By closing in on the viewer, the films have further questioned the role of distanced modern death.

This safe distance is also questioned by many post-classical films, which often refuse to re-control death at the end of the story. For example, the revived army of mummies in *Dawn of the Mummy* is unstoppable and all-consuming in a cannibalistic manner. The apocalyptic tendency that has taken over since the late 1960s and early 1970s defies tamed death, as Russell (1995: 2, 174–76) argues, and also defies the security provided by closures. The monsters' final deaths either no longer exist or solve anything, as the alienation of death causes more problems than it solves. This highlights the move away from the classical films, where closures were delivered and the viewer's security was guaranteed. Grønstad argues that although conservative closure with death still appears as a desired destination or fulfilment of the story, it is often forbidden in post-classical (and digital) films, which prefer to create a spectacle of dying and death that never ends. These films deny death's role as a natural ending for the story: 'The texts end technically, but not structurally', Grønstad formulates (Grønstad 2003: 230–35). Instead of explaining death, these films explore and make visible death's spectacular and taboo nature. An open ending where not all of the monsters are killed places the emphasis on spectacles of death. In these films, final deaths become separate incidents; rather than conflict resolutions, they are new narrative turning points. In fact, in denying closure, such apocalyptic films also withhold resolution by death.

In addition, the post-classical films started to offer more personalized relationships with the monsters and invited the viewer to create a similar relationship with the undead, especially with vampires. The hospice and palliative care movements had directed more attention to the relationship the living had with the dead and dying. It is in this vein that *Bram Stoker's Dracula* presents the possibility of a more personalized relationship with the embodiment of death. The narration of this film does not focus solely on the vampire hunters – the vampire and his (female) victims create important narrative perspectives for the story, too. Thus, the monstrosity is shown to be constructed by the narrative solutions and perspectives, at least partially. Whereas the monsters are not necessarily evil in themselves, it could be that the violent solutions of those hunting the monsters might be as questionable as the actions of the monster.

Whereas in the classical era, scientists and authorities were the heroes of the stories, in the post-classical era their right to define how death should be managed was questioned. In these films, death starts to be encountered by regular people, who have no means of dealing with the returning dead. The films thus show how rationalized death can diminish the human capability to encounter death. Since the dying process is managed by professionals, either by medical staff or the commercial funeral industry, people have little direct experience with death. In this sense, the rationalization of death has turned against itself: as a side effect, modern society has created an irrational fear of death and dying. Quite simply, these films question the professionals' promised ability to handle death as controlled. *The Return of the Living Dead* reveals that the dead are sentient beings who continue to suffer after they have been declared dead. By now, the treatment of the dying and the dead had also started to raise public concerns. By claiming some power to define death by ordinary people, the invisibility of modern death has lost some of its power.

Chapter 6

Digitalized Living Dead

Although the post-classical and digital eras share several characteristics, some important changes have come about in the production modes, such as the transnationalization of production and film industry ownership in the 1990s, which have further emphasized Hollywood's global role. The advent of digital cinema has also affected the technology and the aesthetics. Marie-Laure Ryan (2004: 30) holds that since the invention of cinema as a mass medium in the early twentieth century, the digital revolution is the second most important change, not only because of the different modes of production and reception, but also because it enables new possibilities and effects in terms of the contents that can be produced. Horror, too, could now concentrate on special effects, which have become ever more impressive with the rise of new technologies and digital features. The benefits of digitalization in creating and developing cinematic spectacles have led to a renaissance of the genres of magical realism, including horror, fantasy and science fiction.

During the post-classical era, death events went to the other extreme compared with classical Hollywood's hidden death. An excess of dying raises the question of the meaning of death events in the narration. For example, Sobchack argues that cinematic death has become casual, technologized and ironic. No longer does death have a 'moral agenda or a critique of violence'. Instead, without blinking an eye, the action scenes produce more dead bodies within a few seconds than some of the classical films do during the whole film. This representation of wanton death also has its cultural functions, one of which, says Sobchack, could be found in the liberating potential of exaggerated death images (Sobchack 2000: 120–22). Too much on-screen dying can diminish death's capability to incite fear in the viewer and, therefore, render it commonplace.

Death events have thus been normalized in terms of film narration at the same time that the undead have gained new life in cross-generic event films. These characters include the romantic vampire of *Twilight* (2008), the action mummy's adventures in *The Mummy* (1999) and the video game zombies of *Resident Evil* (2002). Death and embodiments of death are not necessarily horrifying anymore. Violent undeath has crossed the boundaries of R-rated films. For example, both *Twilight* and *The Mummy* are marketed for younger audiences, whereas *Resident Evil* has positioned its zombies in the R-rated category.

Similarly, as death has become a normalized and excessive phenomenon of Hollywood films, and not limited to violent genres, such as horror, it could be argued that the Western twenty-first century has been obsessed with death in general. Many scholars agree that late-modern societies are facing a new era regarding both death-related practices and the cultural consciousness of death (for example, Lagerkvist 2013; Howarth 2007). In today's world, death is often a mediatized event, as political murders, terrorist attacks, accidents, natural disasters, individual tragedies and imagined deaths are part of everyday news narration and popular culture. Also, social media, including Facebook remembrances, YouTube videos and various webpages dedicated to discussions about death or remembering the dead, reveal not only a revival in the discourse of death, but also a rather obsessive relationship with it.

When discussing ordinary death, public debates continue to focus on end-of-life issues. Animated embodiments of the undead on-screen correlate with our fears about how death in old age (as a result of degenerative diseases) might come later than death of the mind. For example, zombies can be compared to Alzheimer's patients – victims of an increasingly common disease, which causes dementia and affects a person's mental capabilities. From 1987 to 1991, Alzheimer's disease was ranked as the 11th leading cause of death, whereas in 2011 it already ranked at number six (Hoyert 1996; Hoyert & Jiaquan 2012: 3–4). At the metaphorical level, then, the body can continue to live on after the person inside has died, similar to the zombies of *Resident Evil*, for example. In the film, a group of soldiers are sent to investigate what happened in a mysterious and catastrophic attack inside an underground research facility called the Hive. The group discovers that not only have the personnel died, but also they have become undead. The soldiers seek answers from the Red Queen, the master computer (with artificial intelligence), which chose to shut down the Hive. The Red Queen explains that the living dead creatures are there because of a spreading T-virus:

> Even in death, the human body still remains active. Hair and fingernails continue to grow. New cells are produced. And the brain itself holds a small electrical charge that takes months to dissipate. The T-virus provides a massive jolt, both to cellular growth and to those trace electrical impulses. Put quite simply, it reanimates the body.

In other words, death and dying can conquer the realm of the living in the everyday world of the viewer, not only through Alzheimer's, but also through the constant fear of other terminal illnesses. Zombie films, where death is connected to illnesses via the theme of infection, address these fears directly. *Resident Evil*, too, narrates surviving in the death-filled story world.

Concerns about the quality of life near death have also intensified debates on the right to die, mainly focusing on the issues of assisted suicide and euthanasia. These debates are in no way new to Western and American culture, but since the nineteenth century they have become central to modern perceptions of death, where first medicine and later jurisdiction took the power from religion to manage death and define it as public policy (Lavi 2005). Whereas medical science has prolonged life and, in some cases, even found ways to maintain life technologically, the ethical questions related to a dignified death have increased.

David Bennahum is among those who note that the public discourse on death currently concentrates on the right to life and the right to die. The debate has found its way to the Supreme Court: do we have the right to refuse medical care or the right to commit assisted suicide and euthanasia (Bennahum 2003: 7)? Regis A. DeSilva finds that death is no longer a matter solely between doctor and patient – it has become part of legal disputes, ethics committees, public advocacy groups and wide public discussion. Real-life end-of-life cases are debated in the media as well as in the Supreme Court (DeSilva 2009: 25–33). The sympathetic monsters and the animated out-of-control bodies of living dead films continue to encourage us to be open to different sides of these debates. Indeed, as Colavito (2008: 18) argues, the horror of the digital era is about the helplessness in tackling the 'breakdown of absolute truth'. No longer can science lay claim to know how to deal with death. Everyone needs to find their own ways of coping with it.

In this chapter, I will discuss how the digital films concentrate on different personalized ways to cope with death and survive in a death-filled world. First, I will discuss how in the digital mummy series death is dealt with by humour and trivialization. In these films, death becomes almost an abstraction as it is robbed of its usual horrifying role. Second, I will discuss how the recent zombie films, such as *Resident Evil*, create such an excess of death images that along with the characters' journey through the death-filled research facility, the viewer's role also takes on an element of survival. The viewer is forced to create his/her own means of taking responsibility for the images and, therefore, respond to them. Third, I will discuss how many digital vampire stories, such as *Twilight*, highlight the individualized right to form an intimate relationship with the undead and death. In all of these films, obsessive and excessive images of death respond to the continuing and self-reflective generic desire to encounter death through fantasizing possibilities.

6.1. *The Mummy* and Aesthetics of Trivial Death

Mummy films, in particular, have enjoyed a revival in the digital age. Ever since the 1940s, these films have been either highly repetitious or individual attempts to recreate the genre. Digital possibilities have given ancient Egypt and mummified bodies a new lease of life. The tombs are open once again. The digital mummy has been branded in the action-based *The Mummy* (1999) and its sequels *The Mummy Returns* (2001) and *The Mummy: The Tomb of the Dragon Emperor* (2008), and they are not the mummy's only screen revivals. Such films as *Legend of the Mummy* (1998) and *Tale of the Mummy* (1998) have also taken advantage of the new possibilities to create detailed images of dead, yet somehow preserved, bodies that manage to resist the decaying process.

The new mummy films exploit the developments in special effects and digitalization. In *Tale of the Mummy*, the monster character can transform into constantly reshaping shrouds, while in *The Mummy* series the skeleton army of mummies is able to climb walls. Almost 70 years between the classical and the digital Hollywood mummy films bring to the fore Hollywood's aesthetic and technical changes. In the 1930s, the height of know-how was represented by painstaking make-up skills, which created the mummy's preserved skin and took hours to achieve (Cowie & Johnson 2002: 64). By the end of the century, Imhotep as a decomposing skeleton with the remains of shroud and flesh and his bodily limits and facial features could be expanded on in amazing ways.

Once resuscitated, Imhotep wants to regain his former human appearance. Instead of opting for a well-preserved body, he starts with a decaying body, which he renews step by step from bits and pieces of other humans. In this sense, the digital mummy resembles decaying zombies – who consume the flesh, skin and organs of humans – and bears a resemblance to vampires, who can renew themselves with the lives of others. The regeneration of his body is followed in great detail throughout the film. *The Mummy* represents a fairly early stage of large-scale digital effects, which play with the technological possibilities of spectacle, especially when they are '*about* bringing forms to life', as is argued by Stephen Keane (2007: 59, 61). However, the digital age is not content with pure recreation alone: the recreated body is more than that of the classical mummy. The body is more flexible, able to change its form fluidly. By the end of the film, Imhotep is no longer a walking corpse, but a man who is able to transgress the limits of the normal body by, for example, opening his mouth unnaturally wide and blowing out a sandstorm that almost kills the protagonists. His transformation goes far beyond the cycle of degeneration and recreation by turning the mummy's body into a constant becoming.

The Mummy of the digital age brings colour and graphicness to the story, not only to the mummy's body, but also to the lost world of ancient Egypt, which the film brings alive on the screen. Its prologue returns to ancient times, and in the shadows of pyramids the film narrates the story of the love and death of Imhotep, the pharaoh's high priest, and Anck-su-Namun, his lover and the pharaoh's mistress. The secret lovers defy the orders and murder the pharaoh. As part of the punishment, Imhotep's priests are mummified alive, and Imhotep is cursed to an undead's fate for all eternity. The evil site stays undisturbed for 3000 years, protected by the Magi, descendants of the pharaoh's sacred bodyguards, before the revival of the mummy by the modern treasure hunters. As Simpson argues, the marketing of the film promises to make the new version bigger, better and more of a spectacle, evident in the ways in which the mummy becomes a global threat (Simpson 2004: 89–91). Indeed, the digital mummy's curse promises that he will become 'a plague upon this earth'.

The Mummy could be called, as Simpson continues, a horror event movie, attracting mainstream audiences while still playing inside the horror genre. The film has an established big-budget director and box-office actors; it concentrates on stylistic and technical effects and simple stories. By marketing the film with the reputation of an earlier story, but in relation to multi-generic practices, such an event horror film sells the movie to an audience wider than the ordinary horror devotees (Simpson 2004: 85–87). Indeed, the film is a happy crossover between genres, combining monsters familiar from horror stories, a love story, comedy elements, action scenes and adventure. Of note is the influence of the popular Indiana Jones series, which is clearly seen in the character of Rick O'Connell, an American hero who is a young and comical version of Indiana Jones. This newly found comedy identity for the mummy films represents the change in the wider public understanding of mummies. As Day (2006: 94–95, 115–17) argues, the endless repetition of predictable stories consigned mummies to humorous contexts and to juvenile and children's culture, such as the Disney film *Under Wraps* (1997) where a group of children revive a mummy, or the indie comedy *Bubba-Ho-Tep* (2002) where Elvis fights a mummy at a nursing home.

At the same time, the character of the mummy has been positioned further away from scientific debate. Similarly, as in *Dawn of the Mummy*, this film concentrates on tomb raiders and other non-professionals in terms of dealing with death. Even Evy, who is educated in ancient Egypt and represents knowledge, has aims and uses methods that are not necessarily scientific, but individual. Evy wants to find Imhotep's grave in order to establish her professional position as an Egyptologist, but instead of following traditional archaeological methods, she hooks up with Rick, a tomb raider. She is also ready to bend the rules when needed. When Rick accuses her of stealing a book, she bypasses the criticism: 'According to you and my brother it's called borrowing.' Furthermore, the Westerners ignore the local knowledge of the Magi and end up bringing devastation to the world. The film suggests that non-Westerners have a greater respect for death, whereas the Westerners who have lost this respect do not consider the possible consequences of their actions. For Westerners, death has become a trivialized issue and this relationship with death is addressed for the viewer in several ways.

Indeed, this film also aims to control death, similarly to earlier mummy films, but instead of using science and knowledge, it robs death of its power by trivializing it. Simpson (2004: 85) argues that event movies, such as *The Mummy*, establish 'an ironic distance between the product and the consumer by evoking familiar generic conventions and then mocking, subverting, or lampooning them to produce self-conscious humour obvious to all but the most naïve of viewers'. For example, just before bringing the mummy alive, Evelyn argues, 'It's just a book. No harm ever came from reading a book', which ironically refers to the classical film's opening scene.

Furthermore, in the humorous action scenes, death is not abjected through horror but through punchlines and comedy. The death of the commander inspires punchlines such as 'you just got promoted' rather than expressions of grief and loss. The added laughter and irony cancel out any potential anxiety connected to the violence caused by the living. Even the final sequence, where the mummy, his lover Anck-su-Namun and the mummy army are killed by the protagonists, uses laughter and stylized dying to ease moral questions. For example, while Eve and Rick try to find a way of making Imhotep mortal with an ancient spell, she orders him to keep the mummy busy. When Imhotep throws Rick against a pillar, it allows him to reassure Eve 'No problem'. Death also appears abstract and meaningless to the main characters. Rick argues, 'I only gamble with my life, never my money', and Evy threatens, 'You better think of something fast, because if he turns me into a mummy you're the first one I'm coming after'.

The Mummy analyses the meaning of death in terms of excess. The film includes several death events and some quite direct images of death in many of its action scenes. In the beginning, a long fight scene takes place in the desert where Egyptian Bedouins fight treasure hunters who are searching for undiscovered tombs. Before even introducing the main characters, the film presents several violent deaths and digital effects. It is not yet explained what the fight is about, and still the scene lasts for several minutes. This scene appears to justify the criticism that digital effects can be seen as a disruption to the narration, or as Keane says, that these effects are 'designed to be noticed'. They can be regarded as spectacles, or 'visual excess' without meaning and, as such, inferior to 'narrative' events. Although now considered part of the narration, such effects as the digitalized death scenes still highlight their spectacular nature (Keane 2007: 56–63). And such spectacular violence, according to Hilary Neroni (2005: 2–6) and Raphaëlle Moine (2008: 193), has both non-verbal and non-narrative qualities.

Non-narrative elements concentrate on the excess of death at the discursive level in a way that either stops or at least significantly slows down the construction of the plot. Verstraten argues that all films include excess, but in classical films excess was often momentary and rare, and the emphasis was rather on sound narrative logic. Digital films more openly embrace moments of non-narrativity, replacing psychological, temporal, spatial and causal motivation with an excess of formal cinematic aspects. In other words, attention is drawn to the style, not to the story. In a way, non-narrative moments constitute a return to the initial visual spectacle of cinema, which existed before the classical storytelling of Hollywood (Verstraten 2009: 155–68).

Although the sublime, as in the mother/daughter scene in *Night of the Living Dead*, includes excess as well, the difference to the non-narrative excess pertains to questions of morality. The sublime positioning encourages the viewer to recognize the anxiety related to the scene, whereas non-narrative moments can provide a viewing position that helps to avoid moral questioning. Thus, non-narrativity brings a different logic and viewer relationship to the living dead films, which makes excessive death commonplace and meaningless. This strategy is used in *The Mummy* when the deaths are caused by the living. These scenes take their models of death and dying from action and adventure films, rather than earlier horror films. The intention is not to cause horror or terror in the viewer. The scenes where the Egyptian Bedouins fight treasure hunters, the Magi (protectors of the mummy's tomb) fight treasure hunters, and the treasure hunters and the Magi fight Imhotep's human slaves and army of mummies, are filled with fighting, explosions, fast-moving sequences and cuts from one fight scene to another. The deaths caused by the living are clearly numerous, but they are stylized in a way that focuses the viewer's attention on fast-cutting and fast-moving images, sounds and colours instead of moral questions of the fight.

Thus, the scenes represent the protagonists as good characters who are compelled to use deadly force. The 'good' killings are excused partly as self-defence and partly as a duty to return the mummy to his grave. Also, their action-style killings do not appear as brutal as those perpetrated by the mummy. The deaths caused by the mummy follow the logic of horror films. They are carefully constructed and can be divided into two categories: deaths before and after the mummy's revival. The film opens with an ancient death scene where the viewer witnesses the murder of the pharaoh, the suicide of his reluctant lover, Princess Anck-su-Namun, a ritual of high priest Imhotep (alias the mummy) trying to bring her spirit and body back to life, and – as punishment for these crimes – the mummification of his still-living priests, and Imhotep himself being cursed and buried alive with flesh-eating bugs. The scenes are connected with an impressive soundtrack that further highlights the dramatic tone of the events.

These ancient deaths are crimes and punishments of passion, clearly intended to impress and stir the viewer. For example, both the transformative and final deaths of Anck-su-Namun are shown through the silhouettes of a body pierced with a sword. While the actual dying is hidden, the shadow of the dying body resembles the wall paintings in ancient Egyptian style. Such framing mystifies the death instead of horrifying or alienating the viewer from the scene, allowing them to empathize with Imhotep and Anck-su-Namun's passion and love. Deaths related to ancient crimes produce fantasized images of violent death. These scenes also reveal the self-conscious and self-referential nature of post-classical and digital death. As Freeland (2000: 256) puts forward, violence and death have become an exaggerated, unavoidable and maybe even self-evident part of horror narration. Deaths have always been part of the narration, and the newer films tend to borrow and comment on earlier treatments. In this opening scene, the shadows cast on the walls and the hiding of the act of death are used to give dying an 'ancient' touch, which makes it mysterious.

In contrast, deaths caused after the mummy's revival do not mystify death, but address the physical excess of dying. Deaths related to warnings, curses and punishments are filled with painful images and the terrifying effects of violent death. The mummy's return brings his curse and revenge upon those who open his tomb. Deaths, whether the result of entering the tomb, the ten plagues of Egypt or flesh-eating bugs, are brought to the living because of their curiosity and greed. However, these deaths are bypassed quickly after their warning function has become clear, and the narration focuses on the deaths of four American treasure hunters instead, who are liable for opening the mummy's casket. All four meet their end with the mummy, who consumes their bodies and leaves the corpses for the viewer to behold. The actual scenes of violent death remain hidden from view probably due to age-limit reasons, but they are either served through impossible objective shots or through consequences, which leave all the consumed corpses with terrified expressions. In addition to the physical anxiety that the scenes invite, these deaths create emotional anxiety, for the viewer is familiar with the characters (unlike in the anonymous deaths of action scenes). Furthermore, there is no added humour to level the tension. Not only are viewers forced to witness the violent deaths, but they also experience the deaths through character engagement and sensual violent images.

Although *The Mummy* partly reinforces the terrifying effects of the undead monster and the power of his curse, the approach in this film is rather adventurous and humorous, filled with amusing characters, accidents and punchlines. This is, therefore, a blockbuster rather than an explicit horror-genre film, mixing several genre traditions and creating a merry hybrid for the viewer. Also, the different types of death in *The Mummy* show that there is no single dominating approach to digital death scenes. The spectacles of death, which are non-narrative, self-conscious and self-ironic, highlight the fabricated and unrealistic nature of cinematic death events. Grønstad argues that the constructed nature of violence intervenes in the viewing and makes those watching aware of their viewing process. They do not witness violence as such, but encounter filmic or generic violence which is represented as part of the story and is intrinsic to its themes and aesthetics (Grønstad 2003: 323–24).

The digital films are openly conscious of the fabricated nature of their death events, but the viewer relationship needs to be re-evaluated as well, as the films assume a viewer with generic knowledge.

6.2. Discomforting Position of the Viewer in Zombie Apocalypses

All living dead films address their audiences both implicitly (through the fictive world) and explicitly (transgressing the boundaries of the story world), yet *Resident Evil* (2002), in particular, demands a particularly challenging type of viewer participation. It refuses to give the viewer any hiding room from death. The demands of viewer participation are built into the multimedia phenomenon, because the film is based on a Japanese video game, which belongs to the genre of survival horror. As Richard J. Hand describes, the players participate in a role game, trying to survive disastrous events in a hostile environment. In such games, role-playing participation is especially stressed. While a film cannot be as interactive as a game, the film version of *Resident Evil* still strives to emphasize the participating role of the viewer on the journey with the main character, Alice (Hand 2004: 117–27).

Similar to the first-person shooter games where a player is intrinsically linked to the character he/she is playing, the film aligns the viewer with Alice. At the beginning of the film, the viewer and Alice are put in the same situation. The story starts with her waking without any clear memories. She is clearly confused – not sure where or who she is. The viewer who also does not know what has happened, or is about to happen, understands and even shares her confusion, but at the same time starts to fear for her. The horror conventions make the viewer anticipate that something is wrong. In this introductory scene, this feeling is heightened by a pervasive atmosphere of threat. When Alice walks around the house, the conventional omens of the horror genre occur: a swarm of birds flies off, a sudden gust of wind raises leaves off the ground and seems to close in on Alice and so on. However, as it turns out, there is no monster to explain these omens yet; the monsters are still locked up within the research facility. Such (automatic) reactions, including responses to surprising sounds, movements or increasing tension, do not arise solely from direct engagement with a character, but rather from the character's environment as well (Smith 1995: 100–03). Horror's generic conventions of suspicion and mood are used here to induce a feeling and fear in the viewer that something terrible is about to happen to Alice.

Later, in the research facility, noticing one of the corpses floating in a water tank, Alice studies it. When she turns away, the viewer witnesses the corpse suddenly open her eyes and reveal her undead nature for the first time. From this moment on, the viewer knows that Alice is in danger. In this case, the viewer is invited to participate in the events together with Alice, both emotionally and physically. Together with a morally positive evaluation that is slowly being created about Alice, allegiance with her becomes more and more encouraged. Although she is capable of acting violently, Alice seems a sympathetic character and her intensions appear moral, which makes the viewer most likely able to share her cultural values and to become allied with her.

From the opening images of the film, the narration slowly increases our trust in Alice's competence to deal with a terrifying situation, whereas her vulnerability and humanity is highlighted by a sense of her being lost in Wonderland. Like the viewer, Alice is trying to make sense of emerging monsters, but as a true heroine she retains the upper hand. However, during the escape, she briefly gives in to violent revenge that is not motivated as a right or positive solution. Earlier in the film, the survivors have been betrayed by her friend and sham husband. When Alice catches up with the traitor, she does not leave him to the zombies, but violently kills him – a live person, not a zombie – as an act of personal retaliation, not as a means of survival. At this point, the viewer is forced to witness an act of murder, which shatters both the image of Alice as a morally good character and potential ally. The scene contrasts to the final death of Dracula in the classical film, where the narration distances the viewer from Van Helsing in the end, and thus protects the viewer from feeling responsible for his violent actions. In *Resident Evil*, however, the narration stays with Alice to the end, despite her increasingly violent behaviour.

This puts the viewer in an uncomfortable position. Ingebretsen argues that it is extremely important in monster narrations that defensive violence is justified by the monsters' actions and the distress they cause. The responsibility cannot be given to an individual (or the viewer), as the death of the monster 'cannot be my fault', but rather the whole community is culpable, which has only reacted to the threat as it sees fit (Ingebretsen 2001: 171–75). Similarly, most horror films thrive on the American myth of the moral necessity of violence, justifying the use of even reciprocal and vengeful violence when it can be seen as maintaining the existing (or preferred) social order and as producing peace and harmony (see also Cawelti 2004: 155–57; Giroux 2002: 231; Russell 1995: 194). In living dead films, too, the living dead are destroyed in the name of morality, survival and ontological purification. However, ethical questions linked to this myth become more important in the post-classical and digital eras. Even if the killing of a monster as a solution is interpreted positively and it is desired by both the characters and viewer, it still does not erase the ethical problems that arise from violent acts. The living, including Alice, are still responsible for their own actions, just as the viewer is responsible for their desire to wipe out the living dead, and the undead are responsible for their monstrous deeds.

In *Resident Evil*, the viewer is forced, at least momentarily, to ponder how ethical it is to kill the living dead. In the film, the true victims are the zombified workers of the underground research facility. They are victims of both the corporation they work for, and of people who oppose the corporation. The key to victimization in both cases is the film's multinational Umbrella Corporation. The corporation has the public profile of a provider of everyday commodities for Americans. However, beneath the surface, the company produces military, viral and terrorist products. In its greed for money and power, the corporation, as a cynical image of global capitalism, deceives both the consumers who unwittingly bolster immoral corporate action and goals, and its employees who appear to be unaware of the company's role in military technology, genetic experimentation and viral weaponry (see also Hand 2004: 130).

In this film, once again, zombies become victimized by a kind of zombie master – the Umbrella Corporation – an evil force behind the events. Thus, *Resident Evil* returns to the topic of slave employees explored in *White Zombie*. Critics such as Fay (2008: 86–87) and Mohammed (2006: 93) have also read the classical zombies as an allegory for modern industrial practice and an alienated workforce. The theme is highlighted in *Resident Evil*, which creates an allegory of the modern factory where the employees work for a large, faceless, transnational company without being aware of the consequences. In a word, they alienate themselves from the work and its ramifications. Their only task is to be productive for a corporation that does not want the nature of the work and working conditions to be made public. Similarly, Jean and John Comaroff argue that the modern zombie allegory can be compared to the immigrant workers of developing countries. The workers have to travel far to work in a multinational factory and produce cheaply manufactured products for Western consumption. In order to make a livelihood, these zombie-like workers have been forced to give up their traditional culture and personal relationships (Comaroff & Comaroff 2002: 780–99).

However, in this film, the workers are also victimized by the protestors who want to bring the Umbrella Corporation down for ideological reasons. The release of the toxic virus that zombifies the workers is caused by a terrorist act carried out by one of the protestors. A similar plot device is used in several other apocalyptic stories where good, but illicit, decisions turn into disaster. For example, the British production *28 Days Later* (2002) sets the events in motion with a group of animal activists releasing infected chimpanzees who then infect humans. In *Resident Evil*, one protestor, Spence, has lost hope in the system. He sees resistance as an impossible dream and deviates from the original plan by agreeing to sell the T-virus to a competing corporation. Spence is after money and argues that 'Nothing ever changes'. His deeds are partially justified by the corporation's unethical attitude, but the effects nevertheless impact on ordinary people. Indeed, while stealing the serum, the toxin is released, and as a consequence, all the employees are killed. However, with the arrival of the investigating team, it becomes clear that every living being (including genetic experiments) has turned into a living dead, now hunting for fresh meat.

After being mistreated by both their employer and the resistance movement, the zombified workers turn against humanity. They carry out the horror genre's conventional monstrous task to destroy at the physical, moral and psychological levels (see also Leffler 2000: 156). Besides preying on the living, they destroy the facility and its research results, causing huge financial losses for the corporation. They turn against both the corporation and the society that have created them. Unlike in classical zombie slave stories, this time the zombified workers successfully take advantage of their terrifying and chaotic undead state to rally against their enslavers.

In the process they reveal how the films are used to narrate the events from the perspective of the living, even in cases where the true victims of the events are the undead. When looked at from the point of view of the living dead, the morality of their transformed existence is evaluated differently. Although in *Resident Evil* this perspective is limited, some other zombie stories explore it further. For example, Romero has launched another series, re-imagining the zombification. In *Diary of the Dead* (2007) and *Survival of the Dead* (2009), the role of the living dead is humanized: these films question whether it is merciful or justified to kill the undead, or whether the killers are the true monsters. In *Diary of the Dead*, a group of students hear about zombies in the news and discuss the trustworthiness of the message. Later, they drive over three people who look like zombies, and the debate intensifies: 'they were already dead, you didn't do anything wrong' and 'we might have just killed three people back there'. With more uncanny and undead bodies, the killing gets easier, yet the similarities between the living and the undead are still recognized. 'Us against them, except they were us'. Thus, digital zombie films, in particular, have started to question the violence used against zombies, and hint that the existence of the undead might be as worthy as the existence of the living. This forces the viewer to re-evaluate his/her accustomed attitudes to otherness and conventional positioning in the stories.

Furthermore, the digital zombie apocalypses challenge the protected position of the viewer on other levels too. Also in these films, violence, action and spectacles of death create several excessive moments where the viewer is challenged to participate in the film at an embodied level. In *Resident Evil*, whose narration has borrowed pacing, effects and techniques from the gaming world, spectacles of death highlight the role of experience and immediate responses to the story – both rewards and punishments of the choices taken (for crossing the borders between the gaming industry and cinema, see Keane 2007: 11, 99–100; Lukas 2009: 221–22, 230). There are no narrative solutions to distance viewers from the violent scenes and to protect them from disturbing images. As Grønstad (2003: 161) reminds us, violence both engulfs and distances viewers, who are, therefore, left alone with their own reactions to such excessive images.

In *Resident Evil*, intensive death scenes include some that do not lead to zombification. Instead, in these scenes it is the computer, Red Queen, who kills part of the team in order to protect herself. The team members who try to shut down the master computer are trapped in the hallway outside the Queen's chamber. The deadly laser beam cuts the team into pieces, one at a time. The viewer is forced to watch the beam enter the bodies and kill the victims instantly. When the beams are turned off, the viewer is positioned to look into the victims' staring yet unseeing eyes, just seconds before their bodies fall apart. At these moments, film narration attempts to force viewers to become an integral and active part of the film, and to recognize their part in it. They are reminded that the characters do not do the dirty work by looking for the viewer (as was the case in classical films, in particular), but the viewer has their own gaze, which is the reason for the film's existence.

The last of these hallway deaths, in particular, underlines the role of death as a digitalized spectacle, making the most of the effects of an explicit showing of death. The viewer is able to see the deadly laser beams form a dense matrix that surrounds the last person standing in the hallway. When the beams pass through him, one of the other team members manages to shut down the computer. For an intensified moment, the viewer stares at the perfect figure of the soldier, before it becomes clear that the shutdown has come too late. Laser imprints become visible on the soldier's face when the body starts to disintegrate into tiny parts that fall to the ground. At this moment of death, the film concretely returns the viewer's gaze, not only through the moment's intensity, but through the stare of the dead. The intensity of the feared and private moment of death forces extreme images of the human body and drives the realization that such extremeness can only lead to a viewer's response and to an awareness of this viewing position (see also Dixon 1995: 33).

This demands 'response-ability', as Marco Abel calls it, from the viewer. He argues that excessive images have shifted the emphasis from the signification or meanings of death on the affective processes of experience. It is not important what violence does, but how the viewer reacts, or how these excessive images require responses. Consequences are replaced by reactiveness – something that exists even before the images. Violent images thus require that the viewer becomes affected and effectuated by the experiments. This also makes violent images performative, converting them into rhetorical provocations that do not necessarily require moral, cognitive, ethical or pedagogical effects, but they do need the viewer to prove that they are at least capable of being moved by these images (Abel 2007: xii–xiii, 10–14, 86, 181–89).

Although the recognition of the viewer's responsibility and 'response-ability' can appear quite abstract, one of the scenes in *Resident Evil* makes the viewer's responsibility especially explicit. At this point, the zombies have already been released from their confined spaces and they are now hunting down members of the rescue team when one of the soldiers, JD, is dragged to a lift full of zombies. His violent death scene is shown first by using the traditional alignment methods, reaction shots of his horror, subjective point-of-view shots when he realizes that none of the others can help him, and through shots of zombies closing in, biting and tearing him apart. The scene ends with a subjective shot where the last thing JD sees are the zombies' hands crowding his field of vision. With overwhelming excess, this image situates the viewer in the uncomfortable position of a man dying a horrible and painful death. Such positioning of both victim and monster forces corporeal effects, because the participatory cinematic techniques enable the viewer to participate in amoral acts through curiosity, as Shaviro argues. Also, such scenes invite the viewer to become transformed and corporeally affected by these images (Shaviro 1993: 49).

Later, the film returns to JD, and this time the image is not accompanied by screams, but by an unsentimental computer voice-over reviewing the nature of the undead. The camera slowly focuses on the bruised body until it zooms in for a close-up of JD's face. At the same time that we recognize him, JD becomes animated and the first thing he does is gaze back at us, making us realize that it was only a while ago that we witnessed his death – maybe even found pleasure in it. Now we are forced to carry the burden of responsibility for his assaultive gaze at the intimate moment of his death.

At such moments, the film provides no hiding places, and this is highlighted in the closing sequence of the film as well. Alice has managed to escape the Hive, only to be captured by the corporation, which wants to do tests on her survivor's body. The final scene starts with an extreme close-up of an eye that stares directly at the camera, startling the viewer and providing the effect of breaking the narrative space. The camera then slowly pulls back and shows Alice awake in a hospital isolation room. She frees herself from the wires attached to her body and sees a mirror on the wall. At this point, the camera becomes positioned where the mirror is, and when Alice slowly walks to the mirror, she appears to be walking straight into the lens of the camera, staring at the viewer. The viewer's impression of being watched is stressed when Alice tries to look through the lens – wanting to know who is there – and demands to be let out. It is as if the film were speaking directly to the viewer who is gazing at Alice, yet is unwilling to reveal his/her position. Obviously, Alice expects the viewer to take responsibility for what is done to her by begging to know why she has been violated (for the viewer's entertainment). In this way, the film forces viewers to confront their position and enjoyment in terms of the viewing experience.

This is precisely the point that emphasizes the importance of negotiation over death-related images. The death events of the living dead films have always aimed to create a relationship with the viewer. In the classical films, the undead gazed at the viewer and forced them to be both assaulted by this gaze and view events through it. In the transitional films, the characters gazed at death acts together with the viewer. In the post-classical era, the viewer relationship became embodied, as the bodily attacks crossed the textual limits with graphic affectivity and sensuality. With the advent of digital films, the self-conscious and self-referential practices demand not only that the viewers be gazed at or that they participate in the gazing, but also that they acknowledge their own responsibility for these acts. Throughout their history, living dead films have made gazing back visible through violent death scenes and violated corpses, pushing the viewer to take a closer look at death and negotiate over the sociocultural and personal meanings and experiences of death and dying. And while these films can provide fantasies of violent death for the viewer's desires to experience and understand something hidden from and rejected by culture, they also throw the demand for violent on-screen deaths back at the viewer, unveiling the cultural incompetence of dealing with the topic. These films dare to reveal the viewer's problematic – both curious and terrified – relationship to violent death, if not in real life, at least in what roles they play in entertainment and in the media.

6.3. Vampires and Death as Part of Personal Identity

As post-classical vampire films have shown, at the same time as an awareness of death and end-of-life issues has increased, living dead films have commented more explicitly on these debates. This tendency has continued in the digital era; for example, Bill Eagle's television movie *Dracula* (2006) materializes the changing cultural awareness of death, dying and mourning. In this film, Arthur weds Lucy – aware that he has syphilis. Hoping that a vampire might be able to cure his blood, Arthur helps to bring Dracula to England. Dracula, however, does not take kindly to being used: 'You think you can control me, you think I am a man's slave. You'll watch that I take all you loved, your country, your God, and then it is you who dies.' In this statement, Dracula as an embodiment of death highlights the countercultural force that death has in modern society. Despite all efforts, death cannot be controlled and it can be all-consuming.

However, rather than concentrating on the vampire, the film focuses on Arthur as a dying man. He represents modern death: his dying is a long and degenerative process, which affects both the body and mind of a person. Arthur's response to his impending death follows Kübler-Ross (1970) stage theory in which people adjust to the idea of death through five different stages – denial, anger, bargaining, depression and acceptance. Arthur, too, first blames God for his unjust fate and then finds that Dracula could serve as a tool for bargaining and buying more time. When this fails and his wife Lucy is killed as a consequence, Arthur is crestfallen. Only after he is asked to help to fight Dracula does Arthur pull himself together. In the final scene, Arthur sacrifices himself to save others. In other words, he is ready to face death.

Furthermore, Mina is made to represent mourning. She has to bury several of her friends and loved ones during this film, and she is also the only character to talk about mourning openly. After Lucy's funeral, Mina argues: 'We must mourn our loved ones and let them go, so that they may rest in peace.' And in the final scene, after burying her fiancé Jonathan, she argues that she does not want to mourn conventionally. Instead of visiting his grave, she plans to travel to all those places where they were supposed to travel together. The closing scene of the film also suggests that a new relationship is evolving between Mina and John. Life goes on even after death and memories remain.

Dracula concentrates on accepting death and mourning as part of life. Unlike with Arthur, death and mourning do not destroy everything. While fighting death, he cannot save himself, but ends up destroying relationships and the lives of his friends and family. In contrast, Mina becomes an exemplar of how death can be dealt with. Also, she combines the rather modern understanding of mourning as a private issue with the idea of personal variation in mourning that goes against the socially conventional grief rituals. Death has hence parted from the classical film convention of it being managed by medical professionals to become a personal issue that can be accepted as part of public life.

Other vampire films have continued to discuss the personalized relationship with death, and quite often the relationship has been created through women who no longer need a liberator; they want to control their own lives and deaths. Thus, by the beginning of the twenty-first century, the old, Victorian, past-orientated and individual vampire has been replaced, as Erik Butler (2010: 177–84) argues, by vampires who are young, look to the future and desire to be part of (youth-obsessed) society. For example, the popular television series *Buffy the Vampire Slayer* (1997–2003) emphasized women's empowerment and active sexuality, and updated the vampire lore for young (female) audiences. In this series, Buffy, a young American girl, inherits the title of vampire slayer and fights the powers of evil. The television series has been read from a feminist perspective not least because Buffy is a physically and sexually active woman who also chooses to have intimate relationships with vampires (for example, Scott 2003).

A relationship with a vampire can include liberating dimensions. In her empirical studies of *Buffy*'s female fans, Williamson has noticed that women actually find that (sympathetic) vampires offer them options for everyday lives. Not only do vampires represent excitement and adventure, but they also point to contradictions between personal desires and societal constructions. Williamson argues that the unattainable ideal image of what a modern woman should be leads female fans to empathize with the vampire's role as an outcast who never truly fits into society's moulds. According to Williamson, then, vampires offer women 'a means of handling contradictory experiences of self and femininity' and ways of imagining that '"things could be different" and so could the "self"' (Williamson 2001: 103–11).

After *Buffy*, the vampire tradition's gender tensions have continued to be rejuvenated by allowing women to have relations with vampires without punishing them with a transformative, social or final death. In television dramas, in particular, vampires have become popular lovers for independent female characters. In *True Blood* (2008–), the Japanese have managed to produce fake blood, which allows vampires to come out of their coffins and be an open part of society. Centre stage is given to the telepathically gifted waitress Sookie Stackhouse and Bill, a vampire. The two fall in love and become symbols of encountering otherness through each other. Similarly, in *Vampire Diaries* (2009–), two vampire brothers, Stefan and Damon, fall in love with Elena, a high-school student. A love triangle takes place no longer between a girl, a boy and a single monster, but rather between a girl and *two* 'monsters'. In these television series, vampires have become expressions of beauty, youth and humanity. They also depict vampires as perfect partners for humans.

Similar vampire romances take place in the cinematic *Twilight* saga as well. The films, based on the book series by Stephenie Meyer, describe high-school student Bella who moves to live with her father in the small town of Forks in Washington, where she falls in love with Edward, a vampire. Edward is part of the Cullens' 'vegetarian' vampire family, refraining from the consumption of human blood and choosing to live in disguise among the living. The film series includes five films: *Twilight* (2008); *The Twilight Saga: New Moon* (2009); *The Twilight Saga: Eclipse* (2010); *The Twilight Saga: Breaking Dawn Part 1* (2011); and *Part 2* (2012).

The series' narrative perspective focuses on Bella, revealing her personal and intimate relationship with the embodiment of death. Indeed, Bella's romantic attachment to Edward no longer mediates horror, disgust or even anxiety, but rather love. When Bella confronts Edward and demands him to admit that he is, in fact, a vampire, her accepting, trusting and loving view of the vampire addresses a romantic relationship with death. And when Edward is ashamed of his skin of a killer, Bella responds: 'It's like diamonds. You're beautiful.' Edward argues: 'It's camouflage. I'm the world's most dangerous predator.' Edward's acknowledgement of the possibility of his own monstrousness offers dual addressing. His words present the deadly threat, but Bella, too, reassures both him and the viewer with such sentences as 'I trust you' and 'I don't care'.

Because of this social acceptance, in contemporary vampire romances, sympathetic vampires do not need to remain hidden away in the darkness anymore. For example, the Cullens resist daylight and serve as members of society. Edward's father figure, Carlisle Cullen, even works as a doctor at the local hospital. Indeed, he helps the community to fight death instead of bringing it to them. In this film, embodiments of death have become an accepted and normalized part of society and they are able to create personal relationships with the living. In this case, as in many other similar vampire stories, including the television series *Vampire Diaries* and *True Blood*, the embodiments of death are no longer alienated from society, even if the relationships with them often remain ambiguous.

One crucial issue with vampires who want to fit in with society is that they refrain from killing humans. They settle for an intimate relationship without the need to cause premature deaths. Similarly, Edward and his vampire family refrain from feeding on people and, instead, hunt animals. In some other vampire stories, vampires also feed from blood banks, synthetic blood or willing donors whom they do not kill. This 'vegetarianism', according to Sally Miller (2003: 53–56), has affected vampires' self-identity, emotional experiences, physicality and sexuality, because they have started loathing their own bodies and natures. The vampires thus desire to be human instead of monsters.

Along with their identity crisis, vampires have become protective of their human communities. Edward, in particular, is overly protective of Bella. He tries constantly to stave off any possible threat (emotional, physical and social) that Bella could face. To a certain extent, this includes Edward himself, as he claims 'I can't ever lose control with you'. J.M. Tyree also argues that, in some cases, humans have become more than prey, for the vampires have grown protective of their human friends and lovers. Vampires, who used to be faux friends with misleading appeal, have turned out to be true friends in the twenty-first century. These vampires can live ordinary lives and be subjected to typical relationship issues (Tyree 2009/10: 33–38).

In their desire to belong, they are willing to follow social norms, instead of breaking them. Similarly, Edward rebels against his role as a breaker of social norms. As Williamson argues, such predatory vampires as the classical Dracula used to rebel against reason. Sympathetic vampires have continued this rebellious trait, but they rebel against what they are (monsters) and defy the rules of the vampire genre (Williamson 2003: 102). In a similar way, Edward exemplifies death's desire to be part of society, not by force, but by ritualized belonging, and Bella continues to symbolize the need for a closer and individual relationship with death.

However, Bella comes to symbolize more than an intimate relationship with death. She also wants to make an active decision to die herself. After falling in love with a vampire, she spends a lot of time and energy convincing others to believe that she desires to become a vampire herself. This open and even loving relationship with death is highlighted by the way that Bella, at the end of *The Twilight Saga: Eclipse*, justifies her decision to become a vampire:

I've always felt out of step, like literally stumbling through my life. I've never felt normal. Because I'm not normal. I don't want to be. I've had to face death and loss and pain in your world, but I've also never felt stronger and more real, more myself because it's my world too. It's where I belong.

Her desire to choose her own death reflects the topical ethical questions related to death and dying – mainly those of right-to-die debates. Although these debates in the United States have been around since the nineteenth century, it has been certain legal cases – including a prison sentence given to Dr Jack Kevorkian who had assisted in voluntary euthanasia in 1999, and a legal struggle (1990–2005) to stop giving life support to Terri Schiavo – that have invoked wider public discussion. In these debates, the states' duty to respect all life is contrasted with the rights of individuals to make death a personal matter, not a state-led or public one (Ferguson 2007; Lavi 2005).

Post-classical and digital living dead films have highlighted the right of the individual to deal with their own death; for example, in *Twilight*, Bella chooses to encounter death on her own terms, instead of waiting for a 'natural' death. She is afraid of the degenerative process of natural death. She is afraid of growing old and idealizes the forever-frozen state of vampires. Throughout the first four films, Bella begs Edward to change her into a vampire, which leads the films to concentrate on her personal views of transformation. At the end of *Twilight* (2008), Bella argues: 'I'm dying already. Every second I get closer, older.' From this moment on, she starts to undergo her own social death in preparing herself for her impending departure from life.

Both before and after her transformation, Bella spends a lot of time planning how she will be remembered. She makes sure that the people she will be forced to leave behind have good memories of her. The death-awareness movement has highlighted the importance of leaving behind the desired memories, and with the advent of social media and the Internet, new possibilities have opened up to achieve this. Various online services have allowed people to plan their afterlives. They can leave messages for the people they know, plan their own funerals and leave notes of their plans on Internet archives, and they can even continue to live on in the digital domain via online memorial sites. These practices further expand the existential limits between life and death, as Amanda Lagerkvist (2013) argues. Similarly, Bella not only plans her own transformative death, but her social death (or life) as well.

However, as with public debates, Bella's decision is challenged. Edward and her male friend Jacob try to talk her out of becoming a vampire. They cannot come to terms with her active decision, and instead they delay and prevent her from executing this act. Thus, although the series highlights Bella's active role, the story has been accused of eroding feminist goals with its underlying patriarchal values where men, especially Edward, control Bella's actions, and where independent women still do not pose a threat to a dominant male worldview (see, for example, Merskin 2011: 159–75; Mercer 2011; Kokkola 2011: 178–79; Scott 2003: 125, 128). Like other female characters in living dead films before her, even Bella is made to represent a reactive role to death, and powerful male characters can still determine the public outcomes of her desires.

Finally, by the end of *The Twilight Saga: Breaking Dawn Part 1* (2011), she begins her physical transformation process into a vampire. She is dying in childbirth, and only her transformation into a vampire can save her from premature death. The moment when Bella is at risk of dying in childbirth is one of the few depictions of 'natural', yet not realistic, death scenes in living dead films. When she goes into labour, her spine cracks and Edward has to perform a C-section on the conscious Bella without any pain medication. This causes her death. The scene is one of the most violent in the whole series and portrays natural death as a monstrous event. A living death, then, no matter how violating, is the only option left to save Bella.

Edward poisons her body with vampire venom, and the camera's gaze follows as it floods her body and cells. The film's digital effects make it possible to portray the dying process from this internal perspective with the use of realistic images. The viewer is invited to witness the venom flooding Bella's organs and to see into her mind as she screams in agony while her body lies still. The film ends with a scene where Carlisle tries to convince Edward that Bella will make it through the transformation: her hair is regaining colour, her skin is turning white and the cells are rejuvenating. At the same time, the viewer is given access to Bella's mind again. She sees flashbacks of her former life before her heart stops beating. The transformation is complete, her previous life is over and she is ready to be born into the world of the undead. The final image of transformation leaves the viewer with Bella opening her blood-red eyes and gazing back at the viewer who has just shared intimately her experience of death, mimicking several scenes in *Resident Evil*.

In the *Twilight* series, the transformation focuses on the dying person's personal experiences, highlighting her individual right to make decisions concerning her life and death, even when this decision is denied by a society still bound by conventional notions of managing death in terms of technological and medical practices. This film series, then, continues to battle and challenge the limitations of modern death practices – a gradual process that has gained more and more ground thanks to living dead films since (and during) the classical era. These films tend to argue that our relationship with death should be a kind of negotiation process where personalized and emotionalized meanings take precedence over the conventionalized rituals of the modern world.

6.4. Obsessive Interest in Death

Similarly, as the early twenty-first century has seen an increasing cultural interest in, or even obsession with, death and dying, the digitalized living dead films bring death closer to the viewer than earlier films. In these films, the viewer is no longer protected from death or dying, but he/she is either forced or allowed to create a personal, embodied and emotional relationship with them. The digital films appear to have two different, and even contradictory, means to achieve this goal of bringing death closer to the viewer. On the one hand, the viewer's role is exposed through physically and morally uncomfortable positioning when violent deaths and grotesque embodiments of death are exposed on-screen. On the other hand, the viewer is invited to experience death from the perspective of either the undead or their (willing) victims. These relationships are often loving, warm and sympathetic, and thus address a personalized emotional reaction to death.

Furthermore, by this point, vampire, mummy and zombie stories are so used to borrowing features from each other that the chosen way of addressing is not related to any certain monster, but rather the narrative goals of the films. For example, although vampires have taken the domestication of monsters furthest, zombies and the mummies have also been made more human. Not even zombies have been immune to opening up the viewer's access to the monster's viewpoint, as Romero's *Land of the Dead* (2005) shows. In the film, zombies communicate with their expressions, which mimic sadness, helplessness, rage and the need for revenge. Furthermore, the ending stresses the new perspective, for in the final encounter the main character chooses not to kill the zombie leader and says: 'They are just looking for a place to go. Same as us.' Here, the possibility of coexistence arises, when both a human being and a zombie refuse to use violence against each other. Furthermore, in a British independent film, *Colin* (2009), the whole story is narrated from the perspective of the zombified character Colin. Such a change of narrative perspective, where stories become narrated from the inside, through the eyes of both monsters and victims, shows how death-related emotions and expressions are slowly becoming more accepted and integrated into public discourse.

However, some critics have seen this type of domestication of monsters to be the end of their horror careers and as a destruction of their 'original' myth (see, for example, Michel 2007: 392). Related to this debate, Lisa Bode has written on the duality of film reviews on *Twilight: The Movie*. The negative responses consider the film unfavourably because it was made for teenage girls and because it ruins vampire horror with romance. In such a way, these reviewers positioned themselves as culturally superior and rational agents against the affective and uncritical girls. The positive reviews discussed the film as a romance and highlighted the affectivity and 'emotional truth' of teenage desires (Bode 2010: 709–17). Thus, the evaluation of this change is a question of chosen perspective. I agree with Williamson (2003: 101–02) who argues that instead of seeing domestication or feminization as a negative process, the connection with the everyday and mundane should be regarded as further widening complex engagements with monsters.

At the same time as the undead have revealed their potential for good and heroism, elsewhere in the living dead films the living have become more violent and their relationship with death more trivial. The changing perceptions of good and evil, or normal and monstrous, show how important the actions of the characters are, rather than generic conventions, in evaluating their morality. Although the living dead are the ones who threaten the living, they are not the only ones to use violence. The living, too, try to kill these monsters, and such encounters challenge further the limits between humans and monsters, because both motivate violence for their own purposes. Thus, the nature of violence is not more or less moral depending on who is acting (the undead or living). Rather, violence has an ambivalent nature, because by using it, humans may out-monster the monster. Defensive violence contains elements of both the destruction and preservation of humanity (see also Waller 1986: 340, 342, 349; Curran 2003: 51; Punter & Byron 2004: 266; Becker 2006: 49).

In the past, apocalypse and paranoia have been particularly central to zombie films; however, in the digital era, these themes have surfaced with all living dead characters. The digital mummy aims for world domination, and a number of vampire films have made their contributions to the apocalyptic world vision. For example, in *Stake Land* (2010) and *Priest* (2011), the similarities between the zombie and vampire apocalypses are stronger than between aggressive and sympathetic vampires. Indeed, the vampires of the digital era have split more clearly than ever into two distinct categories of evil and sympathetic monsters. The evil vampires continue to discuss themes of decadence and violent death, also represented by their physical appearance. In *Priest*, vampires are animal bodies that grow in pupae in hives. This contrasts to the sympathetic vampires whose bodies are less transformed, even realistic. Also, in such films as *From Dusk till Dawn* (1996), *Vampires* (1998) and *30 Days of Night* (2007), the digital aesthetics create grotesque, animal or even rotting vampire bodies. The function of such physicality is to deny the process where the vampires have become more human (see, for example, Zanger 1997: 22–27; Schneider 2003: 176).

The increasing tendency for apocalyptic narratives, especially in zombie stories, is the focus on survival. This has been linked to the aftermath of the 9/11 terrorist attacks. The fractures in societal infrastructure and increasing feelings of paranoia have made survival themes popular for the contemporary viewer, who is likely to find the onset of an apocalyptic scenario (caused by either terrorism, wars, infections or natural disasters) to be a very real possibility (see, for example, Bishop 2009: 17–24; Bishop 2010: 26). Indeed, *Resident Evil* has been followed by such films as *I Am Legend* (2007), *Zombieland* (2009), *The Crazies* (2010) and *World War Z* (2013), which imagine the lives of survivor groups in a post-apocalyptic world. In these stories, the survivors can only trust themselves to make the right choices. There are no more communal solutions or rules, such as modern death practices, that would create shared or public models of how to act in a certain situation. The creation of new rules in a new situation has become one of the most persuasive elements of zombie fiction. For example, the television series *Walking Dead* (2010–) is based on this constant social negotiation of the survivors, while the zombies' role is to create a threatening death-filled world.

In these narratives, deaths no longer have strong causal reasons. It is more important that they exist as spectacles for eager genre audiences. For example, *Resident Evil* employs apocalyptic visions for exploiting an increasing number of violent deaths and the destructive power of the undead instead of providing any direct social commentary. In comparison, the high frequency of digitalized deaths in *The Mummy* is laced with irony and humour, which trivialize death. By highlighting non-narrative moments with detailed images of dying processes and death events, the digital films demand viewers to become conscious of their own positioning and responsibility. It is up to the viewer to give some meaning to death, if the films refuse to provide it.

In many ways, death has been brought closer to humanity and normality. The monster's viewpoint has become more accessible, and the role of monster has been increasingly occupied by the living. The change does not end there; the viewer, too, has been dragged into the fray. Both the extreme violence and the emphasized human responsibility attempt to force viewers to look at their own viewing positions, understanding and uses of violent death. And while death has been brought closer to the viewer's immediate experience at the discursive level, the triumph of modern death has become somewhat more problematic at the level of the story. Changes in the films' social allegories, in fact, represent one important development. Namely, the protective role of the community and of the traditional social models has diminished throughout, and the characters are now more dependent on their own identities, decisions and actions. Indeed, symbolically, personal survival techniques have become more significant in living dead films. In *Resident Evil*, survival is achieved through violence, in *The Mummy* through humour and in *Twilight* through the loving gaze. In this way, death can be either a horrifying, personal, empowering or liberating experience, depending on the perspective.

Along with a demand for solutions to personal death-related issues, death has returned to the public arena, but it has taken a different tack. Staudt and McIlwain, for example, argue that this renewed awareness and desire to discuss death takes place in the imagined communities of the media, and even more concretely in the virtual communities of the web. It is not only public debates on death-related issues and images of death and dying that have filled the Internet, but also virtual memorial spaces and videos have given death a communal role (Staudt 2009: 3–4, 15; McIlwain 2005: 241–42). These imagined communities have obviously played a role in earlier decades, too, but the opportunity to connect with other Internet users has made these imagined communities more real. This has also led to new types of living dead films and series where the fans, amateurs and professionals create Internet series based on their favourite characters. Such zombie series as *Bite Me* (2010), *Universal Dead* (2010) and *Zombiewood Pines* (2010) go on to discuss survival themes, whereas the vampire series of *Dead & Lonely* (2009), *Blood Light* (2010) and *Vampirism Bites* (2009–12) depict vampires as part of a (tragicomic) mundane world. They engage in the same discussions as the Hollywood films before them, but they do it through a global online network, and through their own social networks and fan communities, opening up the debates on death more and more as a social and public discourse, thus diminishing the controlling influence of authorities to dominate such discussions.

Chapter 7

Transforming Traditions of Rhetoric of Death

Death remains a mysterious event and experience. The vampire of *The Return of Dracula* (1958) sums up our awe of it: 'You only fear the unknown. Only this casing, this clumsy flesh stands between you and me. You are already balanced between two worlds. Eternity awaits you now.' This dual relationship to death – of endlessly defying control and intensifying the desire to master it – is what living dead films are made of. Their explicit encounters with death evolve to both re-mystify and demystify it. Death, well and truly, entices the imagination. These films are one way of trying to imagine and embody the unknown.

I opened this study by introducing the notion of modern death, referring to the mechanisms that American society has used to distance death from the practices of everyday life. While this marginalization was never total, death was transferred to the media and fiction, which have offered public arenas for encountering, imagining and fantasizing about death. Thus, this modern concept of alienating death has been constantly contradicted by the mediatized, and more or less obsessive, relationship with death. As my analysis of the different living dead films from different eras has shown, the fantasized relationship with death is neither simple nor stable. The films have both reproduced the ideological practices of modern death and challenged the possibilities to live up to these ideals, pondering the consequences of such alienation. In this way, the cultural tension between masking and unveiling death has been constantly present in living dead films. By way of conclusion, I want to return to assess how these films and their transgressive potential have both responded to this change and even anticipated and demanded the revival or spectacle of death.

The fantasizing possibilities offered by these films' multilayered narrative structures resonate with the theoretical views which demand that both the actual viewing process and the textual addressing of the viewer be understood in terms of changing and conflicting positions. The characters (monsters, victims, heroes), events and symbolical dimensions open up different perspectives to the stories, to death and the uses of death in cultural discussions. The narrative practices are at times mutually supportive, but occasionally they conflict, hide and reveal different things for different positions, creating a textual multiplicity. Similarly, it is possible for the viewer to be both fascinated by and afraid of death, to be enchanted by sublime images and despise looking, even at the same time. The different addressed positions contribute to the viewer's active role in the viewing process. They are both given the opportunity and required to take some responsibility for the meaning-making and experiences. Also, when addressing is understood as ways in which the film invites and anticipates the viewer to participate in the film affectively and semiotically, it becomes clear that the complexity of the viewing process is further emphasized by the use of a culturally controversial theme – death – as the unifying idea, repository of imagery and source of fascination.

Similarly, as cinematic deaths cannot be isolated and separated from their narrative and generic contexts, living dead films are neither produced nor consumed in a vacuum, but rather in a close relationship to the film industry, genre conventions and the sociocultural background. Changes in the communicative elements and decoding practices of the viewer thus create reciprocal negotiation over the rhetoric of death. The viewing process of the living dead films concentrates on the images and themes of death, which respond to and negotiate with the impossibility of escaping death: there is a cultural need to encounter it. The importance of death is visibly embodied in the undead monster on whom the cause/effect chains, emotional and physical reactions and symbolic references seem to centre. Through their cinematic images, the films successfully give some form and meaning to death. Also, when death is treated at the symbolic and rhetoric level that carries cultural and social significance, deaths and the threat of death reveal a set of values, attitudes and institutional structures.

In terms of the genre's historical development, the basic characters and structures have maintained their position in the continuing struggle between differentiation and standardization of film narration. In fact, the centrality of both the undead monsters and the death events has been highlighted over the years. Some of the most important changes are the viewer's more open access to the monster's perspective and the increasingly spectacular visualization of death scenes and dying processes. Most notably, deaths have become more graphic, violent and extreme. This underlines the constructed nature of death in these films, which tend not to create any sense of cinematic realism around the issue. The deaths have become more fantastic, deconstructed at the level of image, and more physically challenging.

As the continuing use of narration of death shows, or in other words, the transformative, social and final deaths of the undead, death in itself has been dramatic and meaningful since the classical films. However, in the classical depictions, cinematic death used to be something that the image did not concentrate on. Instead, the different deaths were most often narrated through consequences of cause–effect chains. Since the classical films, the viewer has been invited to witness more and more detailed images of violent death, as the framing of death events has changed from off-screen to on-screen, from bypassed to prolonged images, from empty shots to all-revealing shots, and from reactive shots of other characters to their subjective shots when the viewer is allowed to experience the event with and through the characters. In this process, the protective and distancing techniques have become a matter of choice rather than of cultural necessity. This further highlights the films' increasing tendency to place responsibility for the violent images on the viewer, instead of protecting the viewer from these images.

The increasing responsibility put on the viewer is also a question of affectivity. The loaded images both address and demand embodied experiences from the viewer. McIlwain, for example, argues that the increasing images of death in the media are not only about a social critique of alienated death, but also about an invasion of emotions. Death and dying, as well as suffering and mourning, have become acceptable (McIlwain 2005: 68). Similarly, the increased and detailed death images have made the viewer participate in death and dying, which has heightened the function of experiences and embodiments. The framing of death has moved from mediating death to the viewer through alternative and diverse techniques to a position where the viewer is made to encounter embodied images of dying. This process, indeed, embodies the claim that the media has helped death to re-enter the public domain through images and experiences.

Whereas the viewer's opportunities to experience death have been widened by the varied viewing positions, the change in offered character relationships has narrowed the gap between monstrosity and normality, between death and life. In the classical era, the encounters with otherness were mostly about fear of the unknown, where learning about the undead was used as knowledge to destroy them. By the digital era, insight into otherness has been about widening perspectives of humanity itself. Leffler (2000: 163) holds that when a monster is encountered, the limits between human and monster are always reconsidered, and when the main characters meet the monster, the line between them is questioned. In other words, when characters end up producing more and more death, the line between caused death and consuming death becomes blurred, making the alienation of death artificial. Where a monster is depicted as tragic or sympathetic, we can clearly see the questionable nature of the use of violence, regardless of the perpetrator. Angela Curran (2003: 50–51) argues that films with tragic monsters can sometimes be more horrifying to the viewer than films with unsympathetic monsters, because the tragedy unfolds when the monster and other characters cannot understand one another.

Indeed, when the viewer is attached to the story through its characters, the living dead films create experiences that challenge the viewer's understandings of life and death. The films offer different positions for the viewer to experience encounters with (violent) death. Classical stories offered the viewer rather transparent, but still multiple, positions to study and understand death in a manner similar to modern science. In the end, death was neatly put back into its socially accepted place by the authorities. Although the undead monsters of the classical films stirred up this negotiation between the demand for recognition of and alienating tendencies towards death, the solutions of these films recreated the conventional idea of modern death as an ideal sociocultural attitude and response towards it. This observing position has since become questioned, not least because of the viewer's expected participative role. First, the transforming embodiments of death have turned more material and grotesque, pushing the viewer to embody death in more reflexive and intimate ways. Second, the more openly complex alignment processes have given the viewer a more open view into the monstrosity and death as well. And last, when the moral basis of character allegiance became challenged, the viewer had no more places to hide. Through character engagement and by the time of the post-classical films at the latest, the viewer was made to take part in the struggle between enforcing and alienating tendencies of death-related practices. From these varied positions, which highlight the importance of experiences, the marginalization of death appears violent and artificial. In response, death has been given more of a voice and more space.

The monster's voice has been made louder and more self-expressive throughout the history of the living dead films; however, it should be noted that allowing their voices to be heard has always been a possible narrative solution. Just as the classical films were able to access the monster's perspective and voice, the later films can also choose to exclude the monster's vantage point. For example, the digital mummy is not as sensitive as the classical monster. The opening of *The Mummy* (1999) highlights the mummy's perspective and his romantic side, but after being brought back from the grave, his monstrosity and undeadness steal the show. Only at the end does the mummy show his softer side when he mourns for his lost lover. So, while the mummy films increasingly cast the undead in major alignment positions, they also highlight the subtle changes within this general movement, making clear that the post-classical and digital films can also choose to alienate monstrousness.

In the post-classical and digital films, where otherness is intentionally alienated, the monster's affectiveness is often sought from the depiction of their monstrous bodies. In the classical films, the zombies, for example, resemble the human body and form, yet they can be recognized by their clumsiness, expressionless posture and empty, staring eyes. In the transition era, Romero's zombie characters, in particular, took more liberties in their deadly postures. The zombies, in fact, came closer to violated corpses: they were expressionless and clumsy; their bodies bloody and missing organs. This tendency for emphasized grotesqueness comes to a climax in the digital horror films. In *Resident Evil*, colour adds sensationalism to Romero's black-and-white version. The blood and the mutilated organs of the visceral, half-eaten and genetically mutated bodies created by digital effects made the corpses more violated and more imaginative than the viewer could ever experience in everyday life.

The changes in the transforming bodies throughout the history of the living dead films betray the artificiality of these character constructions. These are no realistic dead bodies, but rather imaginative versions of reanimated and transformed corpses – either through excessive grotesqueness or excessive beauty. Pushing the limits of the bodily form on-screen has increased with new advances in film technology. Smith also argues that character recognition has always been constructed and changes necessarily with new cinematic techniques and conventions. Before the sound era and the possibilities of mediating emotions and embodiments through dialogue, silent films relied on overflowing posturing. In contrast, the classical films used rather discreet structures, such as facial expressions or close-ups, including expressionless or suggestive stares of the classical undead. Conventions changed again during and after the transitional era, making continuance and bodily expressions reflexive and stressing the artificiality of characters. This new reflexivity challenges the characters' features and the recognition process, frustrating, amusing and confusing the viewer (Smith 1995: 138, 151).

A similar historical pattern, as suggested by Smith, is recognizable in living dead films where the classical undead created a discreet relationship to corpses and the post-classical and digital on-screen bodily form intentionally exceeded the limits of the human body. At first glance, it would appear that this increasingly constructed embodiment of death seeks to either increase the viewer's distance from the monster or dismiss questions of the shifting borders between humanity and monstrosity. However, whereas domesticated vampires blur these boundaries by being human, the increasingly corporeal undead bring the viewer closer to monstrosity by creating visceral embodiments of death as part of the cinematic experience. This liminality, the closeness to humanness, the becoming bodies of the undead, and the affective and sensual film/viewer relationship all challenge the notions and limits of life and death. The very recognition of the living dead characters as embodiments of death and their transforming bodies confront the idea and definition of modern, alienated and controlled death. They make the central theme of death more concrete in the living dead films. Furthermore, by inviting the viewer to participate in experiencing death, the undead monsters bring the encounter and experience of death into the public sphere.

Also, the allegorical power of the undead has addressed the borders of modern death, by both idealizing and challenging it. First, by bringing impure mummies to life and then taming them, all mummy films deal with the Western desire and ability to control death. The classical *The Mummy* laid out the basic structure in abjecting the mummy and contrasting ancient death rituals with modern Western practices. The transition era film *Curse of the Faceless Man* celebrated the modern practices and the power of science. The post-classical *Dawn of the Mummy* presented the negative consequences of both the professionalization and commercialization of death. The digital *The Mummy* extends this trajectory further by highlighting the trivialization of death. All the ritualized encounters with the mummy are related to the notion of modern death, but they address the idea differently. The distancing, professionalism and scientific approach to death are first idealized, then looked at from the perspective of individuals who are incapable of understanding death and need to find their own means to come to terms with it.

The vampire films have emphasized the limits of a desirable and individualized relationship with death. In *Dracula, The Return of Dracula, Bram Stoker's Dracula* and *Twilight*, sexual desire and death are linked through punishment and liberation. The films also discuss changing ideas about women's sexuality: in the classical films, women need to be protected and placed under patriarchal control; in the transition films, a woman could be given a more active role although her (teenage) sexuality still remained problematic; and the post-classical era has, to a certain extent, turned the original positioning of female sexuality on its head. Sexuality, even if experienced through death, is rewarding for women. In the digital era, desire and sexuality are not punishable. Indeed, if one is willing to embrace it, desire can be empowering. This change in depicting gender and sexuality through death as punishment or as liberation also creates an evolving image of death. At the implicit level, the change suggests that death can be related to expressing one's identity.

In addition, zombie films have discussed death's destructive social force. While *White Zombie* presents zombies as oppressed slave workers, *Night of the Living Dead* features zombies who start a revolution. Furthermore, *The Return of the Living Dead* represents zombies as being conscious of their neglect and the zombies of *Resident Evil* appear to bring these traits of enslaved workers and revolutionary resistance together. In a way, zombies have accepted the revolutionary potential of their monstrous character. At the implicit level, these films can also be seen to be debating the public role of death. The classical films idealize the marginalization of death, whereas the later apocalyptic films acknowledge that violent death cannot be alienated, or otherwise everyone needs to find their own means of survival when encountering death.

It would seem that the exclusion of death from society becomes less of a critical question, as death could coexist and reappear in public contexts. This serves to communicate that death is, indeed, part of the human experience, not something exterior to it. In sum, the narration of living dead films has changed from marginalizing and rationalizing death to a refusal of distancing death and to highlighting its effects. At the same time, the strategies of addressing the viewer at the level of personal experience have gained momentum. Post-classical and digital films deny viewers the secure and detached position of classical and most transition films, pushing them towards participating in on-screen death events physically, emotionally and cognitively. The change in narration correlates with the change in the social role of death. At the start of the twentieth century, the modern and scientific understanding and explanations of death prevailed, but before the end of the century, death had been revived by the individual experiences of the dying and the bereaved without limiting the explanatory functions of scientific or professional voices.

Throughout the decades, living dead films have challenged the boundaries and frontiers of modern death, making evident the constant and pressing human need to encounter, negotiate with and give meaning to death. By creating a modality of death in which death is given form, narrative structure and genre-specific themes, living dead films have participated in death-related social processes, and as a participant in public debates. By questioning the ideals of modern death and pushing the boundaries of its narrative, visual and affective dimensions, living dead films have used socially shared experiences to make death a visceral part of modern existence. Death never entirely left the public consciousness, but it has gladly reasserted its place.

Filmography

Bibliography

Abel, Marco (2007), *Violent Affect: Literature, Cinema, and Critique after Representation*, Lincoln and London: University of Nebraska Press.

Aizenberg, Edna (1999), '"I Walked with a Zombie": The Pleasures and Perils of Postcolonial Hybridity', *World Literature Today*, pp. 461–66.

Altman, Rick (1987), *The American Film Musical*, Bloomington and Indianapolis: Indiana University Press.

Altman, Rick (1995), 'A Semantic/Syntactic Approach to Film Genre', in Barry Keith Grant (ed.), *Film Genre Reader II*, Austin: University of Texas Press, pp. 26–40. (Orig. in *Cinema Journal* 1984, 23: 3).

Altman, Rick (1999), *Film/Genre*, London: British Film Institute.

Ariés, Philippe (1977), *Western Attitudes toward Death: From the Middle Ages to the Present*, transl. Patricia M. Ranum, Baltimore and London: The Johns Hopkins University Press. (Orig. 1974).

Aristotle (1997), *Aristotle's Poetics*, transl. and commented by George Whalley and John Baxter, Montreal, Buffalo: McGill–Queen's University Press. (Orig. c. 335–22 BC).

Auerbach, Nina (1995), *Our Vampires, Ourselves*, Chicago and London: The University of Chicago Press.

Aufderheide, Arthur C. (2003), *The Scientific Study of Mummies*, Cambridge: Cambridge University Press.

Badley, Linda (2010), 'Bringing It All Back Home: Horror Cinema and Video Culture', in Ian Conrich (ed.), *Horror Zone: The Cultural Experience of Contemporary Horror Cinema*, London and New York: I.B. Tauris, pp. 45–63.

Badley, Lisa (1995), *Film, Horror and the Body Fantastic*, Westport, Connecticut and London: Greenwood Press.

Bal, Mieke (1999), *Narratology: Introduction to the Theory of Narrative*, 2nd edn, Toronto, Buffalo and London: University of Toronto Press.

Balio, Tino (1995), *Grand Design: Hollywood as a Modern Business Enterprise, 1930–1939. History of the American Cinema, Volume 5*, Berkeley and Los Angeles: University of California Press.

Barber, Paul (1988), *Vampires, Burial, Death*, New Haven and London: Yale University Press.

Bauman, Zygmunt (1992), *Mortality, Immortality and other Life Strategies*, Cambridge: Polity Press.

Bazin, André (2005), 'The Ontology of the Photographic Image' (orig. *Problèmes de la peinture,* 1945), in *What Is Cinema?,* Hugh Gray (transl.), Berkeley and London: University of California Press, pp. 9–16.

Becker, Matt (2006), 'A Point of Little Hope: Hippie Horror Films and the Politics of Ambivalence', *The Velvet Light Trap,* 57, pp. 42–59.

Behuniak, Susan M. (2011), 'The Living Dead? The Construction of People with Alzheimer's Disease as Zombies', *Ageing and Society,* 31: 1, pp. 70–92.

Bell, Michael E. (2013), 'American Vampires and the Ongoing Ambiguity of Death', *Kritikos,* 10. http://intertheory.org/bell.htm (28 March 2013).

Bennahum, David A. (2003), 'The Historical Development of Hospice and Palliative Care', in Walter B. Forman, Judith A. Kitzes, Robert P. Anderson and Denice Kopchak Sheehan (eds), *Hospice and Palliative Care, Concepts and Practice,* Sudbury: Jones and Bartlett Publishers, pp. 1–12.

Benshoff, Harry M. and Griffin, Jean (2006), *Queer Images: A History of Gay and Lesbian Film in America,* Lanham: Rowman & Littlefield Publishers Inc.

Berenstein, Rhonda J. (1995), 'Spectatorship-as-Drag: The Act of Viewing and Classic Horror Cinema', in Linda Williams (ed.), *Viewing Positions: Ways of Seeing Film,* New Brunswick and New Jersey: Rutgers University Press, pp. 231–69.

Bishop, Kyle (2006), 'Raising the Dead', *Journal of Popular Film & Television,* 33: 4, pp. 196–205.

Bishop, Kyle (2008), 'The Sub-Subaltern Monster: Imperialist Hegemony and the Cinematic Voodoo Zombie', *The Journal of American Culture,* 31: 2, pp. 141–52.

Bishop, Kyle (2009), 'Dead Man Still Walking: Explaining the Zombie Renaissance', *Journal of Popular Film & Television,* 37: 1, pp. 16–25.

Bishop, Kyle William (2010), *American Zombie Gothic: The Rise and Fall (and Rise) of the Walking Dead in Popular Culture,* Jefferson: McFarland & Company Inc.

Bode, Lisa (2010), 'Transitional Tastes: Teen Girls and Genre in the Critical Reception of *Twilight*', *Continuum, Journal of Media & Cultural Studies,* 24: 5, pp. 707–19.

Booth, Wayne C. (2004), *The Rhetoric of Rhetoric: The Quest for Effective Communication,* Malden, Oxford and Victoria: Blackwell Publishing.

Bordwell, David (1985), *Narration in the Fiction Film,* London: Methuen & Co. Ltd.

Bordwell, David (2006), *The Way Hollywood Tells It: Story and Style in Modern Movies,* Berkeley and London: University of California Press.

Bordwell, David, Staiger, Janet and Thompson, Kristin (1996), *The Classical Hollywood Cinema: Film Style & Mode of Production to 1960,* updated edn, London: Routledge.

Bourget, Jean-Loup (1995), 'Social Implications in the Hollywood Genres', in Barry Keith Grant (ed.), *Film Genre Reader II,* Austin: University of Texas Press, pp. 50–58. (Orig. in *Journal of Modern Literature* 1973, 3: 2).

Browning, John Edward and Picart, Caroline Joan (Kay) (2009), 'Introduction: Documenting Dracula and Global Identities in Film, Literature, and Anime', in John Edgar Browning and Caroline Joan (Kay) Picart (eds), *Draculas, Vampires, and Other Undead Forms: Essays on Gender, Race, and Culture,* Lanham, Toronto, New York and Plymouth: The Scarecrow Press, Inc., pp. ix–xxii.

Buckland, Warren (1998), 'A Close Encounter with *Raiders of the Lost Ark*: Notes On Narrative Aspects of the New Hollywood Blockbuster', in Steve Neale and Murray Smith (eds), *Contemporary Hollywood Cinema*, London and New York: Routledge, 166–77.

Burke, Edmund (1990), *A Philosophical Enquiry into the Origin of our Ideas of the Sublime and Beautiful*, Adam Phillips (ed.), Oxford and New York: Oxford University Press (orig. 1757).

Butler, Erik (2010), *Metamorphoses of the Vampire in Literature and Film: Cultural Transformations in Europe, 1732–1933*, Rochester, New York: Camden House.

Card, Claudia (2003), 'Genocide and Social Death', *Hypatia*, 18: 1, pp. 63–79.

Carroll, Noël (1990), *The Philosophy of Horror*, New York and London: Routledge.

Casetti, Franco (1998), *Inside the Gaze: The Fiction Film and Its Spectator* (*Dentro lo sguardo: il film e il suo spettatore*, 1996), Nell Andrew and Charles O'Brien (transl.), Bloomington and Indianapolis: Indiana University Press.

Cawelti, John (1976), *Adventure, Mystery and Romance: Formulaic Stories as Art and Popular Culture*, Chicago: Chicago University Press.

Cawelti, John (2004), *Mystery, Violence and Popular Culture*, Wisconsin: The University of Wisconsin Press.

Charney, Leo and Schwartz, Vanessa R. (1995), 'Introduction', in Leo Charney and Vanessa R. Schwartz (eds), *Cinema and the Invention of Modern Life*, Berkeley and London: University of California Press, pp. 1–12.

Chatman, Seymour (1978), *Story and Discourse*, London: Ithaca.

Chatman, Seymour (1990), 'What Can We Learn from Contextualist Narratology?', *Poetics Today*, 11: 2, pp. 309–28.

Clack, Beverley (2002), *Sex and Death: A Reappraisal of Human Mortality*, Cambridge: Polity Press.

Clover, Carol J. (1992), *Men, Women, and Chain Saws: Gender in the Modern Horror Film*, London: Bfi-Publishing.

Cohen, Jonathan (2001), 'Defining Identification: A Theoretical Look at the Identification of Audiences with Media Characters', *Mass Communication & Society*, 4: 3, pp. 245–64.

Colavito, Jason (2008), *Knowing Fear: Science, Knowledge and the Development of the Horror Genre*, Jefferson, North Carolina and London: McFarland & Company Inc.

Cole, Phillip (2006), 'Rousseau and the Vampires: Toward a Political Philosophy of the Undead', in Richard Greene and K. Silem Mohammed (eds), *The Undead and Philosophy: Chicken Soup for the Soulless*, Chicago and La Salle: Open Court, pp. 183–96.

Comaroff, Jean and Comaroff, John (2002), 'Alien-Nation: Zombies, Immigrants, and Millennial Capitalism', *The South Atlantic Quarterly*, 101: 4, pp. 779–805.

Cook, Pam (1998), 'No Fixed Address: The Women's Picture from Outrage to Blue Steel', in Steve Neale and Murray Smith (eds), *Contemporary Hollywood Cinema*, London and New York: Routledge, pp. 229–46.

Corbin, Carol C. and Campbell, Robert A. (1999), 'Postmodern Iconography and Perspective in Coppola's *Bram Stoker's Dracula*', *Journal of Popular Film and Television*, pp. 41–48.

Corr, Charles A. and Corr, Donna M. (2003), 'Death, Dying and Bereavement in the United States of America', in John D. Morgan and Pittu Lauangani (eds), *Death and Bereavement around the World. Volume 2: Death and Bereavement in the Americas*, Amityville and New York: Baywood Publishing Company, pp. 37–55.

Cowie, Elizabeth (2003), 'The Lived Nightmare: Trauma, Anxiety, and the Ethical Aesthetics of Horror', in Steven Jay Schneider and Daniel Shaw (eds), *Dark Thoughts: Philosophic Reflections on Cinematic Horror*, Lanham, Maryland and Oxford: The Scarecrow Press Inc., pp. 25–46.

Cowie, Susan D. and Johnson, Tom (2002), *The Mummy in Fact, Fiction and Film*, Jefferson: McFarland & Company Inc.

Craig, J. Robert and Smith, B.R. (2003), 'Tracking the Sands of Time: Origin Stories in the Mummy Films', *Journal of Evolutionary Psychology*, 24: 3–4, pp. 172–79.

Crane, Jonathan Lake (1994), *Terror and Everyday Life*, Thousand Oaks: Sage Publications Inc.

Creed, Barbara (1989), 'Horror and the Monstrous-Feminine: An Imaginary Abjection', in James Donald (ed.), *Fantasy and the Cinema*, London: Bfi-Publishing, pp. 63–90.

Creed, Barbara (1995), 'Horror and the Carnivalesque: The Body-Monstrous', in Leslie Devereux and Roger Hillman (eds), *Fields of Vision*, Berkeley, Los Angeles and London: University of California Press, pp. 127–59.

Csabai, Márta and Erós, Ferenc (2003), 'Bodies in Transition, or the Unbearable Lightness of the "Traditionless" Self', in Naomi Segal, Lib Taylor and Roger Cook (eds), *Indeterminate Bodies*, Hampshire and New York: Palgrave Macmillan, pp. 205–18.

Curran, Angela (2003), 'Aristotelian Reflections on Horror and Tragedy in *An American Werewolf in London* and *The Sixth Sense*', in Steven Jay Schneider and Daniel Shaw (eds), *Dark Thoughts: Philosophic Reflections on Cinematic Horror*, Lanham, Maryland and Oxford: The Scarecrow Press Inc., pp. 47–64.

Dadoun, James (1989), 'Fetishism in the Horror Film', in James Donald (ed.), *Fantasy and the Cinema*, London: British Film Institute, pp. 39–62.

Davies, Douglas J. (2002), *Death, Ritual and Belief: The Rhetoric of Funerary Rites*, 2nd edn, London and New York: Continuum.

Davies, Douglas J. (2005), *A Brief History of Death*, Malden, Oxford and Carlton: Blackwell Publishing Ltd.

Day, Jasmin (2006), *The Mummy's Curse: Mummymania in the English-speaking World*, London and New York: Routledge.

De Vany, Arthur (2004), *Hollywood Economics: How Extreme Uncertainty Shapes the Film Industry*, London and New York: Routledge.

Deane, Bradley (2008), 'Mummy Fiction and the Occupation of Egypt: Imperial Striptease', *English Literature in Transition, 1880–1920*, 51: 4, pp. 381–410.

Deleuze, Gilles (1989), *Cinema 2: The Time-Image* (*Cinéma 2: L'Image-temps*, 1985), Robert Galeta and Hugh Tomlinson (transl.), London: The Athlone Press.

Denzin, Norman K. (1995), *The Cinematic Society: The Voyeur's Gaze*, London Thousand Oaks and New Delhi: Sage Publications.

DeSilva, Regis A. (2009), 'End-of-Life Legislation in the United States and the Semiotics of the Female Body', in Sarah Earle, Carol Komaromy and Caroline Bartholomew (eds), *Death and Dying: A Reader*, London: Sage Publications, pp. 25–33.

Diffrient, David Scott (2004), 'A Film is Being Beaten: Notes on the Shock Cut and the Material Violence of Horror', in Steffen Hantke (ed.), *Horror Film: Creating and Marketing Fear*, Jackson: University Press of Mississippi, pp. 52–81.

Dixon, Wheeler Winston (1995), *It Looks at You: The Returned Gaze of Cinema*, Albany: State University of New York Press.

Doherty, Thomas (1995), 'Teenagers and Teenpics, 1955–1957: A Study of Exploitation Filmmaking', in Janet Staiger (ed.), *The Studio System*, New Brunswick and New Jersey: Rutgers University Press, pp. 298–316.

Doherty, Thomas (1999), *Pre-Code Hollywood: Sex, Immortality and Insurrection in American Cinema 1930–1934*, New York: Columbia University Press.

Doherty, Thomas (2002), *Teenagers And Teenpics: Juvenilization of American Movies*, Philadelphia: Temple University Press.

Doka, Kenneth J. (2003), 'The Death Awareness Movement: Description, History, and Analysis', in Clifton D. Bryant (ed.), *Handbook of Death and Dying*, Thousand Oaks, London and New Delhi: Sage Publications, Inc., pp. 50–56.

Dollimore, Jonathan (1998), *Death, Desire and Loss in Western Culture*, London: Allen Lane, The Penguin Press.

Donald, James (1989), 'The Fantastic, the Sublime and the Popular; Or What's at Stake in Vampire Films?', in James Donald (ed.), *Fantasy and the Cinema*, London: Bfi-Publishing, pp. 233–52.

Donald, James and Hemelryk Donald, Stephanie (2000), 'The Publicness of Cinema', in Christine Gledhill and Linda Williams (eds), *Reinventing Film Studies*, London: Arnold, pp. 114–29.

Douglas, Mary (1996), *Purity and Danger: An Analysis of the Concepts of Pollution and Taboo*, London and New York: Routledge. (Orig. 1966).

Draper, Ellen (1988), 'Zombie Women: When the Gaze Is Male', *Wide Angle: A Film Quarterly of Theory, Criticism and Practice*, 10: 3, pp. 52–62.

Elias, Norbert (2001), *The Loneliness of the Dying* (*Über die Einsamkeit der Strebenden in unseren Tagen*, 1982), Edmund Jehcott (transl.), London and New York: Continuum International Publishing Group.

Elsaesser, Thomas (1998), 'Specularity and Engulfment: Francis Ford Coppola and *Bram Stoker's Dracula*', in Steve Neale and Murray Smith (eds), *Contemporary Hollywood Cinema*, London and New York: Routledge, pp. 191–208.

Evans, Walter (1973), 'Monster Movies: A Sexual Theory', in Barry Keith Grant (ed.), *Planks of Reason: Essays on the Horror Film*, Metuchen, N.J. and London: The Scarecrow Press Inc., pp. 53–64. (Orig. in *Journal of Popular Film*, II: 4).

Fay, Jennifer (2008), 'Dead Subjectivity: White Zombie, Black Baghdad', *The New Centennial Review*, 8: 1, pp. 81–101.

Ferguson, John E. (2007), *The Right to Die*, New York: Chelsea House.

Foucault, Michel (1977), *Discipline and Punish: The Birth of the Prison* (*Surveiller et Punir: Naissance de la Prison*, 1975), Alan Sheridan (transl.), London: Penguin Books.

Freeland, Cynthia A. (1999), 'The Sublime in Cinema', in Carl Plantiga and Greg M. Smith (eds), *Passionate Views: Film, Cognition and Emotion*, Baltimore and London: The Johns Hopkins University Press, pp. 65–83.

Freeland, Cynthia A. (2000), *The Naked and the Undead: Evil and the Appeal of Horror*, Colorado and Oxford: Westview Press.

Freeland, Cynthia (2003), 'The Slasher's Blood Lust', in Steven Jay Schneider and Daniel Shaw (eds), *Dark Thoughts: Philosophic Reflections on Cinematic Horror*, Lanham, Maryland and Oxford: The Scarecrow Press Inc., pp. 198–211.

Freud, Sigmund (2011), *Beyond the Pleasure Principle*, Todd Dufresne (ed.), Gregory C. Richter (transl.), Peterborough, Buffalo: Broadview Editions. (Orig. in *International Psycho-Analytical Library*, no. 4, 1922).

Frow, John (2006), *Genre*, Abingdon and New York: Routledge.

Gaut, Berys (1999), 'Identification and Emotion in Narrative Film', in Carl Plantiga and Greg M. Smith (eds), *Passionate Views: Film, Cognition and Emotion*, Baltimore and London: The Johns Hopkins University Press, pp. 200–16.

Gervais, Karen Grandstrand (1986), *Redefining Death*, New Haven and London: Yale University Press.

Giles, Dennis (1984), 'Conditions of Pleasure in Horror Cinema', in Barry Keith Grant (ed.), *Planks of Reason: Essays on the Horror Film*, Metuchen, N.J. and London: The Scarecrow Press Inc., pp. 38–52.

Giroux, Henry A. (2002), *Breaking in to the Movies: Film and the Culture of Politics*, Malden and Oxford: Blackwell Publishers.

Gledhill, Christine (2000), 'Rethinking Genre', in Christine Gledhill and Linda Williams (eds), *Reinventing Film Studies*, London: Arnold, pp. 221–43.

Goldberg, Vicki (1998), 'Death Takes a Holiday, Sort of', in Jeffrey H. Goldstein (ed.), *Why We Watch: The Attractions of Violent Entertainment*, New York and Oxford: Oxford University Press, 27–52.

Gomery, Douglas (1998), 'Hollywood as Industry', in John Hill and Pamela Church Gibson (eds), *The Oxford Guide to Film Studies*, New York: Oxford University Press, pp. 245–54.

Grant, Barry Keith (1995), 'Experience and Meaning in Genre Films', in Barry Keith Grant (ed.), *Film Genre Reader II*, Austin: University of Texas Press, pp. 114–28.

Grant, Barry Keith (2007), *Film Genre: From Iconography to Ideology*, London: Wallflower Papers.

Greene, Richard and Mohammed, K. Silem (2006), '(Un)dead (Un)certainties', in Richard Greene and K. Silem Mohammed (eds), *The Undead and Philosophy: Chicken Soup for the Soulless*, Chicago and La Salle: Open Court, pp. xiii–xvi.

Grønstad, Asbjørn (2003), *Transfigurations: Violence, Death, and Masculinity in American Cinema*, Bergen: University of Bergen.

Guthke, Karl S. (1999), *The Gender of Death: A Cultural History in Art and Literature*, Cambridge, New York and Melbourne: Cambridge University Press.

Haggerty, George E. (2006), *Queer Gothic*, Urbana and Chicago: University of Illinois Press.

Hall, Stuart (2001), 'Encoding/Decoding', in Meenakshi Gigi Durham and Douglas M. Kellner (eds), *Media and Cultural Studies: KeyWorks*, Malden, Oxford, Melbourne and Berlin: Blackwell Publishing, pp. 166–76. (Orig. in *Culture, Media, Language*, 1980).

Hallam, Elizabeth, Hockey, Jenny and Howarth, Glennys (2001), 'The Body in Death', in Nick Watson (ed.), *Reframing the Body*, Basingstoke and New York: Palgrave, pp. 63–77.

Hallet, Wolfgang (2009), 'The Multimodal Novel: The Integration of Modes and Media in Novelistic Narration', in Sandra Heinen and Roy Sommer (eds), *Narratology in the Age of Cross-Disciplinary Narrative Research*, Berlin and New York: Walter de Gruyter, pp. 129–53.

Hand, Richard J. (2004), 'Proliferating Horrors: Survival Horror and the *Resident Evil* Franchise', in Steffen Hantke (ed.), *Horror Film: Creating and Marketing Fear*, Jackson: University Press of Mississippi, pp. 117–34.

Hansen, Miriam (1991), *Babel and Babylon: Spectatorship in American Silent Film*, Cambridge and London: Harvard University Press.

Hansen, Miriam (1995), 'Early Cinema, Late Cinema: Transformations of the Public Sphere', in Linda Williams (ed.), *Viewing Positions: Ways of Seeing Film*, New Brunswick and New Jersey: Rutgers University Press, pp. 134–52.

Hanusch, Folker (2010), *Representing Death in the News: Journalism, Media and Mortality*, Basingstoke: Palgrave Macmillan.

Hauser, Larry (2006), 'Zombies, *Blade Runner*, and the Mind–Body Problem', in Richard Greene and K. Silem Mohammed (eds), *The Undead and Philosophy: Chicken Soup for the Soulless*, Chicago and La Salle: Open Court, pp. 53–66.

Hayward, Philip (2009), 'Introduction', in Philip Hayward (ed.), *Terror Tracks: Music, Sound and Horror Cinema*, London and Oakville: Equinox Publishing Ltd, pp. 1–13.

Heffernan, Kevin (2002), 'Inner-City Exhibition and the Genre Film: Distributing *Night of the Living Dead* (1968)', *Cinema Journal*, 41: 3, pp. 59–77.

Herman, David (1997), 'Scripts, Sequences, and Stories: Elements of a Postclassical Narratology', *PMLA*, 112: 5, pp. 1046–59.

Hills, Matt (2003), 'An Event-Based Definition of Art-Horror', in Steven Jay Schneider and Daniel Shaw (eds), *Dark Thoughts: Philosophic Reflections on Cinematic Horror*, Lanham, Maryland and Oxford: The Scarecrow Press Inc., pp. 138–57.

Hoberman J. (2003), *The Dream Life: Movies, Media and the Mythology of the Sixties*, New York and London: The New Press.

Horstkotte, Silke (2009), 'Seeing or Speaking: Visual Narratology and Focalization, Literature to Film', in Sandra Heinen and Roy Sommer (eds), *Narratology in the Age of Cross-Disciplinary Narrative Research*, Berlin and New York: Walter de Gruyter, pp. 170–92.

Hoyert, Donna L. (1996), 'Mortality trends for Alzheimer's disease, 1979–91', *National Center for Health Statistics, Vital Health Stat*, 20: 28.

Hoyert, Donna L. (2012), '75 Years of Mortality in the United States, 1935–2010', *NCHS Data Brief March 2012/88*, Centers for Disease Control and Prevention/National Center for Health Statistics.

Hoyert, Donna L. and Jiaquan, Xu (2012), 'Deaths: Preliminary Data for 2011, M.D.', *National Vital Statistics Reports*, 61: 6.

Howarth, Glennys (2007), *Death and Dying: A Sociological Introduction*, Cambridge: Polity Press.

Hughes, William (2000), '"The Raw Yolky Taste of Life": Spirituality, Secularity and the Vampire', *Gothic Studies*, 2: 1, pp. 148–56.

Ikram, Salima (2003), *Death and Burial in Ancient Egypt*, Harlow and London: Longman.

Information Please® Database (2011), *Life Expectancy at Birth by Race and Sex, 1930–2010*, Pearson Education, Inc., http://www.infoplease.com/ipa/A0005148.html (11 February 2013).

Ingebretsen, Edward J. (2001), *At Stake: Monsters and the Rhetoric of Fear in Public Culture*, Chicago and London: The University of Chicago Press.

Jacquette, Dale (2006), 'Zombie Gladiators', in Richard Greene and K. Silem Mohammed (eds), *The Undead and Philosophy: Chicken Soup for the Soulless*, Chicago and La Salle: Open Court, pp. 105–18.

Jahn, Manfred (2005), 'Focalization', in David Herman, Manfred Jahn & Marie-Laure Ryan (eds), *Routledge Encyclopedia for Narrative Theory*, London and New York: Routledge, pp. 173–77.

Jancovich, Mark (1992), *Horror*, London: B.T. Batsford Ltd.

Jenkins, Henry and Karnick, Kristine Brunovska (1995), 'Introduction: Golden Eras and Blind Spots – Genre, History and Comedy', in Kristine Brunovska Karnick and Henry Jenkins (eds), *Classical Hollywood Comedy*, New York and London: Routledge, pp. 1–13.

Johnson, Carol Siri (1991/1992), 'The Limbs of Osiris: Reed's *Mumbo Jumbo* and Hollywood's *The Mummy*', *Melus*, 17: 4, pp. 105–15.

Jones, Miriam (1997), 'The Gilda Stories: Revealing the Monster at the Margins', in Joan Gordon and Veronica Hollinger (eds), *Blood Read: The Vampire as Metaphor in Contemporary Culture*, Philadelphia: University of Pennsylvania Press, pp. 151–68.

Kacandes, Irene (2005), 'Address', in David Herman, Manfred Jahn and Marie-Laure Ryan (eds), *Routledge Encyclopedia for Narrative Theory*, London and New York: Routledge, pp. 4–5.

Kant, Immanuel (1965), *First Introduction to the Critique of Judgement*, (*Erste Fassung der Einleitung in die Kritik der Urteilskraft*, 1833), James Haden (transl.), New York: The Bobbs–Merrill Company Inc.

Kastenbaum, Robert (2003), 'Definitions of Death', in Robert Kastenbaum (ed.), *MacMillan Encyclopedia of Death and Dying*, New York: MacMillan Reference USA, pp. 224–29.

Kawin, Bruce F. (1995), 'Children of the Light', in Barry Keith Grant (ed.), *Film Genre Reader II*, Austin: University of Texas Press, pp. 324–45.

Keane, Stephen (2007), *CineTech: Film, Convergence and New Media*, Basingstoke and New York: Palgrave Macmillan.

Kearns, Michael (1999), *Rhetorical Narratology*, Lincoln and London: University of Nebraska Press.

Kellehear, Allan (2009), 'Brain Death: A Sociological View', in Sarah Earle, Carol Komaromy and Caroline Bartholomew (eds), *Death and Dying: A Reader*, London: Sage Publications, pp. 135–43.

Kindt, Tom (2009), 'Narratological Expansionism and its Discontents', in Sandra Heinen and Roy Sommer (eds), *Narratology in the Age of Cross-Disciplinary Narrative Research*, Berlin and New York: Walter de Gruyter, pp. 35–47.

King, Karen Sisco (2004), 'Imaging the Abject: The Ideological Use of the Dissolve', in Steffen Hantke (ed.), *Horror Film: Creating and Marketing Fear*, Jackson: University Press of Mississippi, pp. 21–34.

Klesse, Christian (2000), '"Modern Primitivism": Non-Mainstream Body Modification and Racialized Representation', in Mike Featherstone (ed.), *Body Modification*, London, Thousand Oaks and New Delhi: Sage Publications, pp. 15–37.

Knight, Deborah and McKnight, George (2003), 'American Psycho: Horror, Satire, Aesthetics and Identification', in Steven Jay Schneider and Daniel Shaw (eds), *Dark Thoughts: Philosophic Reflections on Cinematic Horror*, Lanham, Maryland and Oxford: The Scarecrow Press Inc., pp. 212–29.

Kokkola, Lydia (2011), 'Virtuous Vampires and Voluptuous Vamps: Romance Conventions Reconsidered in Stephanie Meyer's "Twilight" Series', *Children's Literature in Education*, 42, pp. 165–79.

Kramer, Peter (1998), 'Post-classical Hollywood', in John Hill and Pamela Church Gibson (eds), *The Oxford Guide to Film Studies*, New York: Oxford University Press, pp. 289–309.

Kreiswirth, Martin (2000), 'Merely Telling Stories? Narrative and Knowledge in the Human Sciences', *Poetics Today*, 21: 2, pp. 293–318.

Kreiswirth, Martin (2005), 'Narrative Turn in the Humanities', in David Herman, Manfred Jahn and Marie-Laure Ryan (eds), *Routledge Encyclopedia for Narrative Theory*, London and New York: Routledge, pp. 377–82.

Kristeva, Julia (1982), *Powers of Horror: An Essay on Abjection* (*Pouvoirs de l'horreur*, 1980), Leon S. Roudiez (transl.), New York: Columbia University Press.

Kuhn, Markus (2009), 'Film Narratology: Who Tells? Who Shows? Who Focalizes? Narrative Mediation in Self-Reflexive Fiction Films', in Peter Hühn, Wolf Schmid and Jörg Schönert (eds), *Point of View, Perspective, and Focalization: Modeling Mediation in Narrative*, Berlin and New York: Walter de Gruyter, pp. 259–78.

Kübler-Ross, Elisabeth (1970), *On Death and Dying*, New York: Macmillan.

Lagerkvist, Amanda (2013), 'New Memory Cultures and Death: The Digital Memory Ecology and the Quest for Existential Security', *Thanatos*, 2: 2, pp. 8–24.

Landsberg, Alison (2009), 'Memory, Empathy, and the Politics of Identification', *International Journal of Politics, Culture and Society*, 22, pp. 221–29.

Lavi, Shai J. (2005), *The Modern Art of Dying: A History of Euthanasia in the United States*, New Jersey: Princeton University Press.

Leffler, Yvonne (2000), *Horror as Pleasure*, Stockholm: Almqvist & Wiksell International.

Leffler, Yvonne (2001), *Skräck som fiktion och underhållning*, Lund: Studentlitteratur.

Lowenstein, Adam (2005), *Shocking Representation: Historical Trauma, National Cinema, and the Modern Horror Film*, New York: Columbia University Press.

Lowry, Edward and deCordova, Richard (1984), 'Enunciation and the Production of Horror in *White Zombie*', in Barry Keith Grant (ed.), *Planks of Reason: Essays on the Horror Film*, Metuchen, N.J. and London: The Scarecrow Press Inc., pp. 346–89.

Lukas, Scott A. (2009), 'Horror Video Game Remakes and the Question of Medium: Remaking *Doom*, *Silent Hill* and *Resident Evil*', in Scott A. Lukas and John Marmysz (eds), *Fear, Cultural Anxiety and Transformation: Horror, Science Fiction, and Fantasy Films Remade*, Lanham: Lexington Books, pp. 221–42.

Lukas, Scott A. and Marmysz, John (2009), 'Horror, Science Fiction, and Fantasy Films Remade', in Scott A. Lukas and John Marmysz (eds), *Fear, Cultural Anxiety and Transformation: Horror, Science Fiction, and Fantasy Films Remade*, Lanham: Lexington Books, pp. 1–20.

Lupton, Carter (2003), '"Mummymania" for the Masses – Is Egyptology Cursed by the Mummy's Curse?', in Sally McDonald and Michael Rice (eds), *Consuming Ancient Egypt*, London: UCL Press, pp. 23–46.

MacCabe, Colin (1986), 'Theory and Film: Principles of Realism and Pleasure', in Philip Rosen (ed.), *Narrative, Apparatus, Ideology: A Film Theory Reader*, New York: Columbia University Press, pp. 179–97. (Orig. in *Screen*, 1976, 17: 3).

Maltby, Richard (1995), '"Baby Face" or How Joe Breen Made Barbara Stanwyck Atone for Causing the Wall Street Crash', in Janet Staiger (ed.), *The Studio System*, New Brunswick and New Jersey: Rutgers University Press, pp. 251–78.

Maltby, Richard (1998), '"Nobody Knows Everything": Post-classical Historiographies and Consolidated Entertainment', in Steve Neale and Murray Smith (eds), *Contemporary Hollywood Cinema*, London and New York: Routledge, pp. 21–44.

Maltby, Richard (2003), *Hollywood Cinema*, 2nd edn, Oxford: Blackwell Publishing.

Mayne, Judith (1993), 'Paradoxes of Spectatorship', in Linda Williams (ed.), *Viewing Positions: Ways of Seeing Film*, New Brunswick and New Jersey: Rutgers University Press, pp. 155–83. (Orig. in *Cinema and Spectatorship*, 1993).

McClelland, Bruce A. (2006), *Slayers and Their Vampires: A Cultural History of Killing the Dead*, Ann Arbor: The University of Michigan Press.

McGeough, Kevin (2006), 'Heroes, Mummies, and Treasure: Near Eastern Archaeology in the Movies', *Near Eastern Archaeology*, 69: 3–4, pp. 174–85.

McGunnigle, Christopher (2005), 'My Own Vampire: The Metamorphosis of the Queer Monster in Francis Ford Coppola's *Bram Stoker's Dracula*', *Gothic Studies*, 7: 2, pp. 172–84.

McIlwain, Charlton D. (2005), *When Death Goes Pop: Death, Media & the Remaking of Community*, New York: Peter Lang.

McKahan, Jason Grant (2007), 'The Substance Abuse Film and the Gothic: Typology, Narrative, and Hallucination', in Caroline Joan (Kay) Picart and Cecil Greek (eds), *Monsters in and among Us: Toward a Gothic Criminology*, Madison and Teaneck: Fairleigh Dickinson University Press, pp. 117–41.

Medovoi, Leerom (2005), *Rebels: Youth and the Cold War Origins of Identity*, Durham: Duke University Press.

Mercer, Joyce Ann (2011), 'Vampires, Desire, Girls and God: Twilight and the Spiritualities of Adolescent Girls', *Pastoral Psychology*, 60, pp. 263–78.

Merskin, Debra (2011), 'A Boyfriend to Die for: Edward Cullen as Compensated Psychopath in Stephanie Meyer's *Twilight*', *Journal of Communication Inquiry*, 35, pp. 157–78.

Michel, Frann (2007), 'Life and Death and Something in Between: Reviewing Recent Horror Cinema', *Psychoanalysis, Culture & Society*, 12, pp. 390–97.

Miller, Sally (2003), '"Nursery fears made flesh and sinew": Vampires, the Body and Eating Disorders: A Psychoanalytic Approach', in Carla T. Kungl (ed.), *Vampires: Myths & Metaphors of Enduring Evil*, Oxford: Inter-Disciplinary Press, pp. 53–58.

Mitford, Jessica (1963), *The American Way of Death*, London: Hutchinson & Co.

Mohammed, K. Silem (2006), 'Zombies, Rest, and Motion: Spinoza and the Speed of Undeath', in Richard Greene and K. Silem Mohammed (eds), *The Undead and Philosophy: Chicken Soup for the Soulless*, Chicago and La Salle: Open Court, pp. 91–102.

Moine, Raphaëlle (2008), *Cinema Genre* (*Les genres du cinema*, 2002), Alistair Fox and Hilary Radner (transl.), Malden, Oxford and Victoria; Blackwell Publishing.

Morgan, John D. (2003), 'General Introduction', in John D. Morgan and Pittu Lauangani (eds), *Death and Bereavement around the World, Volume 2: Death and Bereavement in the Americas*, Amityville and New York: Baywood Publishing Company, pp. 1–4.

MPAA, *Film Ratings*, The Motion Picture Association of America, http://www.mpaa.org/FlmRat_Ratings.asp (20 March 2010).

Mulkay, Michael (1993), 'Social Death in Britain', in David Clark (ed.), *The Sociology of Death*, Oxford and Cambridge: Blackwell Publishers, pp. 31–49.

NCHS Data (2009), *Leading Causes of Death, 1900–1998*, Centers for Disease Control and Prevention/National Center for Health Statistics, http://www.cdc.gov/nchs/data/dvs/lead1900_98.pdf (21 February 2013).

Neale, Steve (1990), 'Questions of Genre', in Barry Keith Grant (ed.), *Film Genre Reader II*, Austin: University of Texas Press, pp. 159–83. (Orig. in *Screen*, 1990, 31: 1).

Neale, Steve (2000), *Genre and Hollywood*, London and New York: Routledge.

Neroni, Hilary (2005), *The Violent Woman: Femininity, Narrative and Violence in Contemporary American Cinema*, Albany: State University of New York Press.

Nixon, Nicola (1997), 'When Hollywood Sucks, or, Hungry Girls, Lost Boys, and Vampirism in the Age of Reagan', in Joan Gordon and Veronica Hollinger (eds), *Blood Read: The Vampire as Metaphor in Contemporary Culture*, Philadelphia: University of Pennsylvania Press, pp. 115–28.

Nünning, Ansgar (2009), 'Surveying Contextualist and Cultural Narratologies: Towards an Outline of Approaches, Concepts and Potentials', in Sandra Heinen and Roy Sommer (eds), *Narratology in the Age of Cross-Disciplinary Narrative Research*, Berlin and New York: Walter de Gruyter, pp. 48–70.

Nyström, Lisa (2009), 'Blood, Lust and the Fe/Male Narrative in *Bram Stoker's Dracula* (1992) and the Novel (1897)', in John Edgar Browning and Caroline Joan (Kay) Picart (eds), *Draculas, Vampires, and Other Undead Forms: Essays on Gender, Race, and Culture*, Lanham Maryland, Toronto, New York and Plymouth: The Scarecrow Press, Inc., pp. 63–76.

Patterson, Orlando (1982), *Slavery and Social Death: A Comparative Study*, Cambridge: Harvard University Press.

Phillips, Kendall R. (2005), *Projected Fears: Horror Films and American Culture*, Westport, Connecticut and London: Praeger.

Picart, Caroline Joan (Kay) and Greek, Cecil (2007), 'Introduction: Toward a Gothic Criminology', in Caroline Joan (Kay) Picart and Cecil Greek (eds), *Monsters in and among Us: Toward a Gothic Criminology*, Madison and Teaneck: Fairleigh Dickinson University Press, pp. 11–43.

Plantiga, Carl (1999), 'The Scene of Empathy and the Human Face on Film', in Carl Plantiga and Greg M. Smith (eds), *Passionate Views: Film, Cognition and Emotion*, Baltimore and London: The Johns Hopkins University Press, pp. 239–55.

Poole, Adrian (2004), *Tragedy: A Very Short Introduction*, Oxford: Oxford University Press.

Powell, Anna (2005), *Deleuze and Horror Film*, Edinburgh: Edinburgh University Press.

Prince, Stephen (2000), 'Graphic Violence in the Cinema: Origins, Aesthetic Design, and Social Effects', in Stephen Prince (ed.), *Screening Violence*, London: The Athlone Press, pp. 1–44.

Prince, Stephen (2003), *Classical Film Violence: Designing and Regulating Brutality in Hollywood Cinema, 1930–1968*, New Brunswick: Rutgers University Press.

Prince, Gerald (2008), 'Classical and/or Postclassical Narratology', *L'Esprit Créateur*, 48: 2, pp. 115–23.

Probyn, Elspeth (1996), *Outside Belongings*, New York and London: Routledge.

Punter, David (1996), *The Literature of Terror: The Modern Gothic*, Vol. 2, London and New York: Longman Group.

Punter, David and Byron, Glennis (2004), *The Gothic*, Malden, Oxford and Victoria: Blackwell Publishing.

Quart, Leonard and Auster, Albert (2002), *American Film and Society since 1945*, Westport and London: Praeger Publishers.

Rhodes, Gary D. (2001), *White Zombie: Anatomy of a Horror Film*, Jefferson: McFarland & Company, Inc.

Ridell, Seija (1998), 'Beyond the Pendulum: Critical Genre Analysis of Media–Audience Relations', *Nordicom Review*, 1, pp. 125–33.

Ridell, Seija (2006), '*Genre ja mediatutkimus*', in Anne Mäntynen, Susanne Shore and Anna Solin (eds), *Genre – Tekstilaji. Tietolipas 213*, Helsinki: Suomalaisen Kirjallisuuden Seura, pp. 184–213.

Roddick, Nick (1983), *A New Deal in Entertainment: Warner Brothers in the 1930s*, London: British Film Institute.

Russell, Catharine (1995), *Narrative Mortality: Death, Closure and New Wave Cinemas*, Minneapolis and London: University of Minneapolis Press.

Russell, David J. (1998), 'Monster Roundup: Reintegrating the Horror Genre', in Nick Browne (ed.), *Refiguring American Film Genres: Theory and History*, Berkeley, Los Angeles and London: University of California Press, pp. 233–54.

Ryall, Tom (1998), 'Genre and Hollywood', in John Hill and Pamela Church Gibson (eds), *The Oxford Guide to Film Studies*, New York: Oxford University Press, pp. 327–38.

Ryan, Marie-Laure (2004), 'Introduction', in Marie-Laure Ryan (ed.), *Narrative across Media: The Languages of Storytelling*, Lincoln and London: University of Nebraska Press, pp. 1–40.

Saler, Benson and Ziegle, Charles A. (2003), 'Dracula and Carmilla: Mythmaking and the Mind', in Carla T. Kungl (ed.), *Vampires: Myths & Metaphors of Enduring Evil*, Oxford: Inter-Disciplinary Press, pp. 17–20.

Sandler, Kevin S. (2007), *Why Hollywood Doesn't Make X-rated Movies*, New Brunswick, New Jersey and London: Rutgers University Press.

Schatz, Thomas (1981), *Hollywood Genres: Formulas, Filmmaking, and the Studio System*, New York: McGraw–Hill.

Schneider, Ralf (2005), 'Emotion and Narrative', in David Herman, Manfred Jahn and Marie-Laure Ryan (eds), *Routledge Encyclopedia for Narrative Theory*, London and New York: Routledge, pp. 136–37.

Schneider, Steven Jay (2003), 'Murder as Art/The Art of Murder: Aestheticizing Violence in Modern Cinematic Horror', in Steven Jay Schneider and Daniel Shaw (eds), *Dark Thoughts: Philosophic Reflections on Cinematic Horror*, Lanham, Maryland and Oxford: The Scarecrow Press Inc., pp. 174–97.

Schroeder, Caroline T. (2003), 'Ancient Egyptian Religion on the Silver Screen: Modern Anxieties about Race, Ethnicity, and Religion', *Journal of Religion and Film*, 7: 2, http://www.unomaha.edu/jrf/Vol7No2/ancienteqypt.htm (7 January 2013).

Scott, Suzanne (2003), 'All Bark and No Bite: Siring the Neutered Vampire on *Buffy the Vampire Slayer*', in Carla T. Kungl (ed.), *Vampires: Myths & Metaphors of Enduring Evil*, Oxford: Inter-Disciplinary Press, pp. 124–28.

Segal, Alan F. (2004), *Life after Death: A History of the Afterlife in the Religions of the West*, New York: Doubleday.

Serafy Sam (2003), 'Egypt in Hollywood: Pharaohs of the Fifties', in Sally McDonald and Michael Rice (eds), *Consuming Ancient Egypt*, London: UCL Press, pp. 77–86.

Shaviro, Steven (1993), *The Cinematic Body*, Minneapolis: University of Minnesota Press.

Shaviro, Steven (2002), 'Capitalist Monsters', *Historical Materialism*, 10: 4, pp. 181–290.

Shaw, Daniel (2003), 'The Mastery of Hannibal Lecter', in Steven Jay Schneider and Daniel Shaw (eds), *Dark Thoughts: Philosophic Reflections on Cinematic Horror*, Lanham, Maryland and Oxford: The Scarecrow Press Inc., pp. 10–24.

Shaw, Rachel Louise (2004), 'Making Sense of Violence: A Study of Narrative Meaning', *Qualitative Research in Psychology*, 1, pp. 131–51.

Sheller, Mimi (2003), *Consuming the Caribbean: From Arawaks to Zombies*, London and New York: Routledge.

Shildrick, Margrit (2002), *Embodying the Monster: Encounters with the Vulnerable Self*, London, Thousand Oaks and New Delhi: Sage Publications.

Signorotti, Elizabeth (1996), 'Repossessing the Body, Transgressive Desire in "Carmilla" and Dracula', *Criticism*, 38: 4, pp. 607–32.

Simpson, Paul L. (2004), 'The Horror "Event" Movie: The Mummy, Hannibal and Signs', in Steffen Hantke (ed.), *Horror Film: Creating and Marketing Fear*, Jackson: University Press of Mississippi, pp. 85–98.

Simpson, Paul (2005), 'Modality', in David Herman, Manfred Jahn and Marie-Laure Ryan (eds), *Routledge Encyclopedia for Narrative Theory*, London and New York: Routledge, pp. 313–15.

Singer, Peter (1994), *Rethinking Life & Death*, New York: St. Martin's Griffin.

Skal, David J. (1993), *The Monster Show: A Cultural History of Horror*, London: Plexus.

Smith, Murray (1995), *Engaging Characters: Fiction, Emotion and the Cinema*, Oxford: Clarendon Press.

Smith, Murray (1998), 'Theses on the Philosophy of Hollywood History', in Steve Neale and Murray Smith (eds), *Contemporary Hollywood Cinema*, London and New York: Routledge, pp. 3–20.

Smith, Murray (1999), 'Gangsters, Cannibals, Aesthetes, or Apparently Perverse Allegiances', in Carl Plantiga and Greg M. Smith (eds), *Passionate Views: Film, Cognition and Emotion*, Baltimore and London: The Johns Hopkins University Press, pp. 217–38.

Sobchack, Vivian (1995), 'Phenomenology and the Film Experience', in Linda Williams (ed.), *Viewing Positions: Ways of Seeing Film*, New Brunswick and New Jersey: Rutgers University Press, pp. 36–58. (Orig. in *The Address of the Eye: A Phenomenology of Film Experience*, 1992).

Sobchack, Vivian C. (2000), 'The Violent Dance: A Personal Memoir of Death in the Movies', in Stephen Prince (ed.), *Screening Violence*, London: The Athlone Press, pp. 110–24.

Sobchack, Vivian (2008), 'Embodying Transcendence: On the Literal, the Material, and the Cinematic Sublime', *Material Religion*, 4: 2, pp. 194–203.

Soren, David (1997), *The Rise and Fall of the Horror Film*, Baltimore: Midnight Marquee Press, Inc.

Spandoni, Robert (2007), *Uncanny Bodies: The Coming of Sound Films and the Origins of the Horror Genre*, Berkeley, Los Angeles and London: University of California Press.

Staudt, Christina (2009), 'From Concealment to Recognition: The Discourse on Death, Dying and Grief', in Michael K. Bartalos (ed.), *Speaking of Death: America's New Sense of Mortality*, Westport, Connecticut and London: Praeger, pp. 3–41.

Synnott, Anthony (1993), *The Body Social: Symbolism, Self and Society*, London and New York: Routledge.

Thompson, Hamish (2006), '"She's Not Your Mother Anymore, She's a Zombie!": Zombies, Value, and Personal Identity', in Richard Greene and K. Silem Mohammed (eds), *The Undead and Philosophy: Chicken Soup for the Soulless*, Chicago and La Salle: Open Court, pp. 27–37.

Tomc, Sandra (1997), 'Dieting and Damnation: Anne Rice's *Interview with the Vampire*', in Joan Gordon and Veronica Hollinger (eds), *Blood Read: The Vampire as Metaphor in Contemporary Culture*, Philadelphia: University of Pennsylvania Press, pp. 95–114.

Tudor, Andrew (1989), *Monsters and Mad Scientist: A Cultural History of the Horror Movie*, Oxford: Basil Blackwell.

Turner, Victor (2008), *The Ritual Process: Structure and Anti-Structure*, renewed edition (orig. 1969), New Jersey: Aldine Transaction.

Twitchell, James B. (1985), *Dreadful Pleasures: An Anatomy of Modern Horror*, New York: Oxford University Press.

Tyree, J.M. (2009/10), '*Warm-Blooded*, *True Blood* and *Let the Right One In*', *Film Quarterly*, 63: 2, pp. 31–38.

Vargas, Manuel (2006), 'Dead Serious: Evil and the Ontology of the Undead', in Richard Greene and K. Silem Mohammed (eds), *The Undead and Philosophy: Chicken Soup for the Soulless*, Chicago and La Salle: Open Court, pp. 39–52.

Verstraten, Peter (2009), 'Between Attraction and Story: Rethinking Narrativity in Cinema', in Sandra Heinen and Roy Sommer (eds), *Narratology in the Age of Cross-Disciplinary Narrative Research*, Berlin and New York: Walter de Gruyter, pp. 154–69.

Vieira, Mark. A. (2003), *Hollywood Horror from Gothic to Cosmic*, New York: Harry N. Abrams, Inc.

Walker, Matthew (2006), 'When There's No More Room in Hell, the Dead will Shop the Earth: Romero and Aristotle in Zombies, Happiness, and Consumption', in Richard Greene and K. Silem Mohammed (eds), *The Undead and Philosophy: Chicken Soup for the Soulless*, Chicago and La Salle: Open Court, pp. 81–89.

Waller, Gregory A. (1986), *The Living and the Undead: From Stoker's* Dracula *to Romero's* Dawn of the Dead, Urbana and Chicago: University of Illinois Press.

Walter, Tony (1994), *The Revival of Death*, London and New York: Routledge.

Warchol, Tomasz (2003), 'How Coppola Killed Dracula', in Carla T. Kungl (ed.), *Vampires: Myths & Metaphors of Enduring Evil*, Oxford: Inter-Disciplinary Press, pp. 7–10.

Watson, Paul (2007), 'Genre Theory and Hollywood Cinema', in Jill Nelmes (ed.), *Introduction to Film Studies*, London and New York: Routledge, pp. 110–27.

Webb, Jen and Byrnand, Sam (2008), 'Some Kind of Virus: The Zombie as Body and as Trope', *Body & Society*, 14: 2, pp. 83–98.

Weiss, Andrea (1992), *Vampires and Violets: Lesbians in the Cinema*, London: Jonathan Cape.

Wells, Paul (2002), *The Horror Genre: From Beelzebub to Blair Witch*, London and New York: Wallflower.

Williams, Linda (1995), 'Introduction', in Linda Williams (ed.), *Viewing Positions: Ways of Seeing Film*, New Brunswick and New Jersey: Rutgers University Press, pp. 1–20.

Williamson, Milly (2001), 'Vampires and the Gendered Body', in Nick Watson (ed.), *Reframing the Body*, Basingstoke and New York: Palgrave, pp. 96–112.

Williamson, Milly (2003), 'Vampire Transformations: From Gothic Demon to Domestication?', in Carla T. Kungl (ed.), *Vampires: Myths & Metaphors of Enduring Evil*, Oxford: Inter-Disciplinary Press, pp. 101–07.

Williamson, Milly (2005), 'Spike, Sex and Subtext: Intertextual Portrayals of the Sympathetic Vampire on Cult Television', *European Journal of Cultural Studies*, 8: 3, pp. 289–311.

Wood, Robin (1984), 'An Introduction to the American Horror Film', in Barry Keith Grant (ed.), *Planks of Reason: Essays on the Horror Film*, Metuchen, N.J. and London: The Scarecrow Press Inc., pp. 164–200. (Orig. in *The American Nightmare*, 1979).

Wood, Robin (1986), *Hollywood from Vietnam to Reagan*, New York: Columbia University Press.

Wood, Robin (1995), 'Ideology, Genre, Auteur', in Barry Keith Grant (ed.), *Film Genre Reader II*, Austin: University of Texas Press, pp. 59–73. (Orig. in *Film Comment*, 1977, 13: 1).

Wood, Robin (1996), 'Burying the Undead: The Use and Obsolescence of Count Dracula', in Barry Keith Grant (ed.), *The Dread of Difference: Gender and Horror Film*, Austin: University of Texas Press, pp. 364–78.

Wyman, Leah M. and Dionisopoulos, George N. (1999), 'Primal Urges and Civilized Sensibilities', *Journal of Popular Film and Television*, pp. 32–39.

Zanger, Jules (1997), 'Metaphor into Metonomy: The Vampire Next Door', in Joan Gordon and Veronica Hollinger (eds), *Blood Read: The Vampire as Metaphor in Contemporary Culture*, Philadelphia: University of Pennsylvania Press, pp. 17–26.

Zimmer, Katherine (2004), 'The Camera's Eye: *Peeping Tom* and Technological Perversion', in Steffen Hantke (ed.), *Horror Film: Creating and Marketing Fear*, Jackson: University Press of Mississippi, pp. 35–51.

Zimmerman, Bonnie (1996), 'Daughters of Darkness: The Lesbian Vampire on Film', in Grant, Barry Keith (ed.), *The Dread of Difference: Gender and Horror Film*, Austin: University of Texas Press, pp. 379–87. (Orig. in *Jump Cut*, 1981, 24: 25).